PSYCHOLOGY OF BRANDING

PSYCHOLOGY RESEARCH PROGRESS

Additional books in this series can be found on Nova's website
under the Series tab.

Additional E-books in this series can be found on Nova's website
under the E-book tab.

PSYCHOLOGY RESEARCH PROGRESS

PSYCHOLOGY OF BRANDING

W. DOUGLAS EVANS
EDITOR

nova
publishers
New York

Library of Congress Cataloging-in-Publication Data

Psychology of branding / editor, W. Douglas Evans (The George Washington University School of Public Health and Health Services, Washington, DC, USA).
    pages cm
  Includes index.
  ISBN 978-1-62618-817-4 (hardcover)
  1. Branding (Marketing)--Psychological aspects. 2. Brand name products--Psychological aspects. I. Evans, W. Douglas.
  HF5415.1255.P79 2013
  658.8'27019--dc23
                          2013016529

Published by Nova Science Publishers, Inc. † New York

CONTENTS

PREFACE

INTRODUCTION

Why did Sam buy the local craft beer instead of the well-known national brand? Given the choice between two similar products, similarly available and at similar prices, why do we choose one over another? Why does one type of branding persuade us and another doesn't? How does who I am (my personal history, personality, genes) and how I live (my environment and interactions) affect the type of brands I choose? Perhaps some combination of rational and emotional reactions to the beer choices led Sam to choose the craft beer.

This book explores the psychological factors underlying brand choices we make. How we encounter brands (and how often), think about them, feel about them, and how we experience them in *in relation to* competing brands, has a big effect on which ones we choose, and keep on choosing. At the same time, presumably there are neural events occurring when we encounter and mentally respond to brands. These represent ways in which we can explain and understand why people choose and remain loyal to brands. These explanations of branding are related and intuitive. But how does the *psychology of branding* work? This book offers answers to that question.

Brands are all around us and in a sense represent any person, place, or thing to which people attach associations – anything that represents something for someone. This insight has led those trying to improve society, not just to sell products, services, and organizational reputations, to take up the mantle of branding. The branding of social and health behaviors has become widespread and is now a central approach in social marketing – the use of marketing to benefit society rather than the marketer. In an earlier volume, my co-editor Gerard Hastings and I noted that "that by learning about concepts such as brand development, identity and equity we can do for public health what Philip Morris had done for teen smoking." This is exactly what's been happening for some 20 years, and now represents a powerful strategy to change social and health behaviors for the better. Branding is now truly a systemic approach to modifying human behavior for commercial as well as socially beneficial purposes.

This book brings together both theoretical learning and practical experience of commercial and social and health branding from around the world, and demonstrates how one of the most powerful tools of marketing is being successfully adopted and deployed. In 12 chapters, this volume examines the basic psychological mechanisms underlying brands and branding, presents models of psychological reaction to brands, explores the neural basis of brand response, examines case examples of branding across multiple subject areas and sectors of society and the economy, and reviews the evidence underlying the psychology of branding. It also looks towards the future, highlighting key challenges and maps out the research agenda.

The idea that branding has a psychological basis – how we think and feel about the brands that are all around us – is not new, but the science of brand psychology continues to grow and in recent years has expanded into domains ranging from neuroscience to behavioral economics. This book aims to advance the study of brand psychology and improve the quality of brands and brand marketing, whether they aim to sell craft beer or improve the public's health.

PURPOSE AND OBJECTIVES OF THIS BOOK

Brands build relationships between consumers and products, services, or lifestyles by providing beneficial exchanges and adding value to their objects. Brands can be measured through associations that consumers hold for products and services. Through brand promotion, these associations can become established and lead to a long-term relationship between the product or service and consumer. But what are brand associations, and through what psychological processes are they formed? What are the relative contributions of emotions, rationality, personal characteristics, our environments, our brains to forming brand associations? How do our brand associations influence our social interactions and communities? This book asks and explores answers to these questions.

Audience

The primary audience for the book will be business and not-for-profit professionals, marketers, psychologists and behavioral economists, health communicators and social marketers, and researchers working in these fields. The intended audience is professionals who design and execute commercial brands, and those who design and study social and health behavior change programs. It will also be a useful book for advanced (post-graduate level) courses in these fields.

Additionally, the book will be of interest to business professionals and commercial marketers interested in "cause marketing" (i.e., marketing to promote socially beneficial causes), corporate responsibility, and business philanthropy. If the reader already has commercial marketing knowledge, then the book will help in understanding consumer psychology and responses to marketing. It will demonstrate how knowledge about branding products like cigarettes, automobiles, or shoes can be applied to branding social and health behaviors like making sound financial decisions, responsible driving, or safer sex - and the ways in which branding strategies can be adapted to these ends. It will also address challenging questions about marketing and corporate responsibility. How do consumers respond to brands that seek to build reputations as responsible actors? What is the psychology of corporate social responsibility marketing?

Scope

The book will review and clarify the psychological constructs underlying branding, brand development and identification, and the higher order concept of brand equity. Several chapters explore emotional response to branding, including the full range of positive and negative emotional motivators from fear and guilt to joy and love. The relative contributions of rational argument – roughly the functional benefits of a brand in relation to other choices and competitors – are compared to emotional appeals – the social and emotional benefits of a brand and its contributions to other psychological wants and needs of the individual. Authors discuss constructs from social and personality psychology, such as individuals' need for social recognition and uniqueness, and these discussions in turn lead proposed conceptual models of brand psychology. Neural mechanisms of response to emotional appeals and rational brand arguments are examined in experimental work and possibly explanations of brain processing of brand stimulus are proposed.

Case studies will cover a wide range of topics in commercial product and service marketing, as well as social and health topics to demonstrate the wide application of branding and power of brand psychology. The book includes examples from around the world, including brand marketing activities in Europe, the U.S., and other parts of the developed world, as well as South Asia, Africa and other parts of the developing world. These cases demonstrate the many and varied social, economic, and cultural contexts that affect the psychology of branding and research in the field.

Major Themes

There are several major themes that emerge for us from reflections on commercial and social and health branding. The remainder of this volume addresses these themes in the context of underlying theory and case studies of specific branded health campaigns. Many of these themes converge and overlap, and each of the specific chapters have attempt to identify these convergences and their potential significance for future public health brands and research on their effectiveness.

The book is organized into two parts reflecting the current state of research in the psychology of branding. Part I focuses on consumer brand psychology, including the basic concepts of branding, strategies for commercial branding, principles for consumer engagement, and theories of exposure, messaging, marketing, and choice that are typically used to develop and promote brands, and the neuropsychology of branding. Case studies examine experimental work on neural brand response, emotional brand appeals, and cases of product and service branding in the developing world. Part II focuses on social and health brand psychology. This section describes the distinctive characteristics of branding behavior and social and health behavioral choice. Case studies examine major brands in drug abuse prevention, water and sanitation, tobacco control, nutrition and physical activity, HIV/AIDS, and other topics.

In part I, which focuses on consumer brand psychology, we identify the following major themes:

Consumer Engagement. In Chapter 1, Bobby J. Calder describes the basic principles of consumer engagement in brand marketing. He explores the basis of brand marketing in the psychology and evolution of decision making from system 1 to system 2 thinking made popular by Nobel Laureate Daniel Kahneman and colleagues. He compares and contrasts consumer engagement strategies based on functional, emotional and social benefits in the context of system 1 and system 2 thinking.

In Chapter 2, Monique M. Turner, explores the emotional appeals used by brands to build consumer engagement. She describes how emotions can be communicted alongside of functional/utilitarian traits of social issues and products and the effects of emotions on cogntive processing. In the context of the Cognitive-Functional Model of cognitive processing, Turner describes what emotions are, what emotional branding is, and how emotions may be communicated through brand marketing to influence consumer decision making.

Consumer experience and interaction with brands. Chapters 3-5 examine consumer brand experience and the foundations of personal connection and affiliation with brands. Chapter 3, by Sandra Loureiro, discusses these concepts in connection with consumer brand love and positive emotions, and the willingness to give something up, to sacrifice, in terms of time, money or other currency. She proposes a model for explaining how connectedness to a brand can lead consumers to sacrifice. Chapter 4, by Rodoula Tsiotsou and Ronald Goldsmith, discuss the role of the community of consumers in building and maintaining a brand. They propose a model of branding strategy that features two actors, the managers on the selling side and the consumers on the buying side and discuss the relative roles and contributions of each side. Chapter 5, by Ronald Goldsmith and Barbara Lafferty, proposes a brand alliance model and describes how these alliances change consumer attitudes and purchase intentions. They also explore the psychological processes consumers go through in evaluating alliances and suggest implications for the future.

Global Branding. Part I concludes with two chapters related to branding in diverse global settings. In chapter 6, Diallo Mbaye describes retail branding issues in developing countries. He focuses on the internationalization of retail branding and its integration into emerging economies. He identifies innovation opportunities for retail brands in developing countries and areas for future research. In chapter 7, Mei-chun Cheung, Yvonne M. Han, Agnes S. Chan, and Sophia L. Sze describe issues of brand name recognition when brands move from their home to global markets. Then they describe three experiments to examine the behavioral responses and neural mechanisms triggered by brand names to yield new insights into how such names are processed by consumers. They suggest future research on behavioral and neural responses to brands and implications for global branding.

In part II, which focuses on social and health brand psychology, we identify the following major themes:

Setting an agenda for social and health branding. In Chapter 8, W. Douglas Evans discusses the theory of social and health branding, the concept of behavioral branding, provides case examples in which social and health brands have been built on theory, and lays out an education and research agenda for the field. Social and health branding represents an evolution in behavioral theory with significant potential to advance programs designed to promote health and improve society. In Chapter 9, Alec Ulasevich, describes a key concept underlying the theory of social and health branding – competition between behavioral alternatives. He describes the concept of competition as it applies to social and health branding and provides case examples.

Cases of social and health brands in diverse community settings. In Chapter 10, Steven Chapman, James Ayers, Olivier LeTouzé and Benoit Renard discuss the psychology of branding in socially marketed product brands in the developing world. They describe the process of brand creation in these settings, which often involve brands targeted to audiences who are not targets of commercial branding. This chapter describes that process beginning with audience insight and ending with evaluation. In Chapter 11, Michael Hecht and Jeong Kyu Lee discuss the co-branding of the *keepin' it REAL* and D.A.R.E. America drug abuse prevention programs and how this effort evolved into a true brand alliance. They examine how brand alliances can create compelling sales points and build positive brand images/identities in the context of substance use prevention. They suggest implications for future social and health brand alliances. In Chapter 12, Nicholas Goodwin defines and describes the concept of a brand community, and notes that building brand communities will help ensure the success of social and health brands. He examines the global evidence and experience of brand communities in both the commercial and public sectors. He discusses traditional approaches to branding, marketing and communications, then addresses the disruption caused by new technologies and ideas.

PART 1: CONSUMER BRAND PSYCHOLOGY

In: Psychology of Branding
Editor: W. Douglas Evans

ISBN: 978-1-62618-817-4
© 2013 Nova Science Publishers, Inc.

Chapter 1

BRANDING AND THE PSYCHOLOGY OF CONSUMER BEHAVIOR

Bobby J. Calder[*]

Northwestern University, Evanston, Illinois, US

ABSTRACT

Branding is traditionally thought of in terms of high consumer involevment. Persuasive messages are used to influence consumers to think about a product in a conscious, deliberative way. The psychological rationale for this Sys2 branding is developed here. An understanding of this psychology also leads to a strategic alternative to the conventional marketing approach, Sys1 branding.

Keywords: Marketing, System 1, System 2, involvement, influence

INTRODUCTION

What is there to understand about consumer behavior? Someone is offered a product and either chooses to buy it or not to buy it. Their behavior is all that matters. Indeed this is the standard economic view of markets. People's choices reveal their preferences and these preferences predict their subsequent behavior. There is no need to consider why the consumer makes a choice or what goes on inside their heads (Gul and Pesendorfer, 2008). Suppose a company develops a new food product that has very high nutritional value but can be produced at a price that is very affordable even to low income consumers. According to the economic view, consumers will choose to buy the product or not, revealing their preference.

There is of course another point-of-view. Based on an understanding of how consumers think about products, you can employ marketing to influence the consumer. You can turn the product into a brand. Even if the new high-nutrition food product is initially rejected by

---

[*] Kellogg School of Management, Northwestern University, Evanston, Illinois 60201 USA. Email: calder@northwestern.edu

consumers, you can launch a marketing intervention that changes the consumer's thinking and leads to acceptance. This chapter presents a model for understanding consumer behavior in this way, as a way of guiding marketing decisions. Specifically, it shows how two different approaches to branding have a basis in consumer psychology.

APPROACH-AVOIDANCE

Whenever an individual encounters an object (say a product) he or she will be motivated to either approach, move toward, the object or to avoid, move away, from it. And, as formulated by the psychologist Kurt Lewin (1935), often there will be conflict between the two that must be resolved in favor of one or the other.

The most common psychological explanation of *approach-avoidance*, though it has taken many forms, is *hedonism*. People approach things to the extent that they give pleasure and avoid things to the extent that they are painful. A truly ancient idea, hedonism took its modern shape in the eighteenth century writing of Jeremy Bentham, who referred to pleasure and pain as the two masters of all that we do. Pleasure may be construed narrowly around sensory experience, as in food that tastes good, or more generally as feeling positive affect.

Today it is possible to give both a neuroscience and a cognitive account of hedonism. The former refers to actual brain mechanisms, the latter to psychological descriptions of mental processes. These are two different levels of analysis (as with physics and chemistry).

The Neuroscience of Hedonism

The brain has many localized areas of specialization, connected together, as *circuits*, to accomplish certain things. These circuits are part of larger patterns of interconnection throughout the brain. The most important dimension of this connectivity is from bottom (ventral) to top (dorsal), where the former tends to be concerned with processing classifications (such as properties of objects) and the later with evaluating expectatons (Borst, Thompson, and Kosslyn, 2011).

Interestingly, many important circuits are ventral and lie below the neocortex, which is the outer surface of the brain that is phylogenetically newer in that it is responsible for higher-order processes that exist only in mammals, and especially humans, that evolved later than other species. In fact *sensory* processing originates deep in the brain. Taste receptors for instance result in the transduction of external energy into bioelectric signals and connect to an area of the brain stem called the nucleus of the solitrary tract located in the medulla which in turn projects to an area of the thalmus which is the gateway to the neocortex and functions as a less fine-grained control center than the neocortex. The implication of this is that we have no direct consciousness of pure sensation. We cannot actually describe what something actually tastes like. Nor does a sensation have any inherent hedonic value. Sensory information is interpreted by higher levels of processing that leads to *perceptions* about what something will be like.

Marketers concerned with product design often try to describe sensory effects by seeking to reduce the impact of higher-order perception (Meilgaard, Carr, and Civille, 2006). A common technique is to expose people to a product in controled circumstances where they receive as little non-sensory information as possbile. They may for instance taste a sample of product "blind," without being told anything about it. Special pannels of people are trained to use a basic vocabuary to describe the product with words that do not reflect perceptual interpretations. With wine a pannelist might describe a sample as having more body (mouthfeel) or even as "chalky" but would not be allowed to use obviously perceptual words like "honest." Honest might well be a perception but not a description of actual taste. Even chalky is dubious in that the person is unlikely to really be familiar with the taste of chalk. Nonetheless, such techniques are a tool for relating physical variables to sensory reactions, but only a rough tool. The fact is that pure sensory registration occurs deep in the brain and is then given meaning and value by higher levels.

So, again, no sensation is inherently rewarding in that pleasure comes directly from the object itself. As Berridge and Kringlebach (2011) put it, "Pleasure in never merely a sensation, even for sensory pleasures (p.3). In point of fact there is an endogenous reward system in the brain. It too originates at a subcortical level, neuroanotomically as a subset of nuclei (collections of neurons such as the neucleus accumbens) and pathways in the larger mega-limbic system regulating among other things emotion and learning. It is composed of a number of "hotspots" that when collectively activated make an object rewarding. Biochemically dopamine was thought to be the major neurotransmitter. Recent evidence from rat studies, however, indicates that two diffierent circuits are at work (Smith, Mahler, Pecina, and Berridge, 2010). Dopamine now appears to be central to a circuit that produces *wanting* for an object, an anticipation of pleasure that can rise to the level of craving. It causes motivation and increases the incentive salience of an object. Another circuit relies on opioid neurotransmition and produces *liking*. It causes the warm feeling of pleasure. Wanting is the desire for something, liking is the actual enjoyment of it. Wanting and liking are distinct processes that typically operate together but in principle can function at different levels of activation. It is thought that addictions may be cases where wanting is high even though an object may no longer be liked.

Thus the brain has the specialized capacity to apply a hedonic gloss to some things, resulting in approach or avoidance. This occurs unconciously at a subcortical level and besides wanting and liking also involves learning about what liked things are like. These subcortical circuits connect to higher brain levels such as the orbitfrontal (above the eyes) cortex and people certainly experience liking and wanting consciously. These neocortical regions can influence what is liked. But the basic process appears to have been conserved with evolution and should not be thought of as necessarily a manifestation of uniquely human higher capacities.

The Psychology of Hedonism

From a psychological point of view the most important idea is that of dual-process. The idea that the mind can be divided into parts is ancient (e. g. Plato's reason, spirit, and appetite). The current understanding that has emerged from several different areas of pyschology is that basically there are two processes at work- one might be called *System 1*, the other *System 2*. These terms have been popularized by the Nobel Laureate Daniel Kahneman (2011; Kahneman and Frederick, 2002), but many other labels have been used.

System 1

System 1 is evolutionary older than System 2. It allows for automatic control of behavior and operates fast. When an animal sees a snake and reflexively moves to avoid it, this is System 1 at work. System 1 operates via associations to *cues* in any given context. It's capabilities do not vary much across individuals and does not reflect general intelligence Stanovich (1999). Sytem 1 is, however, very smart in that it is highly adaptive. It allows the processing of large amounts of information in a parallel, versus sequential, manner. Its strength is thus speed and capacity. We would otherwise be overwhelmed by the shere amount of information in any context. As Kahneman emphasizes, System 1 is not only efficient but effortless in that it operates automatically. Since the brain uses a disproportionate share of the body's energy resources, this is thought to be a major advantage of System 1 thinking.

Over the last three decades psychologists have many studies of what is called "priming" to investigate the effect of cues. In a priming study people are exposed to a cue, which they may or may not be consciously aware of, say a word such as EAT. The word serves as cue that affects subsequent reactions by virtue of its associations. In one study, for instance, people were exposed to either a smiling or a scowling face and viewed Chinese ideographs. They liked the ideographs better if they had been primied with the smiling face (Murphy and Zajonc, 1993). Note that this is not persuasion in the classical sense of argumenation (Greenwald, 1992). Indeed there is evidence that exposing people to a sentence ENEMY LOSES, which is positive, has the same effect as the negative individual words (Greenwald and Liu, 1985). People do not process it as a sentence.

Priming can even affect peoples' behavior in a very direct way. One well-known study presented people with sets of words in scrabled order from which they had to assemble meaningful sentences (Bargh, Chen and Burrows, 1996). Although people showed no awareness of this, the word sets contained, for some people but not others, one word associated with being older (e.g., Florida). After the word task, the time it took the people to walk a certain distance was unobtrusively measured. The people who had been exposed to the cues associated with older people moved more slowly than those who had not. The cues primed their behavior. Likewise our own behavior can act as associative cues.

The effects of priming cues can seem trivial and momentary, and they can be, but it should be remembered that they reflect the fundamental way that System 1 operates. A complex network of associations is continuously being activated by cues, many of which are consistently present in commonly encountered situations. Think vegetables at the front of the supermarket. Such associations guide our behavior unconsciously, without any apparent effort. The supermarket seems a healthier place. And if I buy the candy, it is not as unhealthy as it might be. System 1 in fact is sensitive to this very "ease" or "fluency" and uses it as a cue. If one has been exposed to something like a name in the past, even if this is not remembered, when the name is encountered again it is associated with familiarity (ease) and this can itself cue other associations- it must be an important name (Jacoby, Kelley, Brown, Jasechko, 1989). Hence, it is entirely explicable that sales of the Chinese brand "Xi Jiu" (a white alcolol spirit called "baijiu") spiked with the rise of President Xi Jinping. The Chinese character for "Xi" is the same ideograph as the president's surname.

Though it operates outside of our conscious awareness, System 1 is the default mechanism influencing approach-avoidance. Much as this might seem counterintuitive, the evolutionary rationale for why this might be so is quite plausible.

System 2

A stock example of the way System 2 operates is simply to imagine yourself carrying out the following task: $25529 + 822791/ 392 - 39$. Our thinking here is sequential and rule based, requiring conscious control (not to mention paper and pencil). It is linked to general intelligence and makes use of *working memory*, which allows us to hold and focus on information for a period of time while it is being operated on. Working memory is limited in the breadth of its capacity in that it can hold only something like four or five units of information at a given level of abstraction (e. g., comparing the overall styling of different automobiles or the price-feature tradeoffs of different washing machines). It can process information at greater depth using sublevels of the high level units. Information can thus be elaborated in depth but the breath of processing is quite limited. There is furthermore a tradeoff between capacity and the amount of time information is held.

As can be seen from the above consensus overview, System 2 is highly effortful compared to System 1. It processes information is a way that System 1 does not. It focuses attention deliberatively on a small amount of information. In one cute study, for which web videos are poplular, people were asked to watch a group of people in front of an elevator who are passing a ball back and forth (Chabris and Simons, 2009). They were asked to figure the rules of the game the people were playing. At a point during the game the elevator doors open and a gorilla emerges, actually a person in a costume, and thumps its chest. Remarkably many people do not even notice the gorilla in the room. The study makes the point of just how focused System 2 processing can be, even to the point of glaring inattention to things in the situation, in the service of deliberately thinking about something.

We began by noting Kurt Lewin's observation that often there will be a conflict between approach and avoidance that must be resolved in favor of one or the other. Enter System 2. It excells at holding conflicting ideas at the same time and attempting to resolve differences in a systematic way. In other words it can evaluate alternatives. It does this based not only on paying focused attention to relevant incoming information but on retrieving previously formed associations. Associations that become conscious and available for System 2 processing might best be termed *beliefs*. These are the explicit thoughts one has about something while resolving an approach-avoidance conflict.

It appears that System 2 is able to resolve problems that System 1 is not equipped to deal with, a novel situation in which associations are scarce, or a situation in which it is not possible to easily integrate a pattern of cues (such that conflicting responses are activated). In turn, there is considerable evidence that System 2 acts to avoid effortful processing if possible so that once a conflict is resolved it is returned to System 1 automatic control. This is the basis for *habits* (Neal, Wood, and Quinn, 2006). Behavior is not so much goal-directed but routinized in chunks cued directly from the situation. Motivation comes from the context itself and behavior is repeated over time in a mindless way, even if the original System 2 goal is devalued.

One study sited by the Neal et al. is quite illustrative of the relationship between Systems 1 and 2. It looked at college students' frequency of purchasing fast food. It found that students who had a weak to moderate habit of eating fast food, but consciously intended to purchase fast food (System 2), bought more fast food. But students with a strong habit of fast food bought it regardless of their intentions- System 1 at work. In general System 2 is goal directed, and it also regulates behavior to avoid undesirable goals. As with all System 2 processes goal self-regulation is effortful and the resources needed for it can become depleted if this effort is expended at a high level over time (Baumeister and Tierney, 2011).

Comparing the Neuroscience and Psychological Accounts

Although two different levels of explanation are involed, it should be apparent that the two accounts of hedonism offer a potentially complementary picture. While the goal is not premature reductionism, the picture that emerges is that System 2 evolved much later than System 1 with its realization in subcortical circuits. Evolution literally layered System 2 on top of System 1, an adaptation that led to greater ability to control behavior and thereby create more complex environments (Damasio, 2010). Nonetheless System 1 continues to be important for maintaining approach-avoidance behaviors. System 2 intervenes as necessary. While we are nowhere near a compelling account of consciousness per se, behavior can only be understood in terms of both types of processes.

INFLUENCE

Historically social psychology is the branch of psychology that has dealt the most with how peoples' behavior can be influenced given the two types of processes at work. The indispensable construct in this work has been that of *attitude*. Conceived early on (Allport, 1935) as a "mental and neural state of readiness," most researchers today would probably consider it synonymous with "liking" or "evaluating something favorably or unfavorably." The term attitude is useful however in pointing up that we are talking about a theoretical construct that is part of a psychological process involved in resolving approach-avoidance conflicts. As such it is different from a questionnaire rating. An attitude is a disposition to respond that has been created through System 2 deliberation. A disposition that may well be returned to System 1 in the form of an implicit, as opposed to explicit, attitude that via cued associations can guide behavior unconsciously.

Attitudes thus provide a useful target for those seeking to influence people. Influence becomes a matter of changing peoples' attitudes. Much of the early work on attitudes looked at the effects of many variables related to the construction of persuasive messages on attitude change. The effects studied included things like whether one-sided or two-sided messages were used, or differences in the number of arguments in a message. As this work progressed it was realized that attitude change also needed to be understood in terms of how the beliefs, or thoughts, leading to an attitude were processed to create attitude change. At this point a number of comprehensive theories emerged that also included the potential for unconscious System 1 change.

It is instructive to review some of these theories. Petty and Cacioppo (1981) proposed the "Elaboration Likelihood Model" (ELM) in which persuasive messages are processed more through a "central" route or more through a "peripheral" route. With the former people attend to the arguments in the message and enlarge on them with their own thoughts or beliefs. Message elaboration is high. With the later people attend to cues such as the source of the message that are peripheral to the message arguments and do not think as much about the message per se (and do not notice whether the arguments are strong or weak). Message elaboration is low. Which of the two paths to influence occurs depends on a person's ability and motivation. If the personal relevance of the message is low or the person is distracted influence will more likely occur from the processing of peripheral cues. If an individual has a higher appetite for information, need for cognition, than others, the person will be more likely to process the message. Cues may have an impact even with high elaboration, but they will be processed in a more thoughtful, less automatic way.

Chaiken (1980) proposed that people ordinarily process a message in terms of "heuristics," which essentially means by association to cues. But given time, motivation, and capacity, they can engage in effortful "systematic" processing of the messages arguments. If people lack confidence in their attitude, systematic processing will be more likely. Thus heuristic processing is the base line with systematic added if increased effort is possible and justified by lack of confidence in an existing attitude.

Further theorizing (Smith and DeCoster, 2000; Stack and Deutsch, 2004) posits that influence can occur through "associative" processing such that cues trigger unconscious affect-ladden associations that in effect become a message in itself. Previous behaviors can even become "embodied" cues that affect behavior. Such processing occurs without a person's awareness. Influence can also happen through "rule-based" processing which is analytical and effortful. Associative processing is more impulsive, rule-based processing is more reflective. Not only can each type of processing affect behavior, but they also compete with each other, so that the two types of precessing can be opposed to each other.

More recently, Gawronski and Budenhausen (2006) distinguished between "propositional" evaluations concerned with the active validation of beliefs, resulting in an explicit attitude, and "associative" evaluations based on passively cued activation of a network of associations, independent of any assessment of truth or falsity, resulting in an implicit attitude. The two types of attitudes can affect each other, there is interplay between the two processes, and people have some conscious awareness of their implicit attitudes. To the extent that something is encountered in varying contexts, implict attitudes may not be very stable. Both types can be differentially affected by cues and messages.

Though developed largely independently, taken together the above theories suggest how to approach the question of influence from a System 1/System 2 perspective. There are two paths to persuasion. One is to present people with strong arguments designed to get them to use System 2 to actively reason about the information in the message and to retrieve their own related beliefs into working memory. The other, equally valid, path is to focus on the context of the influence attempt to identify cues that can be introduced into it that lead to associations that affect behavior unconsciously through System 1. The first path may seem obvious but consider the psychological account of it developed here. Relying more on System 2 is not something that people automatically do. Using System 2 to scrutinize arguments is effortful. The person has to be motivated and involved in order for System 2 resources to be committed. If they are not, or the person is already confident in their attitude, the balance will shift toward the default of System 1 processing. In this case influence via the System 1 path may make more sense (despite the seeming obviousness of using persuasive arguments). And it may be that even if System 2 is active, System 1 may also be active so that it potentially competes with System 2.

Suppose, for example, that a car rental company wanted to market their services to consumers. They might obviously use advertising messages to convey that they are the biggest rental company, with the biggest fleet, with the most variety of automobiles, and so on. And renting automobiles may be important enough for frequent business renters that their consumers will process messages using the System 2 path. But what about infrequent, non-business renters? They may not expend the cognitive resources to process the messages in this way no matter how clever or creative the advertising is. A better approach for this target consumer would be to look for cues that could influence System 1 processing. Designing the rental locations and materials around the color yellow could be such a cue. Using yellow as a cue would influence people if they associated yellow with taxis and taxis with the most common way of paying to use a car.

SYS2 AND SYS1 BRANDING

Marketers traditionally have thought about branding along the following lines. Branding is a matter of persuading target consumers to think about your product positively. Mere awareness of the product is not enough. Consumers must know about the product and have feelings about it. You have to convince the consumer that your product produces a meaningful benefit, that it satisfies a goal. And convince them that your product is in this respect different from competitive products. To do this you first focus on a key attribute or feature of the product that is most important or visible to the consumer. Marketing activities, including advertising messages, are used to influence the consumer's thinking about this attribute. At a minimum it is necessary that the consumer understands and accepts the functional benefit of the key attribute. The functional benefit is the critical thing that the product does for the consumer. But ideally the consumer should feel an emotional connection to the product on top of this cognitive understanding. And the ultimate objective on top of this is to get the consumer to see a connection to their self-concept as an expression of who they are as a person. To use a stock example, Harley-Davidson is a great brand because the company has convinced older men that, whereas other bikes are merely wellmade, the rumble of the Harley engine means the power to feel freedom and a sense of belonging to a group that rebels against the confines of ordinary life. In the parlance of marketing, the brand has laddered-up from the functional to the emotional to the social benefit of buying a Harley. In short, a great example of Sys2 branding, with probably some Sys1 branding around unconscious associations to the rumble and other accoutrements such as the biker clothing.

Another contrast between the balance of Sys1 and Sys2 branding is the marketing for the package delivery service UPS. An objective of the company has been to attract a wide variety of consumers, to be an automatic choice, chosen without any more thought than using a public service such as the postal service or even the police. Hence the use of the color brown for trucks, uniforms, and materials- associations to basic, grounded, routine, public service. And in the recent past advertising was intended not so much to persuade as to cue these associations with a television spokesperson who was obviously not a TV personality drawing simple diagrams of routes on a whiteboard with a brown marker. Print ads that showed the same diagrams. A logo in the form of an official seal, a brown shield. The slogan- "What can Brown do for you today?"

Marketing in the form of cues, rather than strong persuasive arguments, designed to elicit intended associations with little if any conscious reflection. More recently this Sys1 branding campaign has been followed by Sys2 branding, a campaign more narrowly targeted at business customers. The messages contain information about UPS's expertise and passion for logistic as a technical business discipline.

As another striking example of Sys1 branding consider the Tiffany brand. Older consumers already have positive attitudes toward the brand. Marketing needs to provide cues that trigger unreflective habit. How powerful is the Tiffany blue box and the vault like stores with their associations to luxury, pride, taste, and appreciation? The box can be saved and passed down to children, a gift in the same box it originated in, timeless, another association. Ads feature not just specific merchandise but cues- each day a Tiffany's ad is on the top right of page three of the New York Times. Price? Another cue. Younger consumers are primed with the cues over time.

Let's return to the company that has a new food product that has very high nutritional value but can be produced at a price that is very affordable even to low income consumers. The product is high in protein, but maybe it is not palatable.

Fortunately, blind sensory taste tests indicate that this is not the case- the product is good for you and tastes good. So Guten is introduced in Mexico with the obvious Sys2 marketing- great price, great taste. It dramatically fails. Research reveals that consumers believe that the product tastes bad, it is nothing like real meat. How could this be? Remember that sensory input has no intrinsic value, it is colored by the reward system and beliefs. Subsequent research showed that consumers believed that, whereas it was important traditionally to the family for the mother to cook in order to have "family time," mothers' now felt that they did not want to cook everyday because of the expense and time involved. Guten was rejected as a poor substitute for traditonal cooking that did not have the advantage of prepared foods, even though in fact it was already cooked and only needed to be heated. Given this attitude, people thought it tasted bad as well.

The company was faced with two marketing alternatives. Persuade consumers that Guten was the solution to traditional cooking without the disadvantages of time and expense. Sys2 branding. Or face the fact that consumers did not want to think about the product, let alone figure out its benefit.

The solution: Package the product as a prepared food in a variety of forms, Fajitas, Picadillo, Cortadillo, Fajitas en Salsa Verde, Fahitas en Salsa Tiaquepaque. The packaged form cueing time saving and reduced work. The price cued inexpensive prepared food (not cheap, fake traditonal food). Using older women in the community to demonstrate the product cued another association- socially acceptable. Another cue associating the product with acceptable change took the form of a purchase reward program supporting local schools, "Apoya a la comunidad." Sys1 branding created a successful product.

THE FUTURE OF BRANDING

Marketers, either of commercial products or socially innovative products, have long faced a dilemma. An attractive strategy, indeed the best practice, is to use persuasive messaging to build a brand, which can lead to a customer base with positive attitudes toward the brand and even habitual usage. But this Sys2 branding strategy often is very difficult. It requires high involvement on the part of consumers. Such involvement is an objective of the strategy but it is not necessarily obtainable. In many cases low involvement is difficult to overcome. Traditional advertising is a waste of resources, but is viewed as the only alternative to doing nothing.

This dilemma is only exacerbated by increasing market competition and the growing difficulty of reaching consumers with persuasive messages. Organizations feel the need to create even stronger brands. Often the objective now is brands that engage consumers beyond even meaningful product benefits, brands that connect with important life goals (Calder, 2008; Calder, Isaac, Malthouse, 2013). Engagement goes beyond hedonism to even larger questions of meaning. If achievable, such engagement is a highly desirable objective. But the fact remains that any Sys2 branding effort requires consumer involvement that may not be forthcoming and that may run counter to consumer psychology.

Marketing needs greater realization of Sys1 branding and acceptance of it as a valid marketing strategy rooted in consumer psychology. This is not a question of below-the-line tactics. Sys1 branding and Sys2 branding should be viewed as major strategic alternatives.

REFERENCES

Bargh, J., Chen, M. and Burrows, L. (1996). Automaticity of social behavior : Direct effects of trait construct and stereotype activaton on action. *Journal of personality and social psychology,* 71, 230-244.

Bausmeister, R. and Tierney, J. *Willpower.* New York : Penguin.

Berridge, K., and Kringelbach, M., (2011). *Building a neuroscience of pleasure and well-being. Psychology of well-being: Theory, research, and practice*, 3, 1-29.

Borst, G., Thompson, W., Kosslyn, S., (2011). Understanding the dorsal and ventral systems of the human cortex. *American psychologist,* 66, 624-632.

Chabris, C. and Simons, D., (2009), The invisible gorilla. New York : Crown.

Calder, B. (2008). *Kellogg on advertsing and media.* New York : Wiley.

Calder, B., Isaac, M., and Malthouse, E., (2013). *Taking the customer's point of view : Engagement or satisfaction.* Cambridge, MA: Marketing Science Institute.

Chaiken, S., (1980). Heuristic versus systematic information processing and the use of source versus message cue in persuaton. *Journal of personality and social psychology*, 39, 752-766.

Damasio, A. (2010). *Self comes to mind : Constructing the conscious brain.* New York : Pantheon.

Gawronski, B. and Bodenhausen, G., (2006). Associative and propositional processes in evaluation : An intergrative review of implicit and explicit attitude change. Psychological review, 132, 692-731.

Greenwald, A. (1992). Unconscous cognition reclaimed. *American psychologist*, 47, 766-779.

Greenwald, A. and Liu, T. (1085). Limited unconscious processing of meaning (abstract). *Bulletin of the psychonomic society*, 23, 292.

Gul, F., and Pesendorfer, W., (2008). The case for mindless economics. In A. Caplin and A. Schotter (Eds.), *The foundations of positive and normative economics* (pp. 3-41). New York: Oxford University Press.

Kahneman, D. (2011). Thinking fast and slow. New York: Farrar, Straus, Giroux.

Kahneman, D. and Frederick, S. (2002). Representativeness revisited : Attribute substitution in intuitive judgement. In T. Gilovich, D. Griffin, and D. Kahneman (Eds.), Heuristics and biases. Cambridge : Cambridge University Press.

Jacoby, L., Kelley, C., Brown, J., and Jasechko, J., (1989), Becoming famous overnight : Limits on the ability to avoid unconscious inférences of the past. *Journal of personality and social psychology*, 56, 326-338.

Lewin, K. (1935). *A dynamic theory of personality*. New York : McGraw Hill.

Meilgarrd, M., and Carr, B., Civille, G. *Sensory évaluation techniques*. CRC, 2006.

Murphy, S. and Zajonc, R. (1993). *Affect, cognition and awareness. Affective priming with optimal and suboptimal stimulus exposures,* 64, 723-729.

Neal, D., Wood, W., and Quinn, J. (2006), Habits- a repeat performance. *Current directions in pyshcological science,* 15, 198-202.

Petty, R. and Cacioppo, J., (1981). *Attitudes and persuasion*. Dubuque, IW : Brown.

Smith, E. and DeCoster, J., (2000). Dual-process models in in social and cognitive psychology : Conceptual intégration and links to underlying memory systems. *Personality and social pyschology review*, 4, 108-131.

Smith, K., Mahler, S., Pecina, S., and Berridge, K., (2010). In M. Kringelbach and K. Berridge (Eds.), *Pleasures of the brain* (pp 27-49). New York : Oxford University Press.

Stanovich, K., (1999). Who is rational? Studies of individual différences in reasoning. Mahwah, NJ: Lawrence Elrbaum.

Strack, E. and Deutsch, R., (2004). Reflective and impulsive déterminants of social behavior. *Personality and social psychology review*, 8, 220-247.

In: Psychology of Branding
Editor: W. Douglas Evans

ISBN: 978-1-62618-817-4
© 2013 Nova Science Publishers, Inc.

Chapter 2

EMOTIONAL BRANDING: WHAT, WHEN, AND WHY

Monique Mitchell Turner[*]
The George Washington University
School of Public Health and Health Services
Department of Prevention and Community Health, Washington, DC, US

ABSTRACT

The effects of, and importance of, emotional branding how long been documented and touted by marketing professionals. Yet, it is still the case that that marketers pitch emotional branding as "in lieu of" functional branding. Likewise, emotional processing of marketing products and messages is pitched as "in lieu of" cognitive processing. In this chapter I will clarify that emotions can be communicated alongside of functional/utilitarian traits of issues and products. I will also clarify the research on the effects of emotions on cognitive processing. As such, I address what emotions are, what emotional branding is, how emotions are communicated via marketing materials and the impact of emotions on cognitive processing.

Appraisal theorists maintain that all emotions are initiated by individuals' appraisal of, in this case, brand positions as they relate to personal well-being and the things that are most cared about, and that these appraisals affect the consequences of emotions (Parrot, 2004). Arnold explained "to arouse an emotion, the object must be appraised as affecting me in some way, affecting me personally as an individual with my particular experience and my particular aims" (1960, p. 171). A message or event triggers a particular predominant emotion which in turn affects the response to the stimulus.

Emotional branding is "a consumer-centric, relational and story-driven approach to forging deep and enduring affective bonds between consumers and brands (Thompson, Rindfleisch, and Zeynep, 2006). Lynch and de Chernatony argued that brands based on emotive traits such as trust, reassurance, reputation or image are seen as more durable and less likely to suffer from competitive erosion (2004).

It is clear that emotions may be infused into brands based on their underlying appraisal patterns being represented and thus frame audience processing. How such emotions actually influence message processing direction and depth is addressed by the Cognitive-Functional Model (CFM; figure 1). The CFM is based on the premise that the

---

[*] 2175 K Street NW, Suite 700, Washington DC, 20037. Email: mmturner@gwu.edu

effects of messages are mediated by cognition (Chaiken, 1980; Petty and Cacioppo, 1986). The emotion induced by a message will guide the depth and direction of message processing. Once emotions are evoked, individuals seek out information in a message to satisfy emotion-relevant goals. Depending on the emotion induced by the message, whether it is an approach or an avoidance emotion, and the presence or absence of reassuring cues in the message, discrete emotions can conditionally trigger systematic or heuristic message (Nabi, 1999, 2002).

Keywords: Emotion, emotion and cognition, social marketing, emotional branding

INTRODUCTION

The effects of, and importance of, emotional branding how long been documented and touted by marketing professionals. Yet, it is still the case that that marketers pitch emtoional branding as "in lieu of" functional branding. Likewise, emotional processing of marketing products and messages is pitched as "in lieu of" cognitive processing. In this chapter I will clarify that emotions can be communicted alongside of functional/utilitarian traits of issues and products. I will also clarify the research on the effects of emotions on cogntive processing. As such, I address what emotions and moods are, what emotional branding is, how emotions are communicated via marketing materials and the impacts of both moods and emotions on cognitive processing of marketing materials.

EMOTIONS AND EMOTIONAL BRANDING

Emotions. Despite the common use of the terms emotion, mood, feeling and affect as synonyms, they should not be treated as such. Each is a distinct, but related, term and they each play a unique role in branding. Affect is the most primitive of the three terms and is often used as an umbrella term (Bagozzi, Gopinath, and Nyer, 1999). Affect has valence (positive, negative) and intensity (weak, strong), but does not have a particular target and thus is less intense and less focused. Mood involves "more or less well-formed set of beliefs about whether, in general, we are likely to experience pleasure or pain -- positive or negative affect -- in the future" (Batson, Shaw and Olson, 1992, p. 299). Moods tend to be longer lasting, more general, and lower intensity (see Mitchell, 2001) than emotions. Emotions, however, are discrete and specific. Emotions have a target and tend to be more intensely experienced than moods (though the intensity depends on what emotion one is experiencing). Emotions are considered to be mental states of readiness triggered by cognitive appraisals of events, have a phenomenological tone that is accompanied by biophysiological changes, are expressed physically in the body, and usually results in actions that are a human's way of coping with the emotion (see Bagozzi et al., 1999). Appraisal theorists believe that emotions are caused by individuals' appraisal of events in the environment as they relate to personal well-being and the things that are most cared about, and that these appraisals affect the consequences of emotions (Parrot, 2004). Emotions are personal--Arnold explained "to arouse an emotion, the object must be appraised as affecting me in some way, affecting me personally as an individual with my particular experience and my particular aims" (1960, p. 171).

As an example, let's take the brand promotion surrounding breast cancer awareness. Let us imagine that I see televised commercial featuring strong women participating in a 60 mile walk to fight breast cancer. The TV commercial shows the women with hands in the air, completing the long walk, hugging each other, and feeling strong. When I see the ad I experience, overall, positive affect. More specifically, it puts me in a positive mood that is of moderate to low intensity and usually lasts the length of the commercial. But, the ad does not cause a specific emotion. Now, imagine that this same TV commercial is viewed by a person who is a breast cancer survivor and who also has completed that 60 mile walk. Such a woman might experience specific and targeted emotions—hope and pride.

Emotional Branding. Unlike the paradigm surrounding traditional marketing, that of "features and benefits" (Schmitt, 1999), emotional branding is "a consumer-centric, relational and story-driven approach to forging deep and enduring affective bonds between consumers and brands (Thompson, Rindfleisch, and Zeynep, 2006). Lynch and de Chernatony argued that brands based on emotive traits such as trust, reassurance, reputation or image are seen as more durable and less likely to suffer from competitive erosion (2004). Brands are about developing emotions *with* the audience (emphasis mine). Utilitarian traits of products may be consistent across the competition—but, emotions may not be, and the most successful brands understand this well. Luther (2006) proposed that the purpose of emotional branding is to "forge strong and meaningful affective bonds witht eh consumers and, in doing so, become a part of their life stories, memories, and an important link in their social networks" (p. 3). Although some have pitted rational and analytical consumers against emotional and sensory consumer against one another—this should not be the relevant comparison. In fact, people are emotional *and* cognitive, and are so at the same time. Later on in this chapter I will discuss the relations between emotions (and moods) and cognitive processing of marketing materials and brands.

Imagine a brochure describing a computer that outlines its features and the benefits of those computer features. The brochure might emphasize the computer's speed, storage capacity, graphics, real-to-life colors, and overall user friendliness. This brochure tells you what you get, that is what benefits you earn, by owning this particular computer. What the computer does not do is build a relationship with you. It does not communicate the *emotional benefits* of owning the computer. In other words, emotional brands also communicate about features and benefits—but, in a different light. Now, imagine an ad for this same computer. This ad reveals a cool, relaxed guy behind the computer putting together a fantastic graphics presentation of his last vacation with his family. You can see he has stored hundreds, maybe thousands of pictures and videos on his computer—but, they are all organized easily. The presentation he has created is vivid to be sure—but, he is also able to put it together easily by simply moving his finger across the trackpad. He leans back, pleased with his awesome creation. He is relaxed, happy, and competent. This latter brand promotion strategy also communicates benefits of a product. But, this is communicated in a sensory way creating an emotional image of what kind of person owns such a computer as well as the emotions experienced by the computer owner. The brand communicated here builds a relationship between the computer and the owner. Indeed, people who use i-mac computers do not say "I own an i-mac"; rather, they say "I am an apple user". The apple company has built such a strong emotional relationship with their consumers that the consumers define themselves by their use. As discussed by Steve Hayden (one apple ad's copywriter), in Wired magazine stated "Macintosh was always bigger than the product...We thought of it as an ideology, a value set...I'm not making this up. Members of the Mac's original engineering and marketing team told me all about it. They did it by building a sense of belonging to an elite club by portraying the Mac as embodying the values of righteous outsiderism and rebellion against injustice. It started in the early '80s with the famous '1984' TV commercial that launched the Mac, and continued with 'The computer for the rest of us' slogan and several ad campaigns playing on a revolutionary theme." (http://www.wired.com/gadgets/mac/commentary/cultofmac/2002/12/56677). This sensory experience is not only communicated in their TV ads. Apple's brand is consistently and effectively communicated within their apple stores, product packages, print materials, product aesthetic design, and etcetera.

Schmitt (1999) argued for five distinct types of emotional experiences that marketers might consider (he calls them strategic emotional experiential modules [SEMs]): sensory experiences (SENSE), affective experiences (FEEL), creative cognitive experiences (THINK), physical experiences, behaviors and lifestyles (ACT), and social-identity experiences (RELATE). Individually, and in combination, these experiences are created through the various people managing a brand to develop strong affective and emotional ties with consumers. Schmitt's implication is that brands should create a mood or feeling. Importantly, mood does have an important effect on how people will cognitive process brands and the attributes of branded products.

A crucial consideration for marketers, when developing their brands, is what emotional or affective experience do they want the consumers to have? This consideration needs to be thoughtful as distinct mood states and emotional states have unique effects on cognitions and behaviors.

THE COGNITIVE EFFECTS OF MOODS AND EMOTIONS

Moods and cognitions. Research in psychology (e.g., Wegener and Petty 1994) and communication (Dillard and Peck, 2000; Mitchell, 2000) shows that mood is relatively easy to create, and is often created via mediated stories and advertisements. Westermann, Spies, Stahl, and Hesse's (1996) research revealed that when moods are generated via film or stories, the resultant moods are felt more intensely. Therefore, moods aroused by media offerings, in which or by which advertisements are received, may be affected by the aroused emotions (see Turner, 2011a). So, when individuals are exposed to brand promotions (via marketing messages) after watching a television comedy, that message will be processed through the lens of an amused person. A very different reaction to the same message may have been evoked when receiving the message after a sad drama. Likewise, brand promotions themselves might create a mood.

Brands often create moods through the strategic use of music, color, and narrative scenes. Based in classical conditioning paradigms, if people are consistently and repeatedly exposed to a brand and mood inducing stimuli, then over time people will experience those feelings when they see the brand—even in the absence of the mood inducing stimuli. Take the GAP brand for example. If I were to watch GAP ads repeatedly (especially in the late 1990's, early 2000's) I would be exposed to visual stimuli of the blue G-A-P letters while listening to up beat jazzy music and watching ethnically and racially diverse beautiful people dance energetically. The music combined with the visuals is aimed at creating a positive, up beat, happy mood. I feel energized and joyful when I watch these ads. Overtime, if I am consistently and repeatedly exposed to these ads, the GAP brand can cause the feeling even in the absence of the commercial.

Brands do not always aim to create a positive emotional experience though. In social marketing (relative to commercial marketing), particularly, there may be times where a negative state is warranted. For example, take the case of drinking and driving. When developing a branded campaign intended to decrease that behavior, it is sensible that the campaign team would want people to experience a negative affective. In fact, of 137 ads regarding drinking and driving that aired between 1987 and 1992, DeJong and Atkin noted that appeals to fear and anger were "frequent themes" (1995, p. 69). But, any type of emotional appeal should only be used with the correct audience, at the correct time, in the correct context, and for the correct reasons.

Moods have a variety of effects on outcomes important to marketing and branding. The influence of moods can first be seen in memory and retrieval of information (Teasdale and Russell, 1983). Studies show that people who recalled information in a positive state retrieved more positive words than those who had learned in a negative or neutral state (Isen et al., 1978). Other studies have also revealed encoding effects caused by mood states (see Bagozzi et al., 1999) where happy people learned more happy facts than they did sad facts. Sad participants learned more sad facts than happy facts (Forgas and Bower, 1987). Interestingly, there may also be mood state dependent learning effects where regardless of the valence of the material being learned (or retrieved) people recall information better when the person is again in that mood state (i.e., if I learned the information while happy I will retrieve it better while happy) (Bower and Cohen, 1982). These aforementioned data seem to indicate a relative advantage for creating a positive affective state with brand communications (e.g., the GAP brand, as mentioned earlier); but, other research indicates that negative states are more likely to cause deeper thinking processes. I turn to this research next.

Studies consistently show a link between mood and persuasion with happy people being more prone to attitude change than those feeling neutral or sad. Galizio and Hendrick (1972) studied the effect of music on attitudes and recall, finding that listening to pleasant music made individuals more persuadible to the recommendations of a persuasive communication. In the 1980s and 1990s, research turned to the moderating role that argument cues might play in the relationship between mood and persuasion. Initial studies found that argument quality has a stronger effect on those in a sad mood than it does on those in a happy mood (Bohner, Chaiken, and Hunyadi, 1994; Worth and Mackie, 1987) indicating that happy people are not "thinkers". This implies that if I see a GAP ad (or experience the brand generally speaking) mentioned earlier, and it ignites a happy mood in the viewers, these viewers might be more easily persuasded regardless of the arguments. In other words, the viewers might not carefully engage arguments (or even think of the arguments) such as "I can buy similar khaki pants for a less expensive price elsewhere." or "I could purchase similar clothes at an outlet store instead of paying full price." Notably, Hullett (2005) reported, through his meta-analysis on the topic of mood and persuasion, that there is a lack of agreement as to why the aforementioned interaction occurs. Thus, most of the discussions in this area of research have centered on the theoretical mechanisms of mood as a moderator of the relationship between argument quality and attitude (see Turner, 2011b for review).

Given the argument that systematic processing requires both the ability (I am informed enough, smart enough, and focused enough to do the thinking) and the motivation (I care enough) to dedicate cognitive resources to the task (from Dual processing models, such as the Elaboration Likelihood Model [Petty and Cacioppo, 1981] and the Heuristic Systematic Model [Chaiken 1980]) Worth and Mackie concluded that a happy mood interferes with individuals' ability to process information systematically. They argued that positive mood activates other concepts to which people have attached positive meaning making it difficult to process other kinds of information (cf. Bower 1981). The explanation was founded on research suggesting that positive affective states increase the accessibility of positive material in memory (Bower, Monteiro, and Gilligan 1978), make positive events seem more likely (Erber 1991), and make people more optimistic (Forgas and Moylan 1987) relative to those in a negative mood (see Bagozzi et al, 1999 for a review of the role of moods and emotions in marketing).

Mackie and Worth's (1989) claim that mood is a distraction interfering with the ability to process a message carefully led them to propose that participants in a positive mood would engage in less systematic processing in limited exposure conditions, but engage in more systematic processing in unlimited exposure (because it increases ability). Although the data were consistent with their predictions, the study's methodology has been subject of criticism (Bohner, Crow, Erb and Schwarz 1992).

To illustrate this theoretical explanation, let us take a new example. Nike ads rarely directly communicate about the features of their running shoes in their ads. In this case, communicating the features would be the arguments to be considered (How does this shoe rate compared to other running shoes?). Rather, they create an emotional experience. The ads show empowered and strong people who "just do it". The ads cause a positive mood in people—general feelings of hope, pride, and strength. Thus, the research I reviewed earlier suggests that the ad causes a positive mood. The positive mood activates other concepts that the viewers have have attached positive meaning to. For me, the ads make me think about my last run, how free and energized I felt. The ads make me recall running track and cross-country in high school and what a wonderful time in my life that was. The ads activate all kinds of attached memories, senses, and feelings. Scholars have suggested that this process makes it difficult for me to process arguments, such as, "other companies sell good shoes also". Thus, while I am in this mood state I may be more persuaded to buy the Nike brand and not even consider the arguments. To make the issue more confusing though, not all scholars agree with this explanation for why a positive mood affects persuasiveness.

As a different explanation, Bohner and colleagues (1992) asserted that persons in a positive mood lack the motivation to process persuasive messages systematically. The lack of motivation hypothesis is also inherent to Schwarz's (1990) feelings-as-information model, asserting that a happy mood informs individuals that the environment is safe and thus reduces their motivation to scrutinize information. In conditions believed to be safe, happy individuals tend to rely on general cognitive structures (e.g., scripts, stereotypes) and to think and act in broad, flexible, creative, and open ways. A negative mood, however, would alert people that a problem has arisen and that they need to be more systematic and attentive. The feelings-as-information model proposes that information processing is tuned to meet situational requirements that are signaled by moods (Clore and Parrott, 1991). Accordingly, moods often become dissociated from their targets and get misattributed to salient features of the situation. Pleasant mood also signals that systematic information processing is unnecessary because no problem awaits solution. A number of studies have explicitly tested the ability versus motivational deficits hypotheses, generally finding that people in positive moods retain their ability to scrutinize persuasive messages but are reduced in their motivations to do so (Bless, Bohner, Schwarz and Strack 1990; Bohner et al. 1992). Smith and Shaffer (1991; and Mitchell et al., 2001) experimentally varied mood, message strength, and outcome involvement to test the hypothesis proposed by Bohner and associates (1992). Their data were partially consistent with the lack of motivation hypothesis and showed that good moods may have disrupted message processing when the message was low in personal relevance, source information preceded the message itself, or subjects were led to believe that their moods were stabilized by a drug. Thus, Smith and Shaffer's (1991) study, as well as Hullett's (2005) meta-analysis of research in this area, are more consistent with the lack of motivation hypothesis of mood effects. So, in this case the Nike ad does not make me unable of considering arguments about other kinds of running shoes. Rather, it makes me unmotivated to do so.

Wegener and Petty's (1994) hedonic contingency model also states that individuals are motivated to achieve and to maintain pleasant moods (Clark and Isen 1982; Smith and Shaffer 1991). Yet, there is an important difference within the hedonic contingency model: The model argues that individuals in pleasant moods scrutinize the mood-altering implications of tasks before investing effort because many tasks are of negative or neutral valence, and therefore threaten their happy state (Wegener and Petty 1994). The hedonic contingency model posits that happy people process tasks expected to be pleasant (and hence not expected to threaten their mood) more systematically than tasks expected to be unpleasant (Wegener, Petty, and Smith 1995). Hedonic contingency proposes that happy people engage in more mood management behaviors than do sad people; one way they may do so is by avoiding processing information that is a "downer," such as counter-attitudinal or depressing topics. However, if communication does not threaten the current pleasant state, happy people would show no such topic avoidance. People in a negative mood, conversely, need not consider the hedonic consequences because they have no pleasant dispositions to maintain. Wegener and Petty (1994) wrote: "Consider a person in a very sad mood. For this person, the range of available activities would be almost entirely more positive (or less negative) than the person's present mood… engagement in almost any activity would tend to make a sad person feel better (and thus more rewarded)" (p. 1035). So, the hedonic consequences of a persuasive message are proposed as an additional moderator of the effect of both, argument strength and mood valence.

My earlier examples were mostly tied to positive mood and emotional states, thus, I will turn to an example of purposefully communicating negative mood states. Imagine a drinking and driving advertisement that begins by showing a car crash caused by a drunk person. A young woman in the other car has died. Ambulances and fire trucks race to the scene. The ad turns to quickly and dramaticly depicting all the life events the woman misses out on because she was killed by a drunk driver. So far, the ad has framed communicated fear and anxiety, sadness and hopelessness. Then, the ad visually reverses all the events and shows the drunk person calling a cab instead. Visually, the ad un-does all of the negative events that were caused and ends by communicating hope that you (the viewer) will make a better decision to not ruin others' lives. What the aforementioned research indicates, first, is that people in negative moods are likely to consider arguments—especially if it takes their mind away from the sadness-causing event. In this case, the viewer carefully considers the arguments toward taking a cab instead of driving after having alcoholic drinks. Because the viewer wants to avoid negative feelings, she will avoid thinking about the negative scene, carefully consider the options, and opt toward the hope revealed at the end of the ad.

In other words, this research explains how emotional branding may affect the ways that people think about the product(s) being marketed. Emotions are inextricably tied to our cognitive processes making us more or less likely to think, recall, and elaborate upon— depending on the positive or negative state that we are experiencing. But, to say that one is feeling "positive" or "negative" is oftentimes too general. Next, I turn to specific emotions that people experience and how that is tied to emotional branding.

Emotion and cognition. Clearly, emotions may be infused into brand promotion stragegies based on the underlying appraisal patterns being represented and thus frame audience processing. Brands, and the marketing products that comprise brands, can affect moods, but, also trigger a particular predominant emotion which in turn affects the response to the brand. There are at least four dimensions that can be communicated through brands (and in any particular message key to the brand) to create a discrete emotion: pleasantness (i.e., valence), control (who has control in a situation, a human or a situation?), responsibility (if a human has control in the situation, was that person you or another person?), certainty (how certain are you of the cause of the event from which the emotion arose from?) (Smith and Ellsworth, 1985). Table 1 includes a breakdown of 8 different emotions and their underlying appraisals. Although brand managers speak of creating "positive" experiences for their consumers, the appraisal tendency view of emotions is much more specific. First, although the overall image of a brand must be positive—the communications surrounding the brand may sometimes involve negative emotions (I'll discuss this further later in the chapter). Second, the pertinent question is not whether to create an emotional experience—this I take to be obvious. The pertinent question is "what kind of emotional experience should be created?"

Brands with distinct emotional flavors have distinct effects on audiences. Nabi's (1999) Cognitive-Functional Model (CFM) explains the effect of discrete emotions on information processing, attitude change, and recall. The CFM predicts that emotion caused by a persuasive message will guide the how deeply individuals will process that message and what information they will pay attention to; individuals will seek out information in the message that satisfies emotion-relevant goals. The CFM also posits that the primary distinction among discrete emotions is whether they are "approach" or "avoidance" emotions which cause different levels of message attention and processing. I talk about the relationship between emotional branding and processing of branded messages subsequently.

How such discrete emotions actually influence message processing direction and depth is addressed by the CFM (Nabi, 1999). The CFM is based on the premise that the effects of emotional messages are mediated by cognition (Chaiken, 1980; Petty and Cacioppo, 1986). The emotion induced by a message will guide the depth and direction of message processing. Once emotions are evoked, individuals seek out information in a message to satisfy emotion-relevant goals. Depending on the emotion induced by the message, whether it is an approach or an avoidance emotion, and the presence or absence of reassuring cues in the message, discrete emotions can conditionally trigger systematic or heuristic processing of the brand (Nabi, 1999, 2002). Nabi (1999) proposed that uncertainty about the inclusion of reassuring information within the message will trigger closer message processing for individuals experiencing avoidance emotions, which would then cause the persuasive outcome to be more dependent on argument quality.

Table 1.

Cognitive Appraisals Leading to Emotions:

Discrete Emotion	Approach/ Avoid — Do we move toward the emotional experience or away from it?	Relational Theme — The thematic experience.	Valence — How pleasant is the emotional experience?	Certainty In cause — How certain are we of the causes of the emotional event?	Control / Agency — Who/what is in control of the emotion causing event? Was it caused by human agency or situational circumstances?	Responsibility — Who is ultimately responsible for the outcome?	Action Tendency — The behaviors (likely) invoked by the emotion.
Fear	Avoid	Imminent harm.	Unpleasant	Uncertain	Situational	Either[1]	Fight or flight.
Sadness	Avoid	Irrevocable loss.	Unpleasant	Uncertain	Could be Situational or human	Other	To withdraw oneself (or into oneself).
Guilt	Avoid	Having transgressed a moral imperative.	Unpleasant	Certain	Human	Self	Expiate, atone, or make reparations for the harm done.
Anger	Approach	Demeaning offense against me and mine.	Unpleasant	Certain	Human	Other	Attack on the agent deemed responsible.
Hope	Approach	Fearing the worst, yearning for better.	Pleasant	Uncertain	Situational	Either	Moving toward the yearned-for outcome.
Pride	Approach	Enhancement of one's ego identity by taking credit for a valued object or achievement.	Pleasant	Certain	Human	Self	To point publicly at the source of the pride.
Happy	Approach	Progress toward realization of our goals.	Pleasant	Certain	Human or situational.	Self or other.	Sense of pleasure and security in the world—desire to maintain this state.

The CFM predicts that individuals experiencing an avoidance emotion (i.e., fear or guilt) who expect reassurance from apparent cues in the message will have low motivation, and will peripherally process the message for cues to alleviate the fear or guilt, for example. Theoretically, the interaction of emotion type and reassurance within the message determines the type of processing and persuasive outcomes of avoidance emotions and does not affect emotions with approach tendencies. Individuals who experience an avoidance emotion (*i.e.*, fear or guilt) and expect reassurance from apparent cues in the message will have lower motivation to process the message carefully. They will, therefore, peripherally process (*i.e*, with less depth) the message for cues to alleviate the fear or guilt. This processing and perception of goal fulfillment, or lack thereof, will lead to message rejection or acceptance—based on these superficial cues. Thus, any resulting decisions may be more susceptible to misguided influence. However, messages that elicit approach emotions will lead participants to examine the message more closely relative to avoidance emotions. Hence, receivers should process the message with greater depth and, assuming reliable information in the message, have increased accuracy in perceptions.

DISTINCT EMOTIONAL BRANDS

The appraisal based framework of emotions (Lazarus, 1991) has implications for how emotions are created through brands. The same issue, communicated through different lenses, will create different distinct emotions. Table 1 shows the different appraisals that are consistent with different emotions. Let's take an example from public health social marketing. If a brank communicates that lung cancer is unpredictable (i.e., low certainty), stressful (i.e., unpleasant), and life threatening, the audience will likely feel anxiety and fear with relation to lung cancer. However, communicating that lung cancer is a horrific disease (unpleasant) definitely (high certainty) caused by other people (that is, smokers) who unjustly choose to smoke (other responsibility) in the presence of others would be more likely to cause anger than anxiety. Emotions are also categorized by core relational themes, which have different action tendencies directing cognition and behavior (Lazarus, 1991). Table 1 also depicts the core relational theme for a variety of emotions important to branding scholars and practitioners in both the commercial and social marketing arenas. These core relational themes and associated action tendencies associated with particular emotions can then guide cognition and behavior. Take the example of the Truth brand. Truth was a counter-culture brand. The Truth campaign communicates that lung cancer can lead to death (one Truth ad shows a street scene filled with body bags of former smokers who died). Truth ads also depict smoking as being caused by big business (caused by others—not by the self). And, people who smoke are being manipulated by big business (they are doing these harmful actions purposefully). Thus, the Truth brand takes an interesting turn in communicating smoking cessation. Instead of communicating the fear and anxiety that may be inherent to lung cancer, they communicate the anger that future smokers might feel about the attempted manipulation that is occurring. The ads empower youth to stand up against being manipulated. This emotional frame works well because anger causes the desire to retaliate—or get revenge. And, in this case the retaliation would be against the tobacco companies.

Fundamental to brands conveyed in these formats is the notion of framing (2003). A frame is a perspective infused into communications that promotes the salience of selected pieces of information over others and influences the responses individuals will have to the product at hand (Nabi, 2003). Frames influence individuals' views of problems and their necessary solutions. Message frames stimulate access to certain information, beliefs, and/or inferences (Cappella and Jamieson, 1997). Elaborating on the more general notion of frames and recognizing the emotionally charged nature of emotional messages, Nabi (2003) posited the emotions-as-frames model in which emotions are conceptualized as frames through which incoming stimuli are interpreted. She argued that certain message features are likely to evoke various discrete emotions (Table 1). These emotional experiences moderated by individual differences (*e.g.*, prior knowledge and attitudes) influence information exposure and attention in the environment, which ultimately generate emotion-consistent decisions. In my last example, instead of taking a fear frame, the Truth brand employs an anger frame. The Truth brand makes salient the actions of the tobacco companies.

Emotional brands frame the kinds of choices they want consumers to make. Looking at some of the examples I provided earlier in this chapter, we can see evidence of this framing of choices. Nike frames the choice of their running shoes as a choice to be strong and a choice to be someone who "does it". GAP frames the choice to wear their clothes as a choice to be "cool, energetic and fun." Apple computers frame the choice to own their computers and tablets as a choice to be "rebellious, relaxed, and interesting" while choosing a different computer is "boring and status quo".

Here and elsewhere (Turner, 2011a) I make the distinction between communicating an emotion and someone *actually experiencing* that emotion (O'Keefe, 2003). When I discuss a particular kind of emotional appeal, I mean to discuss a type of ad or brand that includes particular message features. Simply because these features are included in brand promotions does not mean that the brand will necessarily evoke the specific emotion attempted. There are several reasons that emotional appeals fail to actually evoke the intended emotion (see Turner, 2011a). First, if audience involvement is not high enough, the message might not strike a responsive chord. Second, if the message communicates the emotion in an overly dramatic, i.e., intense, form it might cause defensiveness, source derogation, or message rejection (Rains and Turner, 2007). That is, emotional appeals need to evoke emotion without causing an overt recognition that emotion is purposefully being manipulated to cause persuasion (Bessarabova, Turner and Fink, 2007). Third, the targeted emotion might be inappropriate for the specific target audience. This third issue is vital for brand effectiveness. Excellent brand managers know their audience at a deep and psychological level. And, they communicate the emotional benefits that their target audience really cares about. Finally, the emotional appeal might be inappropriate for the topic. Message receivers might see the message as being alarmist if the intensity of the emotion attempted does not match the severity of the issue. Aaker et al. (1986) stated well "One problem with the Aad-focused research is that little effort has been expended in making distinctions between different execution strategies…three equally liked commercials-one using slapstick humor, another employing a serious informative copy, and a third with warm, sentimental copy-may be effective in completely different ways, as may two equally disliked commercials-one which is considered boring and the other irritating. (p. 365)." I address distinct types emotional brand strategies next.

Fear. Imagine a PSA showing a young man sitting on a motel room bed waiting for the cash he just earned for meth by pimping out his teenage girlfriend. If you are in the intended target audience (adolescents who might consider trying the use of meth "just one time") such a PSA might cause fear and anxiety about using the drug. This scene actually does play out in a PSA developed for the Montana Meth Project (see http://www.montanameth.org). Fear appeals are persuasive messages that intentionally arouse fear to motivate behavior change in people (Witte and Allen, 2000). The primary component making a message a fear appeal (versus some other kind of emotion) is that it conveys a relevant threat to the audience (Rogers, 1983). Perceived threat has two components: perceived susceptibility to the threat (e.g., I believe that I could end up addicted to meth) and perceived severity (e.g., people can die from drug overdoses) of the threat.

Fear appeals are the most commonly used type of any emotional appeal (Freimuth et al., 1990). They have been applied across health topics (dental care, cancer, hearing loss, condom use, HIV/AIDS) and marketing topics (life insurance) as well as political topics (fighting the war on terrorism). The implication is that fear appeals are effective across topics and arenas. LaTour and Zahra (1989) discussed the ethics of using fear appeals in marketing, arguing that the overuse of fear appeals in advertising campaigns can be dangerous and that perhaps advertisers should focus on stimulating energy in target audiences, and not focus on creating tension and anxiety. LaTour and Zahra do not, however, discuss the realm of using fear appeals for public health messages which leaves readers to wonder whether the context, in this case commercial versus pro-social (public health), makes a difference in the ethical use of fear appeals.

Although there are several theories proposing the mechanisms by which fear appeals work, the dominant model is Witte's Extended Parallel Processing Model (EPPM; 1992). According to the EPPM, the evaluation of a fear appeal initiates two appraisals of the message—appraisal of the threat followed by an appraisal of the efficacy of the recommended response—which results in either danger control processes or fear control processes (Witte, 1992, 1994). The initial appraisal of the threat consists of the individual's assessing the severity of the threat (i.e. the degree of harm that could possibly be experienced if that threat occurred) along with his or her perceived susceptibility (i.e. one's expectancy of being exposed to the threat). When perceived threat is low (i.e. trivial or irrelevant), there is no motivation to process the message any further; efficacy is not evaluated and there is no response to the fear appeal. However, if the target audience assesses the threat they will be motivated to pay attention to and process the message which leads to the second appraisal (Witte, 1992, 1994).

Threat motivates action, but, perceived efficacy determines what action will be taken. Specifically, people will either be motivated to control their fear (e.g. by ignoring the message and engaging in defensive or maladaptive behavior) or control the danger (e.g. by adopting the recommended behavior; Witte, 1992). Perceived efficacy is composed of two dimensions: perceived response efficacy and perceived self-efficacy (Witte, 1992; also see Bandura's social cognitive theory, 1994). Perceived response efficacy regards individuals' perception that if they perform the advocated behavior, the response will be effective (Bandura, 1997). Self-efficacy is a person's beliefs about his/her ability to perform a behavior; it is the extent to which people feel confident that they can perform the behavior, regardless of circumstance.

According to the EPPM, if perceptions of efficacy are greater than perceptions of threat, people will be motivated to control the danger of the threat and the message will be accepted (Witte, 1992). However, threat outweighs efficacy, the motivation to process the threat will be misdirected into fear control processes. As a result, it is important that the threat and efficacy messages be correctly balanced to motivate individuals to properly process the threat and seek adaptive behavior to avoid it. Overall, the general consensus in the current literature on fear appeals is that strong fear appeals work best when accompanied by equally strong efficacy messages (Witte and Allen, 2000). One pharmaceutical company uses fear as a way to brand its HIV medications. One of its ads includes images of sharks in the water, with the message "Don't take a chance -- stick with the HIV medicine that's working for you." Another ad communicated "Will the HIV medicine make my skin or eyes turn yellow?" Given what we know of the EPPM, the idea here is to ignite fear in HIV infected persons regarding what will happen if they do not take their current meds. This threat appraisal will motivate the viewers to pay closer attention to the message and assess their own efficacy with regard to taking the medicine. If the viewers assess that they are capable of accessing and taking the medincine, and that the medicine works for them, then they will have a strong efficacy appraisal. In this case, their sense of efficacy will be stronger than their sense of fear. This will lead the viewers to keep with the HIV medicines developed by the pharmaceutical company and not their competitors.

Witte (1994) implicitly contends that fear appeals are effective for any segment of a target audience as long as the message components were tailored to that audience. For example, attempts to cause fear of lung cancer in adolescents may be improbable because there is such a lack of immediacy of that outcome for that age group. Therefore, as evidenced in smoking cessation messages, appraisals of severity and susceptibility might be higher for adolescents if the message discusses topics that they immediately consider severe-such as social outcomes. Indeed, we often see anti-smoking messages that are targeted at kids discuss outcomes like yellow teeth, bad breath, or generally being un-cool (see for example, Worth, 1999).

Guilt. Guilt appeals typically have two components: the material that evokes guilt (via drawing attention to some discrepancy between the receiver's standards and the receiver's behavior) and the appeal's recommended action or point of view (O'Keefe, 2002). Message receivers are expected to become aware of the discrepancy, feel guilty or anticipate they will feel guilty if they act in such a manner, and then engage in the recommended behavior(s) to ameliorate the resultant/anticipated guilt.

One of the most famous brands that employed guilt with great sophistication was Jif peanut butter. By communicating that "Choosy moms choose Jif" the implication was that "Moms who do not care that much about their children choose other brands of peanut butter." In this way, Jif communicated the anticipated feelings that moms would experience if they failed their children by purchasing a "less than" product.

Huhmann and Brotherton's (1997) content analysis of the use of guilt appeals in magazine advertisements find that guilt appeals were employed as often as humor appeals and sexual appeals. Their data also reveals that guilt appeals are used in every magazine genre and that the actual appeal to guilt appears in both the ad copy as well as the visuals.

Consider the following Australian televaised PSA: A little boy about age 2 is holding his mother's hand as he goes up the escalator in a large train station. Suddenly, the hand is gone and the boy is alone. He is confused and distraught about where his mother went. As tears well up in his eyes the voice over says "If this is how your child feels if you leave them for a minute, imagine if they (sic) lost you for life?" The idea here is that the message will make mothers who smoke realize that their personal behavior harms the life of another person who they value. As such, they are living below their own moral standard. If the intended audience perceives this moral gap then they may also feel guilty about their smoking behavior. And, guilt is noted to impel behavior change.

There is no theory specifically regarding guilt appeals (though the CFM considers guilt as one of the avoidance emotions; see Table 1); but, in recent years a number of scholars in both the social marketing and commercial genres have examined the underpinnings of guilt's success and failures. Pinto and Priest (1991) examined the effect of low, moderate, and high guilt-appeals on purchase intentions finding that as the intensity of guilt messages increased, felt guilt was expected to increase until it peaked, at which point felt guilt would decrease (i.e., an inverse U relationship). Pinto and Priest found that high intensity guilt appeals aroused anger at the source of the message, but, did not create guilty feelings. Both Pinto and Worobetz (1992) and Coulter and Pinto's (1995) studies achieved comparable results: Consumers' emotional responses, their attitudes toward advertisements and brands, attributions about the companies promoting the brands, and purchase intention for ads depending on the intensity of the guilt appeal. These studies imply that a moderate level of guilt communicated in ad copy is more effective than either intense guilt or subtle guilt. Their data also supported a linear effect of guilt-appeals on feelings of anger such that as more guilt was communicated in the ad copy, more anger at the source was experienced by the participants.

Studies in the social marketing domain (where financial profit is a non-issue), though, show little evidence of an inverse-U relationship between guilt appeals, feelings of guilt, and other outcomes such as attitude change. Lindsey (2005) investigated the effect of guilt appeals in helping an unknown other by signing up for the bone marrow registry. Participants were randomly assigned either to a control group, naturalistic guilt appeal, or a highly intense guilt appeal. Lindsey hypothesized that guilt appeals would affect guilty feelings, thereby impacting behavioral intentions. Her data were consistent with predictions in the main. There is an important distinction among the studies in marketing and the studies conducted with health behaviors, namely, whether the message is pro-social or commercial. With marketing or advertising appeals, there is an inherent conflict of interest in these types of messages, which ultimately seek to sell a product or service. Other types of guilt-inducing persuasive messages, especially within the health communication domain, are seen as simply pro-social and without profit-motive. Guilt appeals might cause guilty feelings if the topic advocates helping others or helping oneself. What is unknown, though, is whether guilt appeals in the pro-social domain cause anger. It could very well be that guilt appeals in the pro-social domain cause guilt and therefore lead to increased persuasiveness and also to the unintended effect of angry feelings. Such an effect would have important implications for the long-term or repeated use of such appeals in the pro-social domain.

Anger. Although some evidence suggests wide use of anger appeals in political advertising (cf. Brader, 2006) and a common theme in drinking and driving ads (DeJong and Atkin, 1995) they are possibly the least studied of all kinds of emotional appeals.

Anger appeals are messages that intentionally communicate a demeaning offense to the audience or to those they care about (Lazarus, 1991). Anger appeals communicate that a negative event, caused intentionally by another person, must be paid attention to and taken care of. Nabi (1999) describes anger as: "...a generally elicited by situations in which either obstacles are perceived to interfere with goal oriented behavior or demeaning offenses..." (p. 297).

Some people have argued that many climate change brand positions has been a position of anger. For example, take just one of Greenpeace's 2007 climate change videos. In the ad, an angry child speaks sternly to adults about climate change. The message copy clearly employs the features of anger: The harm caused was caused by adults (human agency), unfairly and knowingly, these adults causing global harm could have acted differently, and the causes of the climate change problem are certain. For example, the child in the video states "This (scientific evidence) proves without a doubt that the earth is getting warmer...this is caused by things you (adults) do...You are either for my future or against it...You are either a friend or an enemy...You had your chance to fix this problem."

Turner's (2007) Anger Activism Model (AAM) proposes that anger appeals are most effective if induce high levels of anger at the issue addressed in the message and if the audience has strong efficacy beliefs in their ability to gain redemption. Thus, anger appeals are most effective for pro-attitudinal audiences; that is, anger appeals motivate people but are unlikely to change people who have a negative attitude. If the audience already has a positive attitude toward the topic, anger should strengthen their attitudes, motivate them to engage in message-relevant thinking, and ignite intentions to engage in activities that are typically viewed as difficult to execute (e.g., organizing a club vs. joining a club). Conversely, if individuals view the issue unfavorably receivers' anger will be targeted at the message source. Audiences who read a counter-attitudinal anger inducing message will perceive it as a personal affront. In this case, as anger increases, persuasiveness will decrease.

The AAM was based upon research showing that (a) angry people *can* show constructive behaviors such as focused attention on persuasive arguments (Mitchell et al., 2001); (b) will make use of accessible and relevant heuristics (Moons and Mackie, 2007); (c) have the ability to discriminate between weak and strong arguments (Moons and Mackie, 2007); and (d) show intentions to engage in behaviors that are difficult to execute (Turner, 2007). However, it is simultaneously the case that angry feelings have been shown to lead to unconstructive outcomes such as (a) the optimism bias in risk perception (Lerner and Keltner, 2000); (b) the distortion of likelihood estimates (DeSteno et al., 2004); (c) decreased trust (Dunn and Schweitzer, 2005), (d) hostility (Baron, 1977); and (e) increased stereotyping (Bodenhausen, Sheppard, and Kramer, 1994). The AAM argues this distinction in effects is caused by the intensity of the angry feelings experienced by the message receivers and the strength of their efficacy beliefs in remedying the problem.

The AAM posits a unique interaction effect between efficacy beliefs and intensity of anger generated by a persuasive appeal. When efficacy beliefs are strong, anger has a linear effect on attitudes, cognitions, and intentions. But, when efficacy beliefs are weak, anger was posited to have a curvilinear effect on these outcomes. Although Turner (2007) specifically suggested that this curvilinear effect would be an inverse-U, her recent data actually shows a u-shaped relationship of anger on outcomes under weak efficacy conditions (Turner, Bessarabova, Hambleton and Sipek, 2007). This u-shaped curve shows that as efficacy decreases, so does the motivating powers of anger—until anger reaches a high enough state where the anger itself is the motivator.

Humor. Humor appeals are not easily defined because they do not necessarily cause one discrete emotion. Humor appeals can affect joy, surprise, or even hope dependent upon the type of humor employed (i.e., sarcasm versus slap-stick) and the target audience. Suffice it to say that humor appeals are persuasive appeals that purposefully use positive affect, through the use of humor, to connect positive feelings with the issue being addressed in the message. Monahan (1995) explained that there are at least two types of positive affect appeals—both of which apply to humor appeals: a) positive benefit appeals and b) heuristic appeals. Positive benefit appeals are those that employ positive feelings to directly communicate about the emotional, psychological, or experiential benefits of complying with the message. Heuristic appeals are those appeals that use "…a more indirect approach to target individuals who do not have the time, skill, or motivation to evaluate the attributes and benefits of a particular campaign." (Monahan, 1995, p. 83).

Examples of humor appeals abound in both social and commercial marketing. An example from McDonald's corporation shows a cow on a trampoline in the middle of a field. The copy reads "the real milkshake". The ad is clearly in line with McDonald's overall positive brand image.

One company that has strategically, consistently, and effectively used humor to create brand image is Etrade. By using a talking baby who provides financial advice, the brand image is fun and lighthearted—not what one expects from financial advisors. In this way, the brand uses joyous emotions caused by humor to connect their audience to the brand. The ads communicate "We are not so serious and boring. We have a sense of humor." In this way, the brand uses irony to build a relationship of fun and levity between the company and its consumers. Thus, E-trade effectively uses irony to lighten up their image. In 2012 the E-trade superbowl ad was one of the top 10 best liked ads by consumers (www.nielsen.com).

Studies reveal that both individual and message variables influence the effectiveness of humor, including: prior attitude (Chattopadhyay and Basu, 1990), need for cognition (Zhang, 1996), self-monitoring (Lammers, 1991), argument strength (Cline and Kellaris, 1999), and source reactions (Lyttle, 2001). More recent research, however, suggests that gender-related individual differences might be a meaningful moderator of the effect of humor on persuasive outcomes for topics that are threatening. Conway and Dubé (2002) predicted that, for threatening topics, humor appeals will be more effective for high-masculinity individuals compared to appeals with no humor. This prediction stemmed out of the research suggesting that highly masculine people are particularly averse to experiencing distress (i.e., sadness and fear). Conway and Dubé (2002) conducted two experiments with different health topics: sunscreen use to prevent skin cancer in a first study, condom use to prevent AIDS in another study. In both studies, men and women high in masculinity exhibited greater intent to engage in the preventive behaviors recommended in the humor appeal compared to the no-humor appeal. No difference emerged for low-masculinity individuals.

In the case of humor appeals, the question might actually be "do they work?" Or, "what outcomes do humor appeals affect?" Early reviews of the humor literature concluded that no consistent evidence exists to support humor's persuasive effect (e.g., Sternthal and Craig, 1973), though they did reveal that particular types of humor affect perceptions of the message source. Weinberger and Gulas' (1992) review of humor advertisements led to the following conclusions: (a) humorous ads attract more attention than non-humorous ones, particularly when the humor is related to the product or issue; (b) humor does not help with comprehension of the ad; (c) humor enhances source liking, but is unlikely to affect credibility judgments; and (d) humor may be persuasive for feeling-oriented products (e.g., clothes, perfume) or low involvement products (non-durable consumer goods).

Other Positive Brand Strategies: Warmth, Pride, and Hope. Clearly, humor appeals are not the only branding strategy that uses positively valenced emotions. The marketing community has decades of examples of materials evoking warmth, pride, and hope. Unfortunately, the dearth of theorizing about, and systematic research on, these strategies leaves me wanting.

Although the McDonald's corporation is known for using a variety of positive appeals, they may be best known for building a brand on feelings of warmth. McDonalds evokes recollections of family traditions, all-American ideals, and the goodness that exists in people. One classic McDonald's ads consistent with this brand image Ronald Mcdonald teaching a boy to ice skate with the help of some Bambi-like animated characters. In the ad, the boy can not skate well and falls on the ice. Ronald sees the boy alone on the ice and picks him up and whirls him in the air. These positive feelings are also communicated in the various slogans McDonalds has used over the years including "You deserve a break today", "I'm lovin it", "We love to see you smile" and "The simple joy of McDonalds." The brand builds a relationship that communicates caring between McDonalds and the patrons. The feeling is that McDonalds cares that you are busy, cares that you smile, and cares about your friends and family. McDonalds corporation hopes that their patrons sees McDonalds as part of the fabric of the family unit.

For audiences to experience pride they must take some credit for the positive event and experience some form of ego-enhancement (Lazarus, 1991). Pride, an ego-focused emotion, may cause people to want to "show off" or to show with confidence their pride. Aaker and William's (1998) examination of pride appeals (relative to empathy) tested message this message copy "Acing the last exam. Winning the big race. Receiving recognition. Ohio Flag Beer. Celebrating life's accomplishments." (p. 245). Hope differs from both pride and warmth in that it is caused by higher levels of uncertainty. Thus, although it is still considered a positive emotion—it does have some overlap with fear. For example, the American Cancer Society has a "stories of hope" internet site (http://www.cancer.org/treatment/ survivorshipduringandaftertreatment/storiesofhope/index) where information seekers can read personal stories of cancer survivors' triumphs over cancer and cancer's difficult treatments. Hope appeals focus on yearning for better and compel people to behavior change by persuading them that "A better outcome is out there if you fight for it."

The effect of warmth, pride and hope in advertising is less extensively studied than humor. Though, overall, there is more research on warmth than on humor or hope appeals. Chaudhuri and Watt (1995) hypothesized that a warmth appeal engenders a happy emotional response and De Pelsmacker and Van den Bergh (1997) found that warmth in advertising decreases irritation (though De Pelsmacker and Geuens (1996) found no differences in response between warm and non-emotional ads.). Aaker and Bruzzone (1981), Aaker et al. (1986) and Goldberg and Gorn's (1987) rearch indicated a positive relationship between the warmth in an ad and purchase intention. There is a dearth of studies on the responses of consumers to different levels of warmth appeals. De Pelsmacker et al. (1997) found that higher levels of warmth lead to better recall whereas less humorous appeals were more effective than messages without humor or with high levels of humor; in fact, high levels of humou could lead to feeling of irritation (De Pelsmacker and Van den Bergh, 1997).

Surprisingly few studies have examined the persuasive effects of hope appeals. In 1994, Kinder noted "the consequences for thought and action of the more powerful emotional experiences that may play an important role in political life—anger, fear, *hope*, pride—have so far gone unexplored" (emphasis mine, p. 279). Hope appeals contain language stressing the possibility of desired outcomes and are strategically used to reinforce the beliefs and behaviors of consumers/citizens. Unlike other positive emotions, hope has been theorized to influence motivation, attitudes, and behaviors in meaningful, long-term ways (MacInnis and de Mello, 2005). Marketing scholars have argued that hope's power comes from its ability to bias cognition toward goal achievement; but, these assertions have not been put to empirical tests (but see Chadwick, 2008; 2011).

SUMMARY AND CONCLUSION

Emotional branding is about connecting brands to people (Gobé, 2009). People can find functional, utilitartian, attributes in a variety of products and issues---but, they feel loyal to the brands they relate to. Importantly, marketers do not need to decide whether they will communicate functions or emotions—they can communicate both. Even more importantly, marketers need not pitch the emotional consumer (citizen) against the rational one. Indeed, emotions and cognitions affect each other. Moods and emotions are known to directly impact recall, learning, systematic processing, attitudes, and even behaviors.

The question about emotional branding should not be one of "whether" but rather "whither". In other words, the real question is what type of emotional relationship do you want to build with your key stakeholders? How will you build this emotional relationship? Although I have heard it proffered that only positive emotions should be used—I think that might be too simplistic an answer for the complex world of global brands. The case is that negatively valenced emotions do lead to closer processing of messages and can activate important action tendencies. At the same time, audiences might not want to feel badly every time they see your brand. Additionally, with regard to both fear and anger appeals, messages that only induce the negative state without inclusion of reassuring messages—efficacy appeals—are less effective. Although there have not been systematic empirical studies on the inclusion of efficacy messages with sadness or guilt appeals, my hypothesis is that it will only help effects and not hinder them. The bottom line, then, is that negative messages of any sort have to be accompanied by messages that uplift. We must give audiences a coping route (Lazarus, 1991), letting them know "Our products/ideas will lead you out of this negative state!"

The kinds of emotions that are nurtured with target audiences depends greatly on the context (social versus commercial marketing), the product / issue being marketed, and of course—the target audience. Studies consistently show that the effectivess of emotions on cognitive and behavioral outcomes depends on the characteristics of the audience.

Andy Goodman wrote "Minds tend to follow hearts, so make sure you reach their hearts first. Caring is an emotional and intellectual process, involving both the heart and the mind – and usually in that order. So, if you want your target audience to stop, read, and truly contemplate your message, you have to engage their hearts first" (Goodman, 2002, p. 25).

Practitioners need to understand the distinctions among and between discrete emotions and what outcomes they cause and to whom. The brand manager's question should be "What emotion should I use in particular contexts, with particular audiences for particular reasons?"

REFERENCES

Aaker, D. A., Douglas, M., Stayman, and Hagerty, M. R. (1986). Warmth in advertising: Measurement, impact and sequence effects. *Journal of Consumer Research*, 12 (march): 365-381.

Aaker, David A., and Donald E. Bruzzone (1985 March), "Causes of Irritation In Advertising," *Journal of Marketing*, 49, 47-57.

Aaker, Jennifer and Patti Williams (1998), "Empathy versus Pride: The Influence of Emotional Appeals across Cultures," *Journal of Consumer Research*, 25 (December), 241-261.

Arnold, M. B. (1960). *Emotion and personality: Vol. 1. Psychological aspects.* New York: Columbia University Press.

Bagozzi, R. P, Gopinath, M. and Nyer, P. U. (1999). The Role of Emotions in Marketing. *Journal of the Academy of Marketing Science,* 27, 184-206.

Baron, R. (1977) Human aggression. New York: Plenum.

Bessarabova, E., Turner, M. M., and Fink, E. L. (2007, November) You ain't guiltin' me into nothin':"Guilt adolescents, and reactance. Presented at the annual conference of the National Communication Association, Chicago, Ill.

Bless, H., Bohner, G., Schwarz, N. and Strack, F. (1990) "Mood and persuasion: A cognitive response analysis", *Personality and Social Psychology Bulletin*, 16: 331-345.

Bodenhausen, G. V., Sheppard, L. A. and Kramer, G. P. (1994) "Negative affect and social judgment: The differential impact of anger and sadness", *European Journal of Social Psychology*, 24: 45-62.

Bohner, G., Chaiken, S., and Hunyadi, P. (1994). The role of mood and message ambiguity in the interplay of heuristic and systematic processing. ***European Journal of Social Psychology***, *24*(1), 207 - 221.

Bohner, G., Crow, K., Erb, H. and Schwarz, N. (1992) "Affect and persuasion: Mood effects on the processing of message content and context cues and on subsequent behavior", *European Journal of Social Psychology*, 22: 511-530.

Bower, J. C. (1981) "Mood and memory", *American Psychologist*, 36: 129-148.

Bower, G. W. and Cohen, P. R. (1982). Emotional influences on memory and thinking: Data and theory. In S. Fiske and M. Clark (Eds.) Affect and Cognition. Hillsdale, NJ. Erlbaum.

Bower, G. H., Monteiro, K. P. and Gilligan, S. G. (1978) "Emotional mood as a context of learning and recall", *Journal of Verbal Learning and Verbal Behavior*, 17: 573-585.

Brader, T. (2006) *Campaigning for hearts and minds: How emotional appeals in political ads work,* Chicago, IL: University of Chicago Press. http://www.cancer.org/

Cappella, Joseph A., and Kathleen Hall Jamieson. 1997. Spiral of Cynicism. New York: Oxford University Press.

Chadwick, A. E. (2008). Hope: Explication and operationalization. Paper presented at the annual meeting of the National Communication Association, San Diego, California.

Chadwick, A. E. (2011). Subjective feelings of hope and appraisals: A test of persuasive hope theory. Paper presented at the annual meeting of the International Communication Association, Boston, Massachusetts.

Chaudhuri, A. and J.H. Watt (1995), "An Exploratory Study of Emotional Attributes in Radio Commercials," *Journal of Marketing Communications,* 1, 2, 61-70.

Chaiken, S. (1980) "Heuristic versus systematic information processing and the use of source versus message cues in persuasion", *Journal of Personality and Social Psychology,* 39: 752-766.

Chattopadhyay, A. and Basu, K. (1990) "Does brand attitude moderate the persuasiveness of humor in advertising", in M. E. Goldberg, G. Gorn and R. W. Pollay (eds), *Advances in consumer research 17,* (p. 442), Provo, UT: Association for Consumer Research.

Cline, J. J., and Kellaris, T. W. (1999). Humor and ad memorability: On the contributions of humor expectancy, relevancy, and need for humor. *Psychology and Marketing, 24,* 497-509.

Clore, G. L. and Parrott, W. G. (1991). Moods and their vicissitudes: Thoughts and feelings as information (pp. 107-124). In J. P. Forgas (Ed.) Emotion and Social Judgments Oxford, Egland: Pergamon Press.

Conway, M. and Dubé, L. (2002) "Humor in Persuasion on Threatening Topics: Effectiveness Is a Function of Audience Sex Role", *Personality and Social Psychology Bulletin*, 28: 863-873.

Coulter, R. H. and Pinto, M. B. (1995) "Guilt appeals in advertising: What are their effects?", *Journal of Applied Psychology,* 80: 697-705.

DeJong, W. and Atkin, C. K. (1995). A Review of National Television PSA Campaigns for Preventing Alcohol-Impaired Driving, Journal of Public Health Policy, 16, 59-80.

De Pelsmacker, P. and J. Van den Bergh (1997), "Ad Content, Product Category, Campaign weight and irritation. A Study of 226 TV Commercials," In Marketing: progress, prospects, perspectives. Proceedings of the 26th EMAC Conference. Eds. D. Arnott et al. Warwick, University of Warwick, 382-400.

De Pelsmacker, P. and M. Geuens (1996), "The Communication Effects of Warmth, Eroticism and Humour in Alcohol Advertisements,"*Journal of Marketing Communications,* 2, 4, 247-262.

De Pelsmacker, P. and M. Geuens (1997a), "Emotional Appeals and Information Cues in Belgian Magazine Advertisements,"*International Journal of Advertising,* 16, 2, 123-147.

DeSteno, D., Petty, R. E., Rucker, D. D. Wegener, D. T. and Braverman, J. (2004) "Discrete emotions and persuasion: The role of emotion-induced expectancies", *Journal of Personality and Social Psychology,* 86: 43-56.

Dillard, J. P. and Peck, E. (2000) "Affect and persuasion: Emotional responses to public service announcements", *Communication Research*, 27: 461-495.

Dunn, J. R., and Schweitzer, M. E. (2005). Feeling and believing: The influence of emotion on trust. *Journal of Personality and Social Psychology*, 88, 736–748.

Forgas, J. P., and Bower, G. H. (1987). Mood effects on person-perception judgments. *Journal of Personality and Social Psychology*, 53(1), 53-60.

Forgas, J. P. and Moylan, S. J. (1987). After the movies: The effects of transient mood states on social judgments. *Personality and Social Psychology Bulletin,* 13, 478-489.

Freimuth, V. S., Hammond, S. L., Edgar, T., and Monahan, J. L. (1990). Reaching those at risk: A content-analytic study of AIDS PSAs. *Communication Research, 17,* 775–791.

Galizio, M. and Hendrick, C. (1972) "Effect of musical accompaniment on attitude: The guitar as prop for persuasion", *Journal of Applied Social Psychology,* 2: 350-359.

Gobe, M. (2009). Emotional branding: The new paradigm for connecting brands to people, New York, NY: Allworth Press. http://www.greenpeace.org/usa/en/

Huhmann, B. A. and Brotherton, T. P. (1997) "A content analysis of guilt appeals in popular magazine advertisements", *Journal of Advertising*, 26: 35-46.

Hullett, C. R. (2005) "The impact of mood on persuasion: A meta-analysis", *Communication Research*, 32: 423-442.

Isen, A.M. Shalker, T.E Clark, M.S. and Karp, L. (1978) Affect, accessibility of material in memory and behavior: A cognitive loop? *Journal of Personality and Social Psychology*, 34, 1-12.

Kinder, D. R. (1994). Reason and emotion in American political life. In R. C. Schank and E. Langer (Eds.). *Beliefs, reasoning, and decision making: Psycho-logic in honor of Bob Abelson*. Hillsdale, NJ: Lawrence Erlbaum.

Lammers, H. B. (1991). Moderating influence of self-monitoring and gender on responses to humorous advertising. *Journal of Social Psychology*, *131*, 57–69.

LaTour, M., and Zahra, S. (1989). Fear appeals as advertising strategy: Should they be used? *Journal of Consumer Marketing*, 6, 61–70.

Lazarus, R. S. (1991) *Emotion and adaptation*, New York: Oxford University Press.

Lerner, J. S. and Keltner, D. S. (2000) "Beyond valence: Toward a model of emotion-specific influences on judgment and choice", *Cognition and Emotion,* 14: 473-493.

Lindsey, L. L. M. (2005) "Anticipated guilt as behavioral motivation: An examination of appeals to help unknown others through bone marrow donation", *Human Communication Research,* 31: 453-481.

Luther, T. (2006). Emotional Branding: Where Hearts and Wallets Collide. Luther Media.

Lynch, J. and de Chernatony, L. (2004). The power of emotion: Brand communication in business to business markets. *Journal of Brand Management* 11, 403–419.

Lyttle, J. (2001) "The effectiveness of humor in persuasion: The case of business ethics training", *Journal of General Psychology*, 128: 206-216.

Mackie, D. M. and Worth, L. T. (1989) "Processing deficits and the mediation of positive effect in persuasion", *Journal of Personality and Social Psychology*, 57: 27-40.

Mitchell, M., Brown, K., Villagran, M., and Villagran, P. (2001). The effects of anger, sadness and happiness on persuasive message processing: A test of the negative state relief model. *Communication Monographs, 68*, 347–359.

Mitchell, M. M. (2000). Motivated, but not able? The effects of positive and negative mood on persuasive message processing. *Communication Monographs, 67*, 215-225.

Monahan, J. L. (1995). Thinking positively: Using positive effect when designing health messages. In E. Maibach and R. L. Parrott (Eds.), *Designing health messages: Approaches from communication theory and public health practice* (pp. 81–98). Buckingham, UK: Sage.

Moons, W. G. and Mackie, D. M. (2007) "Thinking straight while seeing red: The influence of anger on information processing", *Personality and Social Psychology Bulletin,* 33: 706- 720.

Nabi, R. (1999) "A cognitive-functional model for the effects of discrete negative emotions on information processing, attitude change, and recall", *Communication Theory,* 9: 292-320.

Nabi, R. (2002) "Anger, fear, uncertainty, and attitudes: A test of the Cognitive-Functional Model", *Communication Monographs,* 69: 204-216.

Nabi, R. L. (2003). The framing effects of emotion: Can discrete emotions influence information recall and policy preference? *Communication Research, 30,* 224-247. http://www.nielsen.com/global/en.html

O'Keefe, D. (2000) "Guilt and social influence", in M. Roloff (ed), *Communication Yearbook 23,* (pp. 67-101), Thousand Oaks, CA: Sage Publications.

O'Keefe, D. J. (2002) "Guilt as a mechanism of persuasion", in J. P. Dillard and M. Pfau (eds), *The persuasion handbook: Development in theory and practice,* (pp. 329-344), Thousand Oaks, CA: Sage.

Parrot, W. R. (2004). The nature of emotion. In M. B. Brewer and M. Hewstone (Eds.), *Emotion and motivation* (pp. 5–20). Malden, MA: Blackwell. Petty and Cacioppo, 1986.

Petty, R.E., and Cacioppo, J.T. (1981) *Attitudes and persuasion: Classic and contemporary approaches,* Dubuque, IA: W.C. Brown.

Pinto, M. B. and Priest, S. (1991) "Guilt appeals in advertising: An exploratory study", *Psychological Reports,* 69: 375-385.

Pinto, M. B., and Worobetz N. D. (1992) "Note on guilt appeals in advertising: Covariate effects on self-esteem and locus of control", *Psychological Reports,* 70: 19-22.

Rains, S., and Turner, M. M. (2007). Psychological reactance and persuasive health communication: A test and extension of the intertwined model, *Human Communication Research, 33,* 241–269.

Rogers, R. W. (1983). Cognitive and physiological processes in fear appeals and attitude change: A revised theory of protection motivation. In J. Cacioppo and R. Petty (Eds.), Social psychophysiology. New York: Guilford Press.

Schwarz, N. (1990) "Feelings as information: Informational and motivational functions of affective states", in E. T. Higgins and R. M. Sorrentino (eds), *Handbook of motivation and cognition: Foundations of social behavior Vol. 2,* (pp. 527-561), New York: Guilford.

Schmitt, B. (1999) Experiential Marketing: How to Get Customers to Sense, Feel, Think, Act, Relate. New York, NY: The Free Press.

Smith, C. A., and Ellsworth, P. C. (1985). Patterns of cognitive appraisal in emotion. *Journal of Personality and Social Psychology, 48,* 813–838.

Smith, S. and Shaffer, D. (1991) "The effects of good moods on systematic processing: 'Willing but not able, or able but not willing?'", *Motivation and Emotion,* 15: 243-279.

Sternthal, B. and Craig, C. S. (1973) "Humor in advertising", *Journal of Marketing, 37:* 12-18.

Teasdale, J. D. and Russell, M. L. (1983). Differential effects of induced mood on retrieval of pleasant and unpleasant events from episodic memory. *Journal of Abnormal Psychology,* 88, 248-257.

Thompson, J., Rindfleisch, A. and Zeynep, A. (2006). Emotional branding and the strategic value of the doppelganger brand image. Journal of Marketing, 70 (Jan).

Turner, M. M. (2007) "Using emotion in risk communication: The anger activism model", *Public Relations Review, 33:* 114-119.

Turner, M. M. (2011a). Discrete emotions and the design and evaluation of health communication messages. In H. Cho (Ed.) *Designing Messages for Health Communication Campaigns: Theory and Practice,* Thousand Oaks, CA: Sage.

Turner, M. M. (2011b). The role of emotion in risk and crisis communication in, K. Doeveling, C. Scheve and E. Konijn (Eds.) *The Routledge Handbook of Emotions and Mass Media.* New York, NY: Routledge.

Turner, M. M., Bessarabova, E., Hambleton, K., and Sipek, S. (2007, May). *Does message induced anger facilitate or debilitate persuasion? A test of the anger activism model.* Presented at the annual conference of the International Communication Association, San Francisco, CA.

Wegener, D. T. and Petty, R. E. (1994) "Mood-management across affective states: The hedonic contingency hypothesis", *Journal of Personality and Social Psychology,* 66: 1034-1048.

Wegener, D. T., Petty, R. E. and Smith, S. M. (1995) "Positive mood can increase or decrease message scrutiny: The hedonic contingency view of mood and message processing", *Journal of Personality and Social Psychology,* 69: 5-15.

Westerman, R., Spies, K., Stahl, G. and Hesse, F. W. (1996) "Relative effectiveness and validity of mood induction procedures: A meta analysis", *European Journal of Social Psychology,* 26: 557-580.

Weinberger, M. G. and Gulas, C. S. (1992) "Humor in advertising: A comprehensive review", *Journal of Advertising,* 21: 35-59.

Witte, K. (1992) "Putting the fear back into fear appeals: The extended parallel process model", *Communication Monographs*, 59: 329-349.

Witte, K. (1994). Fear control and danger control: A test of the extended parallel process model (EPPM). *Communication Monographs, 61*(2), 113–134.

Witte, K. and Allen, M. (2000) "A meta-analysis of fear appeals: Implications for effective public health campaigns", *Health Education and Behavior,* 27: 591-615. http://www.wired.com/

Worth, L. T., and Mackie, D. M. (1987) Cognitive mediation of positive affect in persuasion. *Social Cognition, 5,* 76-94.

Zhang, Y. (1996). The effect of humor in advertising: An individual difference perspective. *Psychology and Marketing, 13,* 531–545.

In: Psychology of Branding
Editor: W. Douglas Evans

ISBN: 978-1-62618-817-4
© 2013 Nova Science Publishers, Inc.

Chapter 3

THE REMARKABLE CONSUMER EXPERIENCE OF BRANDS AS DRIVERS TO A DEEP CONSUMER-BRAND RELATIONSHIP

Sandra M. C. Loureiro

Department of Marketing, Operations and General Management,
ISCTE Business School- Lisbon University Institute, Lisboa

ABSTRACT

This chapter reviews concepts of brand experience, brand connection, brand love and positive emotions, and the willingness to sacrifice in different perspectives. Then a theoretical model is proposed for explaining the mechanism under the extreme connection to a brand that leads to the willingness to sacrifice. The sacrifice for a brand means to give up one's immediate self-interest or interests not related to the purchase and experience the brand for the sake of a relationship with the brand.

The chapter concludes with suggestions to test the model and presents some preliminary empirical results from the first seminal studies.

Keywords: Brand experience, brand love, brand connection, commitment, willingness to sacrifice

INTRODUCTION

Since the 1990s, brands became more and more interesting for consumers, researchers and practitioners. Brands have been regarded from the company owner of the brand, which could also be a celebrity, and from the consumer's point of view. The company creates the identity (Aaker, 1996) of the brand and the consumer builds an image of the brand in their mind (Keller, 1998). The feedback of that image can help brand managers to reduce the gap, if it exists, between brand identity and brand image (De Chernatony, 2001). Therefore, a close relationship between the company, owner of the brand, and the consumer can help managers to define and refine the brand identity and the brand becomes closer to the consumers. Thus, we need to understand how the relationship between the brand and the consumer can be fruitful for both, in other words consumer-brand relationship, and becomes a prolific research field, especially, after the pioneer work of Fournier (1998) proposing the metaphor of human relationship and the Brand Quality model. Since then several studies emerged, for example, brand community (Muniz and O'Guinn, 2001), brand trust (Delgado-Ballester, Munuera-Aleman, and Yagoe-Guillin, 2003), self-brand connections (Escalas, 2004), brand attachment (Thomson, MacInnis, and Park, 2005), brand experience (Brakus, Schmitt, and Zarantonello, 2009), brand love (Batra, Ahuvia, and Bagozzi, 2012), or brand emotional connection (Loureiro, Kaufmann, and Vrontis, 2012). The last three concepts are crucial for the framework presented in this chapter. Therefore, brand experience is the "subjective, internal consumer responses (sensations, feelings, and cognitions) and behavioral responses evoked by brand-related stimuli that are part of a brand's design and identity, packaging, communications, and environments" (Brakus et al., 2009, p. 53). Brand love is "a broad and long-term consumer–brand relationship, with multiple interrelated cognitive, affective, and behavioral elements, rather than a specific, single, transient love emotion" (Batra et al., 2012, p. 6).Regarding brand emotional connection (Loureiro, Kaufmann, and Vrontis, 2012), the concept comprises self-expressive brand and brand attachment, meaning the consumer ' s perception of the degree to which the specific brand enhances one ' s social self and / or reflects one ' s inner self and the deep attachment to a brand.

Even so, more studies are needed to provide insights about the causal relational mechanism between consumers and brands. Moreover, there still is a lack of understanding of the mechanism underlining the extreme commitment to a brand which leads to the willingness to sacrifice for a brand.

Sacrifice is to give up one's immediate self-interest for the sake of a partner or a relationship (Van Lange, Rusbult, Drigotas, Arriage, Witcher, and Cox, 1997). Sacrifice could be a stage for "co-dependency" relationship dissatisfaction and depression (e.g., Jack, 1991; Jordan, 1991; Lerner, 1988). Therefore, research in social psychology has demonstrated the positive role of sacrifice in relationships, including increased satisfaction and a greater likelihood of persistence over time (Van Lange, Agnew, Harinck, and Steemers, 1997; Van Lange, Rusbult et al., 1997; Wieselquist, Rusbult, Foster, and Agnew, 1999). Furthermore, the willingness to sacrifice is a relationship maintenance behaviour utilised by committed individuals (e.g., Van Lange, Agnew et al., 1997). So, the willingness to sacrifice is associated with relationship satisfaction and commitment (Van Lange, Agnew et al., 1997; Van Lange, Rusbult et al., 1997; Wieselquist et al., 1999).

On the other hand, the economic view of sacrifice for a brand lies on price, perceived sacrifice (e.g., Dodds et al., 1991; Teas and Agarwal, 2000), and even in the intention to pay more for the same product (e.g., Zeithaml, Berry, and Parasuraman, 1996), if we consider the consumer behaviour field.Indeed, in the marketing field sacrifice has been analyzed focusing on economic perspective, that is, analyzing the customers' intention to pay more for the same features of the good and service because of the perceived benefits of the brand and to continue their relationship with the brand. In addiction time and effort are also analyzed in previous research. Time and energy investments would include willingness to delay purchase when the brand is unavailable, or the engagement in extended search for the brand (e.g., Monroe, and Chapman, 1987; Dodds, Monroe, and Grewal, 1991; Cronin, Brady, and Hult, 2000). Therefore, in order to go further in understanding the concept of willingness to sacrifice for a brand, the social psychology perspective should be regarded and more research is needed.

The goal of this chapter is to present an overview of the potential process under the extreme connection to a brand. In order to achieve such goal, this chapter is organised in seven sections. Thereby, following the introduction, the first section is dedicated to brand experience; the second section presents brand connection and the third section brand love. Then, the investment model is described in section four. The next two sections are the core of the chapter presenting the concept of willingness to sacrifice for a brand and the framework of its antecedents. The chapter ends with conclusions, implications, and suggestions for further research.

BRAND EXPERIENCE

The 1990s are the turning point in order to consider customer experience as a single and differentiated construct. Holbrook and Hirschman (1982) allude to the "experiential view" of consumption, which involves a steady flow of fantasies, feelings, and fun. In the consumer-product relationship the relation between a consumer and a product is viewed as an accumulation of consumption experiences (Anderson and Fornell, 1994). The consumer's service experience involves the active construction of personally relevant meanings associated with the behaviours, thoughts, and feelings that occur during the consumption (not simply the production) of the service (Padgett and Allen, 1997). Thus, the consumption experience is a term used to represent the sensory and emotional reactions experienced during consumption (Evrard and Aurier, 1996, p. 128).

The consumption experience with products (goods and services) could also be hedonic. Hedonic consumption designates those facets of the consumer behaviour that relate to the multisensory (tastes, sounds, scents, tactile impressions and visual images), fantastic and emotive aspects of one's experience with products (Hirschman and Holbrook 1982). Thus, the cognitive experience (fantasies) influences the affect experience (feelings) and ultimately controls the behaviour experience (fun).

In fact, consumption experience seems to be closely related to positive motivation and emotions. The experience is a goal-directed activity, meeting experiential needs by providing some level of alertness, activity and challenge that enhances quality of life and self-esteem (Csikszentmihalyi, 2000). Schmitt (1999) mentions that experiences occur in response to stimulation and often results from direct observation and/or participation in events. Such events could be real, virtual, or appear in dreams. These statements lead us to brand experiences, which are created in response to stimuli related to the brand during the encounter (e.g., Davis *et al.*, 2000; Padgett and Allen, 1997).

The Schmitt´s (1999) work divided brand experience into two categories: individual and shared experiences. Sense, feel, and thinking experiences are considered as individual experiences. In contrast, act and relate experiences are regarded as shared experiences. Thus, sense marketing appeals to the senses (sensual and tangible aspects of a good or service that appeal to the five senses of sight, sound, scent, taste and touch); feel marketing addresses to the inner feelings and emotions of consumers; think marketing beseeches the consumers' creativity; act experience on the other hand to the affect bodily experience, lifestyle, and interactions of consumers; and relate marketing evokes other people or cultures (Schmitt, 1999; Brakus, Schmitt, and Zarantonello, 2009).

Schmitt (1999) also claims that the development of experiential types resembled the AIDA model, in consumer research, and the hierarchy-of-effects model, in advertising research. It implies that cognitive and affective effects influence behavioural effects. The sense and thinking experience can be identified as fantasies that include all aspects of experientially oriented cognitions (Holbrook, 2000; Schmitt, 2012). Therefore, feel experience emphasizes the various consumption-related affects, fun (or act of experience) refers to the leisure-oriented aspects of behaviour, and the individual experience (i.e., sense, feel, and thinking experiences) influences the shared experience (i.e., act and relate experiences).

Gentile, Spiller, and Noci (2007, p. 397) highlight that experiences originate "from a set of interactions between a customer and a product, a company, or part of its organisation, which provoke a reaction. This experience is strictly personal and implies the customer's involvement at different levels (rational, emotional, sensorial, physical, and spiritual)". In accordance, Meyer and Schwager (2007, p. 118) mention an internal and subjective response that an individual contact directly or indirectly with an organisation (or brand), so "direct contact generally occurs in the course of purchase, use, and service and is usually initiated by the customer. Indirect contact most often involves unplanned encounters with representatives of a company's products, service or brands and takes the form of word-of-mouth recommendations or criticisms, advertising, news reports, reviews and so forth".

Verhoef *et al.* (2009) propose a holistic approach in nature for customer experience which involves the customer's cognitive, affective, emotional, social and physical responses. They refer that "experience is created not only by those elements which the retailer can control (e.g., service interface, retail atmosphere, assortment, price), but also by elements that are outside of the retailer's control (e.g., influence of others, purpose of shopping)" and additionally point out that "encompasses the *total* experience, including the search, purchase, consumption, and after-sale phases of the experience, and may involve multiple retail channels" (Verhoef *et al.*, 2009, p. 32).

Thus, brand experience is a subjective internal consumer response, as well as a behavioural response (Brakus, Schmitt, and Zarantonello, 2009). The first regards sensations, feelings, and cognitions, while the last is due to the brand-related stimuli, such as brand's design and identity, packaging, communications, and environments. Based on such considerations, Brakus, Schmitt, and Zarantonello (2009) propose four dimensions for brand experience: sensory, affective, intellectual, and behavioural. These dimensions contain both individual and shared brand experience.

BRAND CONNECTION

Brand connection is presented by Loureiro *et al.* (2012) as comprising self identification with a brand and brand attachment. Therefore, brand connection is the extent to which a consumer has incorporated a brand into her or his self-concept (Escalas and Bettman, 2003), and it is also related to communal aspects (Keller, 2003), this means that the brand needs to be approved by the social group where the consumer belongs or wishes to belong to.

Brand connection is based on attachment theory, which, in turn, has its foundations on studies of parent – child relationships (Bowlby, 1979) and continues through adulthood to romantic relationships (Hazan and Shaver, 1994), kinships and friendships (Weiss, 1988; Trinke and Bartholomew, 1997). Since the 1990s, several studies have analysed the adequacy of such theory to the context of the emotional attachment between human beings and animals, places, destinations, special objects, brands (e.g., Richins, 1994; Schouten and McAlexander, 1995; Price *et al.*, 2000; Yuksel *et al*, 2010), and even human brands or celebrities (Thomson, 2006). Thomson *et al.* (2005) conducted a study that identified a higher order emotional attachment construct consisting of three factors: affection, passion and connection.

According to Escalas and Bettman (2003, 2005), when the association with a brand (like the associations to a reference group) are used to construct the self or to communicate the self-concept to others, a connection is formed with the brand.

The attractiveness process occurs when the consumer undergoes a mechanism of identification with the group, tribe, or community, which is built on the basis of a shared passion and/or emotion (e.g., Maffesoli, 2004; Carroll and Ahuvia, 2006; Loureiro *et al.,* 2012).

The identification mechanism of an individual consumer and a group expresses the degree of perception of self, both, as an individual and as a member of the group, in relationship with other group members and with the firm/brand. This aspect, therefore, satisfies the double need of the individuals to develop their self-concept and their identification with the social group of belonging (Mael and Ashforth, 1992). In this context, the concept of brand love arises, which is defined as "the degree of passionate emotional attachment a satisfied consumer has for a particular trade name" (Carroll and Ahuvia, 2006, p. 81).

BRAND LOVE

Sternberg (1986, 1986) analysed the theories of love and suggests a triangular theory of liking and loving. The interpersonal triangular theory of love adapted to the consumption contexts considers that brand love is made by dimensions such as passion, intimacy, and commitment (e.g., Kamat and Parulekar, 1997; Keh, Pang, and Peng, 2007). Ahuvia (1993) suggests that consumers can have a real feeling of love toward an object and conceptualises the love feeling as having two dimensions: the real and the desired integration.

Based on the brand-consumer relationship paradigm, Carroll and Ahuvia (2006) indicate that brand love is composed of five dimensions: passion, attachment, positive evaluation of the brand, positive emotions in response to the brand, and declaration of love for the brand. Thomson, MacInnis and Park (2005) also study the brand love phenomenon and present three dimensions: passion, affection, and connexion. Albert, Merunka, and Valette-Florence (2008a, 2008b) propose two main components of brand love that are also to be found in the interpersonal love literature. The seven first order dimensions were capture through exploratory factorial analysis and then confirmed through confirmatory factorial analysis: idealisation (*Rho of Jöreskog*=0.707), pleasure (*Rho of Jöreskog*=0.822), intimacy (*Rho of Jöreskog*=0.771), long duration relationship (*Rho of Jöreskog*=0.707), dream (*Rho of Jöreskog*=0.812), memories (*Rho of Jöreskog*=0.856), and uniqueness (*Rho of*

Jöreskog=0.672) (Albert et al., 2008b). Six of the seven factors have a reliability coefficient superior to 0.7 (good reliability) and one factor has a reliability coefficient of 0.672 which can be judged satisfactory. The seven factors offer a second order solution with two factors labelled Passion and Affection. Albert et al. (2008a) using exploratory correspondent analysis followed by cluster analysis found eleven dimensions underlie brand love: passion, a long duration relationship, self-congruity, dreams, memories, pleasure, attraction, uniqueness, beauty, trust (satisfaction), and a willingness to state this love. However, as they (Albert et al., 2008a, p. 1073) note, they did not find the aspects of attachment and commitment.

Recently, Batra, Ahuvia, and Bagozzi (2012) try to bridge the gaps of previous studies and propose the brand love higher-order prototype model which comprises seven latent constructs: self–brand integration (current and desired self-identity, life meaning, intrinsic rewards, and frequent thoughts); passion-driven behaviours (willingness to invest resources, passionate desire to use, involvement); positive emotional connection (intuitive fit, emotional attachment, positive affect); anticipated separation distress; overall attitude valence; attitude strength (certainty and confidence).

In this vein, the consumers brand lovers desire to use the brand, to invest resources into it, and to interact frequently with it because the brand love has the ability to express the consumers' actual and desired identities and also the ability to connect to life's deeper meanings and important values. The brand love creates positive emotional connections with the brand, which includes a sense of attachment and an intuitive feeling of rightness about the brand. The brand love also creates a feeling of anticipated separation distress and a sense of long-term relationship.

COMMITMENT AND THE INVESTMENT MODEL

The investment model has its root on interdependence theory which analyses the tendency to persist in a relationship (Kelley, 1979; Kelley and Thibaut, 1978; Rusbult and Van Lange, 2003). Interdependence theory explains the persistence in a relationship; therefore, dependence is a core feature.

The investment model presents three factors to explain how an individual (could be a consumer) becomes dependent on their relationship with another person (that we can extend to a brand): satisfaction level, quality of the alternatives, and investment size. The first factor, putting into the context of consumer-brand relationship, should reflect the extension to which a brand fulfils the consumer's important needs.

The quality of alternatives or better the week quality or the inexistence of quality refers to the degree that a consumer's needs (tangibles and intangibles, such as intimacy, self-identification, or even physical characteristics) could not be fulfilled elsewhere (with other brands), this means that the quality of alternative brands in fulfilling the consumer's needs is poor. If the quality of the alternatives is high the consumer will not tend to be committed to the brand. In other words, a consumer will tend to be much more committed to a particular brand if they judge and believe that the quality (tangibles and intangibles) of that brand is high and the quality of alternatives is low.

The investment size is the extent to which the relationship partners (consumer and brand) may put considerable effort into their relationship. The investment increases the costs of giving up the relationship and induces persistency, plus enhances commitment. Commitment in the investment model is the intention to persist in a relationship, feeling attached and involvement in a long-term relationship (Agnew, Van Lange, Rusbult, and Langston, 1998). Thereby, commitment is a consequence of increasing dependence (the consumer wants and needs to persist and has no choice unless persist in the relationship with the brand).

WILLINGNESS TO SACRIFICE

The concept of sacrifice was first developed into the context of close relationships field. Sacrifice is to forgo one's immediate self-interest for the sake of a partner or a relationship (Van Lange, Rusbult *et al.*, 1997) and is associated to a great satisfaction and commitment with the relationship. Sacrifice can be passive (an individual forgoes a desired activity), active (an individual engages in an undesired activity), or both (Rusbult, Olson, Davis, and Hannon, 2001).

Impett, Gable, and Peplau (2005) and Mattingly and Clark (2010) highlight that most empirical research on sacrifice has relied on interdependence theory. According to this theory, sacrifice will be necessary when the partners' interests are at odds, and so, individuals have to decide if they choose their own self-interest or if they are willing to sacrifice. Therefore, individuals undergo a transformation of motivation in which self-interests may be supplanted by the well-being of the partner or the relationship. This transformation of motivation occurs because individuals are committed to their relationship (Agnew, Van Lange, Rusbult, and Langston, 1998). Consequently, if a committed relationship were to end, there would be a threat to the self concept of the involved individuals (Lewandowski, Aron, Bassis, and Kunak, 2006) and of investments made such as time, effort, experienced emotions, mutual social networks, social status, and material resources (Le and Agnew, 2003).

From the classic economic theory, the sacrifice effect of price represents the consumer's evaluation of the amount of money individuals must sacrifice to satisfy their consumption needs. Accordingly, high prices can generate negative purchase probabilities (Erickson and Johansson, 1985). However, consumers can also infer quality information, prestige, and other positive effects from price, which not always leads them to buy the products at the lowest price (e.g., Brucks *et al.*, 2000; Kardes *et al.*, 2004; Völckner, 2008). Following the idea of Dodds *et al.* (1991) and Monroe and Chapman (1987), Teas and Agarwal (2000) propose a construct of perceived sacrifice in which quality and sacrifice perceptions mediate linkages between brand name, store name, and price name and consumers' perceptions of value. Perceived sacrifice is evaluated as monetary sacrifice. In this vein, the sacrifice perceived construct is measured in terms of "unable to purchase some other products that consumer would like to purchase now" and "reduce the amount of money that consumer spend on other things for a while."

In the marketing field it is common to consider the willingness to pay more for the same good or service as an indicator of sacrifice. The preference for a company over others, expressed by the increase volume of purchases or paying a price premium, is a behavioural indicator that consumers are bonded with the company (ZeithamI, Berry, and Parasuraman, 1996). According to Zeithaml (1988), consumers may also incur in nonmonetary sacrifices such as time, effort, and search costs. Therefore, if consumers assemble durable goods, prepare packaged foods, or travel large distances to acquire products, they incur in additional costs that might influence the assessment of the product value. Indeed, even in the conceptualization of brand equity the willingness to pay price premium appear (Aaker, 1996; Keller, 1998; Evans, Price, and Blahut, 2005) as the amount a customer will pay for the brand in comparison with another brand offering similar benefits.

Nevertheless, in the marketing field willingness to sacrifice can be more than a cost sacrifice. In her preliminary study, Loureiro (2012) points out the importance of analyse the individual willingness to forgo a desired activity to continue his/her relationship with the preferred brand and even the willingness to engage in an undesired activity to continue the relationship with the preferred brand. These passive and active sacrifice need to be further explored through qualitative approach (e.g., depth–interviews and focus groups with different consumers profiles).

ANTECEDENTS OF WILLINGNESS TO SACRIFICE FOR A BRAND

Based on Schmitt (1999), the individual experience (i.e., sense, feel, and think experiences) can influence the shared experience (i.e., act and relate experiences) (see figure 1) and so the following hypothesis is formulated:

H1: Individual brand experience has a positive influence on shared brand experience.

Love is regarded as a very complex emotion, probably the most complex of all, that includes various emotions, some of them positive (Strongman, 1998). Several positive emotions that can contribute to explain a very complex state of being: interest, joy, pleasure, happiness, euphoria, victory, intense own satisfaction, delight, and so many others. The Carroll and Ahuvia's (2006, p. 84) brand love scale uses items like "this brand is a pure delight". Albert, Merunka, and Valette-Florence (2008a, 2008b) mention words like "pleasure" and "happy" in the dimension called pleasure in their proposed scale. Hence, delight and even pleasure are central positive emotions in the complex context of love.

However, delight is itself a second level emotion, characterised by a combination of first order emotions (Plutchik, 1980). According to the psychologist Plutchik (1980), who suggests a circumplex model of emotions, there are eight basic emotions that may be resumed into four dimensions with opposite poles (sadness - happiness; surprise - anticipation; acceptance - reject; anger - fear). Combining these basic emotions more complex emotions would arise. According to this theory, a secondary dyad is defined like a combination of two basic emotions which generate a more complex emotion. Thereby, delight would be defined as a secondary dyad comprised of joy and surprise, similar to the Westbrook and Oliver (1991) consumer dimension (pleasant surprise), which comprised pleasure and surprise.

Other emotional theories define delight as a combination of activation and pleasure (Russell 1980) or as a positive affection of high activation (Watson and Tellegen, 1985). Conversely, Richins (1997) identifies the most outstanding emotions in marketing studies related to the consumption, including the delight within the category of "joy". Oliver and Westbrook (1993) point out three emotions associated to the concept of delight: joy, surprise, and interest.

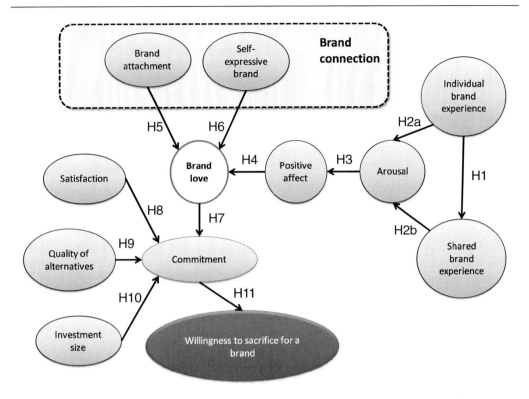

Figure 1. A conceptual model for a deep relationship with a brand: from experience to sacrifice for a brand.

This concept of delight coming from the emotion literature has been assumed by the main researchers on the consumer behaviour. Along these lines, the works of Westbrook and Oliver (1991) and Oliver and Westbrook (1993) show differences in the profile of the consumers as function of their simply satisfied or manifest surprise, or delight with the consumption.

On the other hand, Oliver (1993) demonstrated significant relationships between positive affect (interest and joy) and satisfaction/dissatisfaction responses.

Mano and Oliver (1993) showed different dimensions of positive–negative affect, including moderate arousal positive affect (pleasure), high arousal positive affect (delight), and high nonspecific arousal (surprise). They also found a strong direct effect of arousal on positive affect, with arousal as a direct antecedent of affect and indirect of satisfaction (Mano and Oliver, 1993). Thus, arousal plays an activation role in the emotional process that leads directly to delight and indirectly to satisfaction.

In the service encounter context, Oliver et al. (1997) present a model of consumer delight in which arousal is a function of surprising levels of consumption and delight is a function of arousal and positive affect. They also hypothesize that delight creates a desire for further pleasurable service, i.e., future intentions.

All of the above considerations lead us to consider that a positive brand experience (positive emotional experience), individual experience and shared experience can create activation and a positive affect. Therefore, consumers satisfied with the brand and who also love the brand are expected to be more willing to sacrifice for a brand. Consequently, the following hypotheses are investigated (see figure 1):

H2a: Individual brand experience has a positive impact on consumer´s arousal.
H2b: Shared brand experience has a positive impact on consumer´s arousal.
H3: Consumer's arousal has a positive impact on positive affect.
H4: Positive affect has a positive impact on brand love.

Not only the experience and positive emotions are important antecedents of brand love; to love a brand, consumers need to be attached to it, that is, feel that the brand is irreplaceable and miss it when they do not have the brand. The brand should reflect the consumer inner and social self, in another words, the consumer should be connected to the brand (Loureiro *et al.*, 2012). Given this conceptualisation, the following hypotheses are proposed:

H5: Brand attachment has a positive impact on brand love.
H6: Self-expressive brand has a positive impact on brand love.

Commitment is regarded as a variable at the core of the consumer–brand relationships (Fournier, 1998; Chaudhuri and Holbrook, 2001). As Fehr (1988) demonstrates, commitment is different from brand love and being in love toward a brand can originate commitment. Therefore, the following hypothesis is proposed:

H7: Brand love exercises a positive effect on commitment.

Nevertheless, not only brand love leads to commitment, based on investment model, satisfaction, investment size and the weak quality of alternatives also create commitment. Thus, being committed drives individuals to pro-relationship behaviours such as the willingness to sacrifice (Agnew and Etcheverry, 2006; Agnew *et al.*, 1998; Rusbult and Van Lange, 1996). Nevertheless, sacrifice can leave behind feelings of resentment, guilt, dependence, or ensure other psychological costs (Rusbult and Van Lange, 1996). Thereby, the following hypotheses are formulated:

H8: Satisfaction exercises a positive effect on commitment.
H9: Quality of alternatives exercises a negative effect on commitment.
H10: Investment size exercises a positive effect on commitment.

Therefore, an increased willingness to sacrifice is associated with greater relationship satisfaction and commitment (Van Lange, Agnew *et al.*, 1997; Van Lange, Rusbult *et al.*, 1997; Wieselquist, Rusbult, Foster, and Agnew, 1999). Additionally, committed individuals are more willing to sacrifice than non-committed individuals (Powell and Van Vugt 2003). As such (see figure 1):

H11: Commitment has a positive effect on willingness to sacrifice.

Given the above, we can consider that there are two types of sacrifices (active vs. passive) and two groups of motives for sacrifice (approach vs. avoidance), both are associated with relational variables (Loureiro, 2012). Relationship commitment, defined as the tendency to feel psychologically attached to a relationship and to have a strong desire to maintain the relationship (Rusbult, 1980), is a key factor in drawing motivation and behaviour in interdependence dilemmas. Committed individuals are more dependent on their partners and need the relationship, and so should be more willing to sacrifice the direct self-interest to preserve the relationship (Powell and Vugt, 2003).

Mattingly and Clark´s (2010) studies indicated that activity importance was a significant predictor of the willingness to sacrifice. Thus, the more significance that an individual placed on an activity (the value placed on the activity), the less likely he/she was to sacrifice that activity, and thus, activity may be a stronger predictor of the individuals' behaviour (Loureiro, 2012).

CONCLUSION AND IMPLICATIONS

The transposition of the psychological knowledge from close relationship to the context of the dyadic relationship between a brand and a consumer has evolved since the 1990s. However, the mechanism that explains how consumers relate to brands is not yet well established and understood. Thus, this chapter intends to contribute to go further in understanding this phenomenon, proposing a framework of antecedents of willingness to sacrifice for a brand.

The proposed framework presents the evolving process to a deep commitment to a brand. In this vein, the experience, the connection to the brand, the satisfaction, the weak quality of alternatives, and the investment size are important drivers to lead to a willingness to sacrifice for a brand. A good experience (good sensations, stimulating curiosity, identification with lifestyle and thinking about relationships) can generate positive emotions, such as the complex emotion love. However, brand love is much more than emotions. According to Batra et al. (2012), brand love comprises other important components, such as, passion-drivers behaviours, self-integration to the brand, long-term relationship, and consumer anticipated separation distress. So, the self and social identification with the brand and the attachment mechanism, expressed as brand connection by Lourerio et al. (2012) plays an important role toward brand love.

The direct key factor for the willingness to sacrifice is being committed to the relationship (Van Lange, Agnew et al., 1997; Van Lange, Rusbult et al., 1997; Wieselquist et al., 1999). Therefore, brand love can generate such commitment together with the satisfaction, pro-active investment in the relationship with the brand and weak alternatives (other brands) to fulfil the consumers' needs. As in the fields of human relationship, committed consumers are more dependent on the brand they love and so should be more willing to sacrifice other interests and activities to keep and relate to the brand.

The proposed framework regards two perspectives of sacrifice: economic (willingness to pay more) and psychological (willingness to sacrifice). The economic perspective is more common in the marketing field and is associated to the perceived sacrifice, consumer behaviour intentions or price premium that is, one dimension of brand equity proposed by Keller (1998), Aaker (1996) and Evans et al. (2005). On the other hand, the psychological point of view was not yet assessed in the marketing field. However, in line with Powell and Vugt (2003), in the marketing field, as well as in the psychological romantic perspective of sacrifice, committed individuals should be more dependent on their brands and need the relationship and so should be more willing to sacrifice. The preliminary work of Loureiro

(2012) reveals that consumers tend to avoid activities that they also like to do (e.g., not dinning out, not having a family dinner, or not travelling abroad; also, they refrain from buying some other product, reduce the amount of money spent with family and friends, decrease their relaxation time) for their chosen brand (the brand that they like the most).Thus, the willingness to sacrifice should be a consequence of being in love and committed.

In a managerial point of view, managers should be aware of the importance of providing a good experience (stimulating curiosity and favourable emotions) in the relationship of the brand with their consumers. All products may carry a symbolic meaning associated to the emotions and feelings of interest to the experiential view. The good experience, together with the continued concern in order to communicate the brand identity, leads consumers to feel identified towards the brand, and helps to put the consumer in a state of passion and love. The strengthening of this state leads to the inclination for sacrifice.

Further research should be carried out in order to develop a scale to measure the willingness to sacrifice for a brand. Then, the framework should be tested. Since committed consumers are expected to be more willing to sacrifice, those consumers that belong to a brand community should be the most committed to a brand. Thus, in the future these consumers should provide a good way to understand which activities consumers would forgo because of the brand or would engage (even when they do not want to).

Another important issue is to understand the personality and socio-demographic characteristics of the consumers that are more willing to sacrifice. Consumers will be more willing to sacrifice for some type or category of brands, only more hedonic, iconic brands, or even brand with high equity? It could also be related to the consumer´s personality. Are consumers more likely to be addicted more willing to sacrifice for the brand?

REFERENCES

Aaker, D. A. (1996). *Building strong brands*. New York: The Free Press.

Keller, K.L. (1998). *Strategic Brand Management: Building, Measuring and Managing Brand Equity* (3rd ed.). Upper Saddle River NJ: Prentice Hall.

Agnew, C. R., and Etcheverry, P. E. (2006). *Cognitive interdependence: Considering self-in-relationship*. In K. D. Vohs, and E. J. Finkel (Eds.), Self and relationships: Connecting intrapersonal and interpersonal processes (pp. 274-293). New York: Guilford Press.

Agnew, C. R., Van Lange, P. A. M., Rusbult, C. E., and Langston, C. A. (1998). Cognitive interdependence: Commitment and the mental representations of close relationships. *Journal of Personality and Social Psychology, 74* (4), 939-954.

Ahuvia, A. C. (1993), *I Love It! Towards an Unifying Theory of Love Across Divers Love Objects* (Unpublished doctoral dissertation). Northwestern University, Evanston/Chicago, IL.

Albert, N., Merunka, D., and Valette-Florence, P. (2008a). When Consumers Love Their Brands: Exploring the Concept and its Dimensions. *Journal of Business Research, 61*(10), 1062-1075.

Albert, N., Merunka, D., and Valette-Florence, P. (2008b). The Feeling of Love Toward a Brand: Measurement and Concept. *Advances in Consumer Research, 36*, 300-307.

Anderson, E. W, and Fornell, C. (1994). A Customer Satisfaction Research Prospectus. In R. T. Rust and R. L. Oliver (Eds.), *Service Quality: New Directions in Theory and Practice* (pp. 241-268). Thousand Oaks, CA: Sage Publications.

Batra, R., Ahuvia, A. C., and Bagozzi, R. (2008). *Brand love: Its Nature and Consequences* (Working Paper). Michigan Dearborn University, Ann Arbord, MI.

Batra, R., Ahuvia, A., and Bagozzi, R. P. (2012). Brand Love. *Journal of Marketing, 76*(2), 1-16.

Batson, C. D., Bolen, M. H., Cross, J. A., and Neuringer-Benefiel, Helen E. (1986). Where is the altruism in the altruistic personality?. *Journal of Personality and Social Psychology, 50*(1), 212–220.

Brakus, J. J., Schmitt, B. H., and Zarantonello, L. (2009). Brand Experience: What Is It? How Is It Measured? Does It Affect Loyalty?. *Journal of Marketing, 73* (May), 52–68.

Cronin, J.J., Brady, M.K., and Hult, G.T.M. (2000). Assessing the effects of quality, value, and customer satisfaction on consumer behavioral intentions in service environments. *Journal of Retailing, 76*(2), 193-218.

Brucks, M., Zeithaml, V. A., and Naylor, G. (2000). Price and brand name as indicators of quality dimensions for consumer durables. *Journal of the Academy of Marketing Science, 28*(3), 359–734.

Carroll, B. A., and Ahuvia, A. C. (2006). Some Antecedents and Outcomes of Brand Love. *Marketing Letters, 17*(2), 79-90.

Chang, P.-L., and Chieng, M.-H. (2006). Building Consumer–Brand Relationship: A Cross-Cultural Experiential View. *Psychology and Marketing, 23*(11), 927–959.

Csikszentmihalyi, M. (2000). The Costs and Benefits of Consuming. *Journal of Consumer Research, 27*(2), 267-272.

Davis, R., Buchanan-Oliver, M., and Brodie, R. (2000). Retail service branding in electronic-commerce environments. *Journal of Service Research, 3*(November), 178-186.

de Chernatony, L. (2001). A model for strategically building brands. *Brand Management, 9*(1), 32-44.

Delgado-Ballester, E., Munuera-Aleman J. L., and Yagoe-Guillin M. J. (2003). Development and validation of a Brand Trust Scale. *International Journal of Market Research, 45*(1), 335-353.

Dodds, W.B., Monroe, K.B., and Grewal, D. (1991). Effects of price, brand, and store information on buyers' product evaluations. *Journal of Marketing Research, 28*(3), 307-319.

Erickson, G. M., and Johansson, J. K. (1985). The role of price in multi-attribute product evaluations. *Journal of Consumer Research, 12*(2), 195–199.

Escalas, J. E. (2004). Narrative Processing: Building Consumer Connections to Brands. *Journal of Consumer Psychology, 14*(1 and 2), 168-179.

Escalas, J. E., and Bettman, J. R. (2003). You Are What They Eat: The Influence of Reference Groups on Consumer Connections to Brands. *Journal of Consumer Psychology, 13*(3), 339-48.

Escalas, J. E., and Bettman, J. R. (2005). Self-Construal, Reference Groups, and Brand Meaning. *Journal of Consumer Research, 32*(3), 378-389.

Evans, D., Price, S., and Blahut, S. (2005). Evaluating the truth brand. *Journal of Health Communication,* 10(2), 181–192.

Evrard, Y., and Aurier, P. (1996). Identification and Validation of the Components of the Person-Object Relationship. *Journal of Business Research, 37*(2), 127-134.

Finn, A. (2005). Reassessing the foundations of customer delight. *Journal of Service Research, 8*(2), 103-116.

Fournier, S. (1998). Consumers and Their Brands: Developing Relationship Theory in Consumer Research. *Journal of Consumer Research, 24*(4), 343-373.

Gable, S. L., and Reis, H. T. (2001). Appetitive and aversive social interaction. In J. M. Harvey and A. E. Wenzel, (Eds.), *Close romantic relationships: Maintenance and enhancement* (pp. 169–194). Mahwah. NJ: Lawrence Erlbaum Associates.

Gentile, C., Spiller, N., and Noci, G. (2007). How to Sustain the Customer Experience: An Overview of Experience Components that Co-create Value with the Customer, *European Management Journal 25*(5), 395–410. doi: 10.1016/j.emj.2007.08.005.

Keh, H. T., Pang, J., and Peng, S. (2007). Understanding and Measuring Brand Love. In J. R. Priester, D. J. MacInnis, and C. W. Park (Eds.). *New Frontiers in Branding: Attitudes, Attachments, and Relationships* (pp. 84-88). Santa Monica, CA: Society for Consumer Psychology.

Hirschman, Elizabeth C. and Morris B. Holbrook (1982), "Hedonic Consumption: Emerging Concepts, Methods and Propositions," *Journal of Marketing*, 46(Summer), 92-101.

Holbrook, M. B. (2000). The millennial consumer in the texts of our times: Experience and entertainment. *Journal of Macromarketing, 20*(2), 178-192.

Holbrook, M. B., and Hirschman, E. C. (1982). The Experiential Aspects of Consumption: Consumer Fantasies, Feelings and Fun. *Journal of Consumer Research, 9*(2), 132-40.

Impett, E. A., Gable, S. L., and Peplau, L. A. (2005). Giving Up and Giving In: The Costs and Benefits of Daily Sacrifice in Intimate Relationships. *Journal of Personality and Social Psychology, 89*(3), 327–344.

Jack, D. C. (1991). *Silencing the self: Women and depression.* Cambridge, MA: Harvard University Press.

Johnson, M. D., Herrmann, A., and Huber, F. (2006). The Evolution of Loyalty Intentions. *Journal of Marketing, 70*(April), 122-132.

Jordan, J. V. (1991). The relational self: A new perspective for understanding women's development. In J. Strauss and G. R. Goethals (Eds.), *The self: Interdisciplinary approaches* (pp. 136–149). New York: Springer-Verlag.

Kardes, F. R., Cronley, M. L., Kellaris, J. J., and Posavac, S. S. (2004). The role of selective information processing in price–quality inference. *Journal of Consumer Research, 31*(2), 368–374.

Kamat, V. V, and Parulekar, A. A. (2007). *Brand Love - the Precursor to Loyalty.* Advertising and Consumer Psychology Proceedings (pp. 94-98), Santa Monica.

Kelley, H. H. (1979). *Personal relationships: Their structures and processes.* Hillsdale, NJ: Erlbaum.

Kelley, H. H., and Thibaut, J. W. (1978). *Interpersonal relations: A theory of interdependence.* New York: Wiley.

Lerner, H. G. (1988). *Women in therapy.* New York: Perennial Library.

Lewandowski Jr., G. W., Aron, A., Bassis, S., and Kunak, J. (2006). Losing a self-expanding relationship: Implications for the self-concept. *Personal Relationships, 13*(3), 317-331.

Le, B., and Agnew, C. R. (2003). Commitment and its theoretical determinants: A meta-analysis of the Investment Model. *Personal Relationships, 10*(1), 37-57.

Loureiro, S. M. C., Kaufmann, H. R., and Vrontis, D. (2012). Brand Emotional Connection and Loyalty. *Journal of Brand Management* [online 24 February 2012], 1-15. doi:10.1057/bm.2012.3.

Loureiro, S. M. C. (2012). Brand experience and willingness to sacrifice for a brand. In S.-H. Lee (Ed.), *Proceedings of 2012 Global Marketing Conference - Globalization and Marketing Performance* (pp. 57-74). Seoul: Yonsei University Graduate School and Sogang Business School.

Mano, H., and Oliver, R. L. (1993). Assessing the Dimensionality and Structure of Consumption Experience: Evaluation, Feeling, and Satisfaction. *Journal of Consumer Research, 20*(3), 451-466.

Mattingly, B. A., and Clark, E. M. (2010). The Role of Activity Importance and Commitment on Willingness to Sacrifice. *North American Journal of Psychology, 12*(1), 51-66.

Meyer, C., and Schwager, A. (2007). Understanding Customer Experience. *Harvard Business Review*, February, 117–26.

Monroe, K. B., and Chapman, J. D. (1987). Framing Effects on Buyers´ Subjective Product Evaluations. *Advances in Consumer Research, 14*, 193-197.

Muniz, A. M., and O'Guinn, T. C. (2001). Brand community. *Journal of Consumer Research, 27*(4), 412- 432.

Oliver, R. L. (1993). Cognitive, Affective, and Attribute Bases of the Satisfaction Response. *Journal of Consumer Research, 20*(3), 418-430.

Oliver, R. L., and Westbrook, R. A. (1993). Profiles of consumer emotions and satisfaction in ownership and usage. *Journal of Consumer Satisfaction, Dissatisfaction and Complaining Behavior, 6*, 12-27.

Oliver, R. L., Rust, R. T., and Varki, S. (1997). Customer delight: Foundations, findings and managerial insight. *Journal of Retailing, 73*(3), 311-336.

Padgett, D., and Allen, D. (1997). Communicating Experiences: A Narrative Approach to Creating Service Brand Image. *Journal of Advertising, 26*(4 Winter), 49-62.

Plutchik, R. (1980). *Emotions: A Psychoevolutionary Synthesis*. New York: Harper and Row.

Powell, C., and van Vugt, M. (2003). Genuine giving or selfish sacrifice? The role of commitment and cost level upon willingness to sacrifice. *European Journal of Social Psychology, 33*(3), 403-412.

Richins, M. L. (1997). Measuring emotions in the consumption experience. *Journal of Consumer Research, 24*(2), 127-146.

Rusbult, C. E. (1980). Commitment and satisfaction in romantic associations: A test of the investment model. *Journal of Experimental and Social Psychology, 16*, 172-186.

Rusbult, C. E., and van Lange, P. A. M. (1996). Interdependence processes. In E. T. Higgins, and A. W. Kruglanski (Eds.), *Social psychology: Handbook of basic principles* (pp. 564-596). New York, NY: Guilford Press.

Rusbult, C. E., and van Lange, P. A. M. (2003). Interdependence, interaction, and relationships. *Annual Review of Psychology, 54*(February), 351-375.

Rusbult, C. E., Olson, N., Davis, J. L., and Hannon, M. A. (2001). Commitment and relationship maintenance mechanisms. In J. M. Harvey and A. E. Wenzel (Eds.), *Close romantic relationships: Maintenance and enhancement* (pp. 87-113). Mahwah, NJ: Lawrence Erlbaum Associates.

Russell, J. A. (1980). A circumplex model of affect. *Journal of Personality and Social Psychology, 39*(6), 1161-1178.

Schmitt, B. H. (1999). *Experimental Marketing: How to get customers to sense, feel, think, act, relate, to your company and brands*. New York: The Free Press.

Schmitt, B. (2012). The consumer psychology of brands. *Journal of Consumer Psychology, 22* (1), 7–17.

Solomon, R. C. (1994). *About love: reinventing romance for our times*. Lanham, MD: Rowman and Littlefield.

Sternberg, R. J. (1986). A Triangular Theory of Love. *Psychologist Review, 93*(2), 119-135.

Sternberg, R. J. (1997). Construct Validation of a Triangular Love Scale. *European Journal of Social Psychology, 27*(3), 313-335.

Strongman, K. T. (1996). *The psychology of emotion: Theories of emotion in perspective* (4th ed.). New York: John Wiley and Sons.

Teas, R. K., and Agarwal, S. (2000). The Effects of Extrinsic Product Cues on Consumers' Perceptions of Quality, Sacrifice, and Value. *Journal of the Academy of Marketing Science, 28*(2), 278-290.

Thomson, M., MacInnis, D. J., and Park, W. C. (2005). The Ties that Bind: Measuring the Strength of Consumers' Emotional Attachment to Brands. *Journal of Consumer Psychology, 15*(1), 77-91.

Van Lange, P. A. M., Agnew, C. R., Harinck, F., and Steemers, G. E. M. (1997). From game theory to real life: How social value orientation affects willingness to sacrifice in ongoing close relationships. *Journal of Personality and Social Psychology, 73*(6), 1330–1344.

Van Lange, P. A. M., Rusbult, C. E., Drigotas, S. M., Arriaga, X. B., Witcher, B. S., and Cox, C. L. (1997). Willingness to sacrifice in close relationships. *Journal of Personality and Social Psychology, 72*(6), 1373–1395.

Verhoef, P. C., Lemon, K. N., Parasuraman, A., Roggeveen, A., Tsiros, M., and Schlesinger, L. A. (2009). Customer Experience Creation: Determinants, Dynamics and Management Strategies. *Journal of Retailing 85*(1), 31–41.

Völckner, F. (2008). The dual role of price: decomposing consumers' reactions to price. *Journal of the Academy of Marketing Science, 36*, 359–377.

Watson, D., and Tellegen, A. (1985). Toward a consensual structure of mood. *Psychology Bulletin, 98*(2), 219-235.

Westbrook, R. A, and Oliver, R. L. (1991). The Dimensionality of Consumption Emotion Patterns and Consumer Satisfaction. *Journal of Consumer Research, 18*(1), 84-91.

Wieselquist, J., Rusbult, C. E., Foster, C. A., and Agnew, C. R. (1999). Commitment, pro-relationship behavior, and trust in close relationships. *Journal of Personality and Social Psychology, 77*(5), 942–966.

Zeithaml, V. A. (1988). Consumer Perceptions of Price, Quality, and Value: A Means-End Model and Synthesis of Evidence. *Journal of Marketing, 52*(July), 2-22.

Zeithaml, V. A., Berry, L. L., and Parasuraman, A. (1996). The Behavioral Consequences of Service Quality. *Journal of Marketing, 60*(April), 31-46.

In: Psychology of Branding
Editor: W. Douglas Evans

ISBN: 978-1-62618-817-4
© 2013 Nova Science Publishers, Inc.

Chapter 4

You're Nothing Without Me: What Consumers Contribute to Brands

Rodoula H. Tsiotsou[1] *and Ronald E. Goldsmith*[2]

[1]University of Macedonia, Thessaloniki, Macedonia, Greece
[2]Florida State University, Tallahassee, FL, US

ABSTRACT

"At the heart of most corporate strategies lies a marketing strategy, and at the heart of most marketing strategies lies a branding strategy." This proposal is based on the idea that the three most important assets (i.e., difficult to duplicate) of any company are: (1) its proprietary assets such as formulas, patents, and innovative processes; (2) its brands; and (3) its customers. Thus, brands and branding strategy are key components for any successful business. The value of a brand, however, is not restricted to a name, logo, or symbol, but also includes the community of customers who buy it. This chapter proposes a model of branding strategy that features two actors, the managers on the selling side and the consumers on the buying side. This model shows how the brand unites these actors into a cooperative activity that creates the brand. Branding is the outcome of an interaction between the two parties. Both contribute to the brand and what it means. Our focus is on the consumer side of the model and on the many ways in which consumers comprehend and interact with brands, representing their contribution to the phenomenon called "branding." After all, a "brand" without consumers is not really a brand but a pile of unsold product, suitable only for the recycling bin.

INTRODUCTION

Most discussions of branding are oriented around brand strategy, that is, the way brand managers spend their budgets to position their brands to specific target segments of consumers. Many other discussions of branding describe how consumers react to these strategies. In both instances, the assumption has been that the managerial side is active and the consumer side is passive. That is, the managers do things with their strategy to which the consumer reacts, favorably or unfavorably. In recent years, however, three converging changes have characterized the brand landscape to fundamentally alter this perspective. First, stimulated by the spread and growing sophistication of web-based and mobile phone technologies, consumers have become more and more engaged with brands so that the consumer side has become a more active contributor to the brand creation, alteration, and management process (Allen, Fournier, and Miller, 2008; Bernhoff and Li, 2008). Second, many branding theorists and consultants have begun to advocate changes in managerial practice that share power with consumers and actively incorporate the consumer contribution to the brand (Chiu et al., 2012; Christodoulides, 2009). Third, an increasing number of brand managers have actually begun to embrace the consumer contribution to their brands and to develop new management strategies to incorporate consumer activity into their existing branding efforts (Elliott, 2006; Hollebeek, 2011).

Because of these changes, both managers and researchers need to become more aware of how consumers interact with brands and the psychology underlying consumer brand co-creation. The purpose of this chapter is to describe many of the new developments in this area that reflect the theoretical and empirical research of consumer researchers who study consumer-brand relationships. The chapter begins with brief descriptions of the importance of brands to companies and to consumers. Then, we present a model of the brand creation and management process that reflects the contribution of both marketers and consumers. Next, we present several of the newer approaches to understanding consumer-brand relationships and describe some of the ways in which consumers are changing how they interact with brands. Finally, the chapter closes with some managerial responses to the challenges new consumers present as well as implications for further research.

WHY ARE BRANDS IMPORTANT TO MARKETERS AND TO CONSUMERS?

Along with physical and intellectual property and consumers, brands are the most important assets a company has. Brands are valuable because retailers and consumers trust and prefer them, consumers will pay more to get their preferred brand, their recognizability and availability reduce marketing costs, and the equity in a brand name can facilitate brand and line extensions. In the words of Rust, Zeithaml, and Lemon (2004, p. 111) " ... in large consumer-goods companies like General Motors, brands are the raison d'etre. They are the focus of decision making and the basis of accountability. They are the fiefdoms, run by the managers with the biggest jobs and the biggest budgets." Brand management is the activity that turns commodity products into brands. A way to conceptualize the marketers' contribution to the brand management process is to consider their goals. From the marketer point-of-view, what are the goals of branding?

1. to make the product distinctive and stand out from the crowd
2. to give the product an image or personality (positioning the brand)
3. the brand then takes on an identity describing who the brand is and what it stands for
4. the brand also represents or can represent the company's image and reputation

5. the ultimate goal is to establish a relationship between the company and the consumer that is a source of revenue, but also becomes an important part of the brand itself

From the consumer point-of-view, we can also consider why brands are important. Consumers use brands and the information conveyed by the brand for several purposes beyond the intrinsic benefits the product provides and could be provided by a commodity version.

1. they allow consumers to distinguish one company's product from another company's product
2. this information allows consumers to make judgments of quality, reliability, suitability; the brand can also be a stimulus to prompt purchase in the absence of careful cognitive evaluation
3. they use the brand image to create and display their own self-images
4. the brand's personality permits them to interact with the brand, the company, and other consumers; some consumers will actively co-create the brand
5. they form relationships with the company through the brand that they find satisfying; they may become brand advocates and act independently of the company
6. brands may form the "glue" that permit social interactions among consumers based on them

For both parties, then, brands are important and valuable because they contribute to both parties' achievement of important goals. The benefits of brands to marketers have been long recognized. Branding theorists have traditionally expressed the benefits brands bring to consumers as functional or utilitarian in nature, with some attention given to the self-identity and self-expression benefits some brands could provide (Belk, 1988; Hirschman and Holbrook, 1982; McCracken, 1988, Tsiotsou, 2012). What is new is the more active role that consumers increasingly take in the brand creation process. This role is depicted in the model of the brand creation process.

A MODEL OF THE BRAND CREATION PROCESS

Figure 1 presents a conceptual model of the brand co-creation and management process. The fundamental idea expressed in the model is that a brand is the co-creation of the complementary activities of managers, consumers and other consumers. Managers create brands through the decisions they make as part of the strategy development and implementation process. The elements of the strategy (shown on the left side of the model) consist of the traditional 4Ps of product, price, promotion, and place, and in this model include the additional four decision areas described by Goldsmith (1991): physical assets, personnel, personalization, and procedures.

This aspect of the model is, until recently, the standard approach to explaining brand building and management, described in considerable detail in many books such as Aaker (1996), Keller (2012), and Aaker and Joachimsthaler (2000).

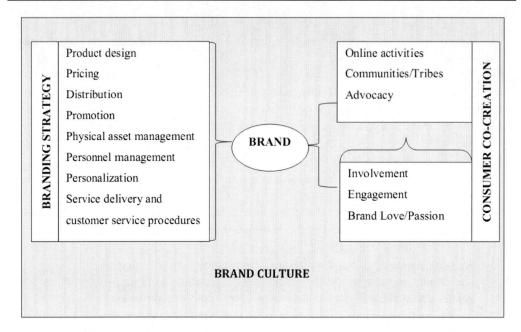

Figure 1. A Brand Co-creation Model.

The right side of the model represents the newer developments in the marketplace whereby brands engage consumers and stimulate emotional attachments that motivate them to actively participate in brand creation in a variety of ways.

The activities of both parties, managers and consumers, facilitate the development of a brand culture. Culture can be used by managers to build the brand via (a) the collaboration and engagement of company employees and (b) via consumers' involvement/engagement, advocacy, and consumer groups' activities. Moreover, managers can use the brand to build the brand culture via (a) associations (brand identity, image and personality) and (b) consumer relationships (e.g., brand attachment and passion).

Several patterns describe the types of brand interactions that consumers can manifest. These patterns can be seen in a relationship continuum as Figure 2 shows and can be ordered in terms of their intensity of consumer feelings toward the brand.

1. Negative Brand Relationship. There is a flip side to brand engagement, the negative reaction to the brand that prompts negative word of mouth and active disparagement and revenge activities. Consumers do not like the brand and they might boycott it (Malaer et al., 2010) and ask from their friends and family to do the same.
2. No Brand Relationship. Consumers buy the brand by habit with little thought. Switching is easy with little emotional content. Low price, coupons, or point of sale marketing can be effective.
3. Brand relationship. Consumers have feelings about the brand and recognize that it has an image and a personality. Consumers use the brand to express self-image. Loyalty is high and brand switching is difficult. Price sensitivity is higher than with no relationship.

4. Strong brand relationship and relationships with other consumers. The consumer has strong positive feelings about the brand so that it forms part of self-image. The brand is an important part of the consumer's life.

Some consumers demonstrate fanatical emotional attachments such as feelings of passion and love, intimacy and dedication towards the brands they have decided to follow. The attachment is so strong that some may express extreme, addictive, and compulsive behaviors (Chung et al., 2008; Tsiotsou and Goldsmith, 2011).

As consumers progress through the types of relationships they can have with brands, from none to passion, they actively co-create the brand by interacting with the marketer and other consumers. Brands become the "excuse" for interacting with other consumers and thus, they can assist in fulfilling their social needs and goals. Nowadays, this last pattern is the most important to branding strategy.

The fourth type of interaction forms the focus of the present chapter. These interactions are the newest and promise to be the most important in shaping future consumer-brand relationships. But why do consumers form strong attachments to brands?

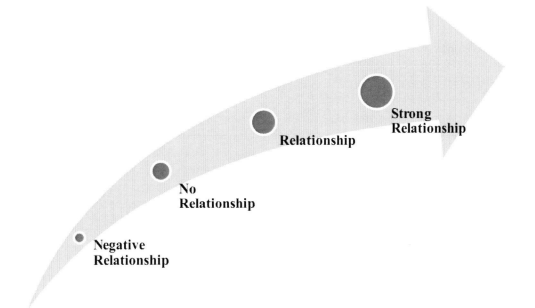

Figure 2. The Consumer-Brand Relationship Continuum.

THE PSYCHOLOGY OF CONSUMER-BRAND RELATIONSHIPS

Marketing and consumer research has a long history of studying consumer/brand interaction. The managerial side of the model is well documented. Based on this body of research, numerous books have been written prescribing branding strategies (e.g., Aaker and Joachimsthaler, 2000), not to mention a whole host of managerial accounts of "how we did it." On the consumer side, the focus of the research was always on how passive consumers reacted to the strategy. One exception to this pattern has been the venerable stream of social communication research that studies how consumers actively spread positive or negative word-of-mouth about brands. This stream of research, however, dealt with how consumers socially interact regarding brands, affecting brand reputation and market acceptance more than it does the nature of the brand itself.

In recent years, research has moved from the consumer-brand transaction/interaction paradigm to the consumer-relationship perspective. Thus, researchers have gradually developed concepts that describe consumer relationships with brands that present consumers as both more emotionally involved with brands than originally assumed and more active in their behavior toward brands. These relationships have the effect of taking some control over the brand away from the brand managers so that consumers increasingly have become co-creators and co-owners of many brands (Allen et al., 2008). The question remains, what explains these consumer activities that effectively transform brands? Why do consumers want to own, co-create, or contribute to the branding process? Researchers have long studied consumer emotional ties to brands, and this stream of research has recently broadened into the study of consumer/brand relationships as it seeks to explain the psychology of this type of consumer behavior. The historical evolution of this stream of research has incorporated the terms, involvement, engagement, and advocacy to describe these phenomena.

Involvement

Historically, researchers used the term *involvement* to describe the type and intensity of consumer interaction with products that could be distinguished from the vague idea of how "important" a product was judged to be by a consumer. Products can be important because they fulfill vital consumer needs. The concept of product importance seems most appropriate for describing functional or utilitarian product benefits, such as the importance of laundry detergent to housewives based on their need to clean clothing. Tires might form a similarly important product for many men concerned with the safety and performance of their cars. Once we add to this consumer-product interaction an emotional component, however, importance alone no longer seems to accurately describe how consumers relate to products. Consumers can intellectually evaluate how important a product is to them, but they can also experience emotional reactions to products that importance does not describe very well. Tires, for example, can elicit emotional responses of pride, power, and masculinity in addition to intellectual judgments of their safety and durability. Emotionally involving products, however, are also deemed by consumers to be important. Thus, all involving products are important, but not all important products are involving. Failure to realize this led to early confusion and debates regarding the nature of product involvement.

Because consumer research already had the concept of involvement with advertising to describe deep cognitive processing of ad messages (see Greenwald and Leavitt, 1984 for a review), it was necessary to carve out a separate concept for product involvement. To clarify the issue, Houston and Rothschild (1978) seem to have been the first to articulate a concept of product involvement distinct from involvement with advertisements by distinguishing situational involvement, response involvement, and enduring product involvement, as three types of consumer interaction with products. *Situational involvement* stems from the "ability of a situation to elicit from individuals concern of their behavior in that situation" (p. 184). Situational involvement thus seems to describe a short term reaction to a situation arising from the interaction of the consumer with the situation. *Response involvement* describes the intensity of cognitive responses to persuasive messages. Finally, Houston and Rothschild (1978) proposed that *enduring product involvement* could be distinguished from the other types of involvement because it describes degrees of the bond a consumer feels toward a product reflecting the strength of the social and personal values expressed by the product and is developed through a history of prior experience with the product. This distinction is important because it separated the concept of involvement from one-off situations and responses to advertising, provided a reason why consumers would become involved with products, and brought in individual differences in consumer values as a defining characteristics of involvement.

Bloch (1986) advanced the concept of product involvement by defining it as "an unobservable state reflecting the amount of interest, arousal, or emotional attachment a consumer has with a product" (p. 77), thus broadening the concept of involvement beyond the reliance on values as the driving motivation and embracing feelings of "enthusiasm and excitement" toward products for whatever reasons the products stimulate these emotions in consumers. Consumers appear to become involved with product categories because they fulfill important needs for consumers. When these needs are largely utilitarian in nature, consumers become experts in the product category by acquiring vast knowledge of the category through experience and study. For instance, homemakers learn which products best solve their problems, thereby becoming very knowledgeable, which then leads them become opinion leaders for others who seek their advice.

When the needs are psychological (symbolic or self-expressive), emotional, or social in nature, consumers become involved in product categories that especially satisfy these needs. Product categories such as movies, clothing, food, automobiles, or sports are examples of categories that consumers become especially involved with because they derive great satisfaction by consuming them. Their satisfactions are less utilitarian in nature and more emotional, self-expressive, or social. Laaksonen (1994, 1999) describes involvement as a sort of personal importance derived from the "psychological linkages" consumers make with product categories that engage their emotions, express their values, become part of their self-concepts, or define their social roles. Consumers enjoy consuming in these categories and therefore actively acquire information about them, become knowledgeable about them, consume them heavily, and become opinion leaders for them (Flynn, Goldsmith, and Eastman, 1996). Hobbies or collections also are an instance of this type of behavior.

Engagement

For a long time, however, enduring product involvement seemed to describe only a consumer response to a product *category* and not to specific brands. Consumers' active involvement with the brand, however, is a necessary condition for value creation and a prime driver of the value creation process (Tzokas and Saren, 1997). Therefore, the next step was to describe consumer involvement with specific brands, which came to be called *consumer brand engagement*. As this blanket term "engagement" became popular among managers, consultants, and researchers, however, it has come to be applied to many aspects of consumer behavior (Hollebeek, 2011). Researchers might refer for example to "advertising engagement," which appears to describe a situation in which a consumer exposed to an ad pays close attention to it, reacts intensively either in a cognitive or emotional way, remembers it, and likely is influenced by the ad to do something. Brand engagement is a widely discussed concept. Bowden (2009, p. 65) reviewed the use of the term and proposed that it could be conceptualized as "a psychological process that models the underlying mechanisms by which customer loyalty forms for new customers of a service brand as well as the mechanisms by which loyalty may be maintained for repeat purchase customers of a service brand." Note that Bowden (2009) seems to focus on the consumption of services in her definition. Emphasizing such related concepts as commitment, involvement, trust, loyalty, Bowden attempts to model the psychological "engagement" process by which satisfaction, trust, and affective commitment lead to loyalty.

Essentially, theorists resort to using synonyms and related terms to convey how they define engagement (Hollebeek, 2011). All the conceptualizations, however, seem to incorporate similar constructs. Consumers are thought to be engaged with an ad, service, product, or especially a brand, when that stimulus invokes their emotions, expresses their values or lifestyles, or helps them express and/or establish social relationships. Engagement seems to be a more specific and at the same time broader type of involvement, in that it is focused on a single stimulus rather than a product category, but also encompasses additional dimensions of cognitive and emotional energy. Trust, commitment, and meaning play a large role in engagement (Bowden, 2009), but so too do feelings of love and even passion. This is why brand engagement seems to be the most critical manifestation of the engagement phenomenon. Brands have personality, they act as symbols for values, they express meaning, and consumers invest emotional energy in what they hope is a reciprocal relationship in which the brand (company) will return their trust, commitment, and maybe even help to give their lives meaning and joy.

Note that traditional customer relationship marketing (CRM) and relationship marketing approached the strategy as one-way exchange with consumers having little opportunity to actively manage their part of the relationship beyond manifesting loyalty to the brand by simply responding to the firm's CRM and relationship marketing initiatives. Brand engagement as the goal of such strategies was limited to managers actively engaging consumers with the brand so that they would be more loyal than unengaged consumers, but leaving engaged consumers little scope to contribute. Beyond the concept of engagement, however, brand theorists have identified a more extreme form of brand engagement that raises the emotional ante for both brands and consumers and expresses the most extreme forms of the consumer-brand relationship continuum.

Brand Love

At the highest level of the consumer-brand relationship is brand love. Consumers do not only develop strong emotional links with brands, but these emotions are transformed to love over time. Thus, consumers do not hesitate to declare their feelings toward the brand and state "I love ... this brand!!!!" Brand love is an interpersonal construct playing a central and relevant role in the consumer-brand relationship. Brand love is considered a rich, deep, and long-lasting feeling (Carroll and Ahuvia, 2006) defined as "the degree of passionate emotional attachment that a person has for a particular trade name" (Carroll and Ahuvia, 2006, p. 81). Although significant in consumer-brand relationships, brand love has attracted only recently research attention in marketing (Albert et al., 2008). Consumers convey their love for a brand as attachment and passion for the brand, love assertions for the brand, and positive evaluations and emotions for the brand (Ahuvia, 2005). Brand love consists of seven core elements: self-brand integration, passion-driven behaviors, positive emotional connection, long-term relationship, positive overall attitude valence, attitude certainty and confidence, and anticipated separation distress (Batra, Ahuvia, and Bagozzi, 2012). Recent evidence suggests that in order to build brand love, the brand should express the individual and social self of the consumer, inspire trust, and consumers should be emotionally attached to them (Tsiotsou and Goldsmith, 2011). However, brand love plays a central role in post consumption consumer behaviors as well which is expressed as positive word-of-mouth and brand loyalty (Batra et al., 2012; Carroll and Ahuvia, 2006) willingness to forgive and pay a price premium (Heinrich, Albrecht, and Bauer, 2010), and resistance to negative information (Batra et al., 2012).

If the story of branding were limited to our understanding of consumer-brand relationships in an environment free of modern Internet-based technology, the focus would be on how marketers could use their strategies to encourage and to maintain brand engagement and love as extensions of traditional branding practice. In the 21st century, however, social technology has changed the environment, empowering consumers and giving them tools they never had before to become more active contributors to the branding process (Uncles, 2008). The impact of social technologies on consumers is difficult to gauge, but it is so pervasive that Chui et al. (2012, p. 1) describe it as a "sweeping cultural, social, and economic phenomenon." Social technologies empower consumers to take more control over brands, to interpret them in new ways, to support and promote them in new ways, to influence how they are viewed by others, and even to shape what the brand means (Chui et al., 2012). In short, consumers are becoming increasingly co-creators of brands and brand cultures. But how do they contribute to the brand? We can identify at least three ways in which consumers have become part of the branding process.

HOW DO CONSUMERS INTERACT WITH BRANDS?

Brands are symbolic entities that assist consumers in shaping and expressing their individual and social identities (Swaminathan, Page, and Gürhan-Canli, 2007). Therefore, there are two types of relationships that consumers might form because the brand exists (Swaminathan et al., 2007; Veloutsou, 2009). The first type is the consumer-brand relationship, which helps individuals express their individual identity; whereas the second type refers to the relationships consumers form with other consumers because of the brand (Veloutsou and Tsiotsou, 2011).

The relationship between consumers and brands could be based on any of the brand features. The brand consists of the symbol, the product, the person, and the firm behind the brand. The emotional and functional brand values form the consumer-brand relationship (Petruzzellis, Romanazzi, and Tassiello, 2011) and define the brand culture. Consumers can form emotional liaisons with the functionality of the brand (Petruzzellis et al., 2011), which derives from the product (Saren and Tzokas, 1998; Whang et al., 2004), the service (Dall'Olmo Riley and de Chernatony, 2000), or other characteristics of an offer, such as the music played in a certain retail outlet (Beverland et al., 2006). Brands have personality characteristics very similar to human characteristics that consumers can relate to and identify with (Aaker, 1997; Blackston, 1992; Fournierand and Yao, 1997; Keh, Pang, and Peng, 2007; Tsiotsou, 2012; Tsiotsou and Veloutsou, 2011). Brands may communicate their offers to customers in an individual or mass manner, while customers can provide feedback and brands can react to that input (Guese, 2010; Veloutsou, 2007). Therefore, it has been suggested that the consumer-brand relationship has an emotional and an informational aspect (Veloutsou, 2007).

In addition, brands act as agents that facilitate other relationships that consumers form amongst themselves. The need of individuals to join others is universal and natural because, consumers as human beings want to belong (McGee-Cooper, 2005). Thus, brands become the excuse that facilitates individuals who desire to form relationships with other individuals sharing similar interests and consumption patterns. The participation in brand communities or brand tribes or brand sub-cultures demonstrates the existence of this type of relationships. These relationships are discussed below.

We can identify at least three ways in which increasing numbers of consumers manifest strong brand relationships in their brand interactions: through their online activities, participation in consumer brand communities/tribes, and brand advocacy activities.

ONLINE CONSUMER-BRAND ACTIVITY

Consumer online brand activities are attracting recent research attention because they have significant impact on brand management and the firms (Christodoulides, 2009; Chui et al., 2012). Consumers gather information about brands online, order/buy brands online and exchange information with other consumers about brands. Electronic word-of-mouth (eWOM) (Goldsmith, 2006: Goldsmith and Horowitz, 2006) and user generated content (UGC) are common activities consumers are engaging online. eWOM is expressed as online consumer-to-consumer interactions about brands (e.g., talking about the watches of Swatch on Twitter) whereas UGC refers to the content produced and uploaded by consumers (e.g., comments and pictures taken from Hilton hotel in Greece). Muntinga, Moorman, and Smit (2011) have named the consumer online brand activities taking place in the social media as COBRAs (from the first letter of each word) and categorize them into three types: consuming, contributing, and creating activities. Consuming is the minimum level of COBRAs and involves consumer participation in brand related activities (e.g., viewing, listening, and watching, following, reading, downloading brand related material). Contributing is the middle level of COBRAs and refers to "user-to content and user-to-user interactions about brands" (p. 17) such as rating brands and commenting on brand-related material (e.g., videos, blogs, pictures, and ads). Creating is the highest level of brand related consumer online activity and includes active production and publication of brand-related content that others consume and contribute to (e.g., creation of blogs and writing articles or reviews about a brand).

Various motives lead consumers to engage in online brand-related activities. Studies show that these motives are different between consumer online brand activities (Berthon et al., 2008; Henning-Thurau and Walsh, 2003; Muntinga et al., 2011). Information about the brand, entertainment, and remuneration have been found to be significant motivations for consuming brand-related content (Henning-Thurau and Walsh, 2003; Muntinga et al., 2011) whereas personal identity, entertainment, integration and social interaction are motives associated with consumers contributing to brand-related content (Goldsmith and Horowitz, 2006; Muntinga et al., 2011). In addition to personal identity, entertainment, integration, and social interaction, empowerment motivates consumers for creating brand-related content (Muntinga et al., 2011).

Brand Communities/Tribes

The literature uses alternative terms to describe the groups consumers form around a brand. Examples include car clubs (Algesheimer, Dholakia, and Herrmann, 2005) and football fan clubs (Abosag, Roper, and Hind, 2012; Alexandris and Tsiotsou, 2012). The most often used terms to describe these groups are brand communities, brand tribes, or brand sub-cultures of consumption (Bazaki and Veloutsou, 2010; Cova and Pace, 2006; Fournier and Yao, 1997; Kozinets, 2001; Schouten and McAlexander, 2005; Veloutsou and Tsiotsou, 2011). Dholakia and Algesheimer (2011, p. 9) define a brand community as "*a collective of consumers organized around one particular brand, which is sustained through repeated online and/or offline social interactions and communication among its members who possess a consciousness of kind, feel moral responsibility toward one another, and embrace and propagate the collective's rituals and traditions.*" However, some academics distinguish brand communities from brand tribes (Bazaki and Veloutsou, 2010; Veloutsou and Tsiotsou, 2011).

Thus, brand communities have been considered as formal brand groups that consist of individuals who join the group willingly and acknowledge their membership of the group. Brand tribes on the other hand are groups of individuals that exhibit tribal behavior (Tsiotsou and Veloutsou, 2011); participants have not necessarily joined the group in some sort of formal manner, but they are demonstrating the behavior (Bazaki and Veloutsou, 2010; Veloutsou and Tsiotsou, 2011). Therefore, brand tribes have a wider membership than brand communities. Although brand tribes are not always so formal, their participants often have a sense of togetherness and belonging (Hamilton and Hewer, 2010).

Consumers differ in their motives to join a group of brand followers (Ouwersloot and Odekerken-Schröder, 2008). Based on the social identity theory, individuals need to interact or even feel strong interpersonal bonds to perceive themselves as members of a group (Brewer, 1991). The brand-group members often have some degree of awareness that they belong to the group and a sense of obligation towards the brand group (Muniz and O'Guinn, 2001). Moreover, group members might influence other group members but not to the same degree (Algesheimer et al., 2005). The members of the brand group differ in their experience, involvement and dedication to the group regarding the time of participation and devotion to brand related activities (Pongsakornrungsilp, 2010). Brand managers need to keep these nuances in the membership of brand communities in mind when seeking to collaborate in the branding process.

Nowadays, brand group followers play a significant role in brand creation and management. Brand communities may take greater control over the associations that characterize the brand rather than the company's brand management team (Muniz and O'Guinn, 2001). Thus, members of the brand group may create value by producing spin off products or concepts that are branded and create a counter brand without the assistance of the company (Cova and White, 2010). The literature suggests that brand tribes can actually work in a manner that is now expected of the company. However, in addition to their positive input, brand groups are capable of developing potentially dangerous opposition to the brand (Cova and White, 2010). Brand hijacking is a contemporary phenomenon of the influence these groups exert over brands (Cova and Pace, 2006). Brand supporters may support a brand that the producer attempts to remove from the market (Muniz and Schau, 2005). Due to the brand group pressure, companies have reintroduced discontinued products in the marketplace.

Brand Advocacy

When some consumers express their brand loyalty, engagement, and emotional attachments to brands in positive, demonstrative ways, they can be said to be *brand advocates*. This type of consumer/brand engagement is the logical outcome of extreme brand involvement. McConnel and Huba (2003) seem to be the originators of the concept of the *customer evangelist*, one who goes beyond spreading positive word-of-mouth about a brand and becomes a true advocate for the brand. According to Huba (2012, p. 46), customer evangelists "not only buy a brand's products or services, but also believe in them so much that they are compelled to spread the word, and voluntarily recruit their friends and colleagues on the brand's behalf. Customer evangelists aren't just buzz spreaders, influencers, 'sneezers' or mavens; they are, by nature, passionate people who are extroverted loyalists." Although few in number compared with the majority of brand loyalists, customer evangelists go to extremes expressing their emotional attachment to the brand in a variety of ways. According to Huba (2012, p. 46), they demonstrate their passion for the brand by:

1. passionately recommending a company to friends, neighbors, and colleagues
2. believe in the company and its people
3. purchase the company's products and services as gifts
4. provide unsolicited praise or suggestions for improvement
5. forgive occasional sub-par seasons or dips in customer service
6. they do not want to be bought, but extol the brand's virtues freely
7. feel part of something bigger than themselves

Creating brand evangelists who actively promote the brand and advocate for it is a worthwhile goal for any brand manager. Doing so turns ordinary brand loyalty into affection and action. Managers can strive to convert customers into brand advocates in a variety of ways (Oracle, 2011). First, they can segment their customers to reveal those most likely to become brand advocates by distinguishing them from the other customers on the basis of their past behavior. Brand advocates reveal themselves through their actions, and when these can be identified, they can form the basis for separating the advocates from the rest. Their "tracks" so to speak, are especially evident in the realm of social technology and social media, where advocates make themselves known by spreading online word-of-mouth, creating positive brand-relevant content such as videos, through their blogs, and leadership in brand communities. Once identified, managers can craft strategies to encourage their feelings for the brand not just through satisfaction, but exceeding satisfaction expectations. Oracle (2011) recommends using technology and management practice to enhance four aspects of a customer's interactions with the firm: focus on the customer's convenience, doing so as swiftly as possible to minimize customer waiting, making all customer interactions relevant to their needs, and exceed industry norms and customer expectations in all aspects of customer service. Treating customers as people, with personal services and respect, listening to their concerns and responding to them proactively, builds relationships that manifest as advocacy.

MANAGERIAL CHALLENGES

Brand managers once sought to capitalize on consumer involvement with brands to increase loyalty. Their managerial tool for doing this was to maintain and enhance customer satisfaction with the brand because this seemed to be the key to why customers were involved. Thus, achieving customer satisfaction by maintaining product quality and service quality was a top priority for most brand management strategies. As it became apparent, however, that some consumers go beyond involvement to engaging with brands because of the emotional ties they formed with them, managers realized that they had to enhance the brand experience itself. Taking satisfaction as a baseline guarantee, brand managers sought ways to further strengthen the emotional ties the form the heart of the engagement concept. For example, an article in the American Marketing Association's *Marketing News* (Sullivan, 2009, p. 20) challenged managers to "Engage Your Target" because "brand engagement - the emotional attachment customers have with a brand - is the ultimate measure of your marketing success because, simply stated, engaged customers are profitable customers." In line with this reasoning, Wayland and Cole (1997) support that the consumer-brand relationship should be the asset of any business, not the customer, while this relationship should be managed and evaluated in the same manner as any other asset (e.g., financial or physical).

The search was on for managerial tools for creating, maintaining, and increasing consumer-brand relationships in order to develop a brand culture that both managers and consumers can embrace. The field lay open for theorists and consultants alike to develop and popularize new ideas. Some consulting companies, notably One-to-One, emphasized customer relationship management as a systematic way to engage customers (Peppers and Rogers 1993). Others, such as Oracle and IBM offered software platforms that managers could use to facilitate engagement. No consensus emerged from this outpouring of ideas, methods, and technology so that, in the words of Robert Passikoff, a consultant cited by Sullivan (2009, p. 20), "'Brand engagement is anything that you do to the brand in any context that ultimately makes people, both emotionally and rationally, feel that the brand better meets the expectations they have for the category' than any other brand."

Brand relationship marketing strategies appear to be anything that managers can do with the brand to increase the connections between the customer and brand because the brand expresses some values of the customer, is part of and expresses a lifestyle, has emotional resonance for the customer, or can be seen as part of the consumer self-concept, helping to define who the customer is and what the customer believes. For example, according to Birkner (2011), managers should determine the philosophy of a brand and what it stands so that customers and identify with it, especially for lifestyle brands that customers see "as a reflection of themselves" or if "consumers aspire to or think of a brand as a representation of themselves" (Birkner, 2011, p. 23).

As new social technologies appeared, however, passing much control over the brand from the marketing manager to the consumer, the new challenge for management became how to adapt management philosophy and practice to the new environment (Uncles, 2008). The ownership of the brand has changed over time and moved from the marketer to the consumer (de Chernatony, 1993). Thus, managers need to re-evaluate their branding strategies, develop new ones that recognize the new role of the consumer and try to take advantage of it. The evolution of consumer-brand relationships from simple involvement through engagement to possibly brand love and advocacy presents managers with new challenges. These parameters should be taken into account when managing brands and designing branding strategies.

The attachment relationship that consumers develop with a brand is very important for companies because, as it has been suggested, a strong emotional attachment with the brand indicates a brand with high brand equity (Christodoulides et al., 2006). As managers adapt their strategies and culture to sharing ownership of the brand with consumers they should do so in a manner that enhances the attachments consumers feel toward the brand.

Consumer/brand relationships present marketers with at least three major management challenges: avoiding alienating customers and converting them into advocates rather than enemies, coping with growing customer power and co-ownership of brands, and using technology to promote positive consumer-brand relationships. In coping with these challenges, brand managers are going to have to adjust their feelings of control over the brand and adopt more cooperative attitudes when working with consumers to manage the brand. In addition, they will have to adopt and implement new technologies to actively engage with consumers by using the technologies that consumers prefer to use. New technologies have changed the way consumers interact with brands and how they express their feelings (negative or positive) toward brands. For example, recent evidence suggests social media can influence brand image, particularly hedonic image, while traditional marketing communications is superior in creating brand awareness and enhancing functional brand image (Bruhn, Schoenmueller, and Schäfer 2012). Managers will have to develop procedures that best utilize the technologies and implement the new strategies of cooperation. And finally, the culture of marketing organizations must change from viewing consumers as a passive "target" to integrate the new, powerful consumer as a partner into the branding process to the comfort and benefit of both parties.

In sum, although managers might have somewhat different motivations from consumers to establish and maintain a brand relationship, analyzing brand relationship strength from the consumer's perspective could help them develop a better and deeper understanding of how to manage the relationship to benefit their company.

IMPLICATIONS FOR RESEARCH

Our chapter provides a number of future research directions that academics could take in order to gain a better understand of the role of consumers in branding. First, future endeavors should try to empirically test our conceptual model of brand co-creation by examining the contribution of each brand strategy element as well as the consumer-brand and consumer-to-consumer relationships. In addition, the role of all these elements in developing a brand culture should be examined.

Second, the full spectrum of consumer-brand relationships as it is presented in our continuum should be studied. Up to recently, most research on branding has been focused on the "brand relationship" stage by studying the role of brand trust, value, and loyalty. "Strong brand relationship" only recently has attracted research attention and there is much more to be done on this area. "No relationship" and "negative relationship" are the less investigated areas that need further investigations in understanding how consumers behave toward the brand in these stages and the effect of these behaviors on the brand. As an example, using the CRM context as their setting, Ashley et al. (2011) describe some obstacles to relationship marketing engagement that mirror to some extent the practices recommended by Huba and the Oracle company to encourage its formation. Research should focus not only on the positive aspects of the powerful consumer, but also on the negative aspects that Ashley et al.'s (2011) research suggests. When consumers resist cooperating with managers, how can managers overcome this non-cooperation or at least mitigate its possible negative impact on the brand?

Third, it will be of great interest to examine when and how a consumer passes from one stage of the relationship continuum to the other. It is important for both, academics and managers, to know what factors act as catalysts in moving the consumer from one stage to the other. For example, we need to understand when and if consumers who have a negative relationship with a brand can build strong positive relationships with it and vice versa.

Finally, due to the evolution of the consumer-brand relationships, we need to understand that branding research has expanded its scope. The unit of analysis in consumer research is no longer limited to the individual level of consumption or the relationship between companies/brands and consumers but extends to the social aspect of consumption, known as the co-consuming (Arnould, Price, and Malshe, 2006).

CONCLUSION

The central thesis of this chapter is that the roles consumers play in the branding process have changed in recent years from largely passive reactions to marketing and branding strategies to active co-creation and co-ownership of brands. This transformation has been facilitated by the growth of social media and social networks. These tools empower consumers so they can interact with other consumers where they can post reviews of brand, describe their interaction with customer service departments and other touchpoints for the brand, exchange information and opinions, create brand relevant online content, and actively interact with brand management through recommendations and comments or by participating in sponsored activities. Consumers also form brand communities and become brand advocates. Consumers want to do these things because they feel the need to express their thoughts and feelings regarding the brand and their consumption of it. For many consumers, brands become important components of their self-image and self-concept. Consumers feel relationships with brands that they want to nourish and publicize. Brands, in this view, are beginning to serve not merely as functional, marketing tools, but as integral elements in the lives of many consumers, thus fulfilling their secondary roles as symbols for consumers that heretofore were one-sided and passively accepted by consumers, but that now have become owned by consumers who are eager to exercise their ownership rights.

Not only has this transformation affected consumers, but managers as well have had to re-conceptualize their role in the brand creation process to accommodate active consumer input. Marketers have traditionally focused on their side of the model, crafting a one-way strategy using the elements of product, price, promotion, and place to position a brand in the marketplace.

Brand management now has to incorporate the ideas that power over brands must be shared with consumers willingly or else it will be seized forcefully by consumers and that traditional branding strategies now have an additional element that accommodates consumer input. The model presented in this chapter tries to express this new way to view brand management.

Finally, the challenges for researchers are to further study the psychology of consumer/brand relationships to reveal as yet unformulated theories that account for these consumer behaviors. In this sense, the study of consumer/brand relationships is just beginning. Not only will consumer behavior theory itself benefit from this work, but brand strategy will be improved as well as managers incorporate new findings into their branding efforts. They will learn how best to make use of the positive consumer input and cope with the negative.

REFERENCES

Aaker, D. A. (1996). *Building strong brands*. New York: The Free Press.

Aaker, J. L. (1997). Dimensions of brand personality. *Journal of Marketing Research*, 34 (August), 347-356.

Aaker, D. A., and Joachimsthaler, E. (2000). *Brand leadership*. New York: The Free Press.

Abosag, I., Roper, S., and Hind, D. (2012). Examining the relationship between brand emotion and brand extension among supporters of professional football clubs. *European Journal of Marketing*, 46(9), 1233-1251. doi: 10.1108/03090561211247810.

Ahuvia, A. C. (2005). Beyond the extended self: loved objects and consumers identity narratives. *Journal of Consumer Research*, 32, 171-184.

Alexandris K., and Tsiotsou, R. (2012). Segmenting soccer spectators by attachment levels: A psychographic profile based on team self-expression and involvement. *European Sport Management Quarterly*, 12(1), 64-81.

Albert, N., Merunka, D. R., and Florence-Valette, P. (2008). "Conceptualizing and measuring consumers' love towards their brands," in *Society for Marketing Advances Proceedings*, 108-111.

Algesheimer, R., Dholakia, U., and Herrmann, A. (2005). The social influence of brand community: evidence from European car clubs. *Journal of Marketing*, 69 (July), 19-34.

Allen, C. T., Fournier, S., and Miller, F. (2008). Brands and their meaning makers. In C. P. Haugtvedt, P. M. Herr and F. R. Kardes (Eds.), *Handbook of Consumer Psychology* (pp. 781-821). New York: Psychology Press.

Arnould, E. J., Price, L. L., and Malshe, A. (2006). Toward a cultural resource-based theory of the customer. In R. F. Lusch and S. L. Vargo (Eds.), *The New Dominant Logic in Marketing* (pp. 320-333). Armonk: M. E. Sharpe.

Ashley, C., Noble, S. M., Donthu, N., and Lemon, K. N. (2011). Why customers won't relate: obstacles to relationship marketing engagement. *Journal of Business Research*, 64, 749-756.

Batra, R., Ahuvia, A., and Bagozzi, R. P. (2012). Brand love. *Journal of Marketing*, 76 (2), 1-16.

Bazaki, E., and Veloutsou, C. (2010). Brand communities, subcultures of consumption, neo-tribes: a melange of terminology. In Christodoulides G, Veloutsou C, Jevons, de Chernatony L and Papadopoulos N., *Contemporary Issues in Brand Management*, Athens Institute of Education and Research (ATINER), Athens, Greece, pp. 163-180.

Belk, R. W. (1988). Possessions and the extended self. *Journal of Consumer Research*, 15(2), 139-168.

Bernoff, J., and Li, C. (2008). Harnessing the power of the oh-so-social web. *MIT Sloan Management Review*, 49(3), 36-42.

Berthon, P. R., Pitt, L. F., and Campbell, C. (2008) Ad lib: when customers create the ad. *California Management Review*, 50(4), 6–30.

Beverland, M., Lim EAC., Morrison, M., and Terziovski, M. (2006). In-store music and consumer-brand relationships: rational transformation following experiences of (mis)fit. *Journal of Business Research*, 59, 982-989.

Birkner, C. (2011). Lifestyle brands make it personal. *Marketing News*, 45(2), 22.

Blackston M. (1992). A Brand with an attitude: a suitable case for treatment. *Journal of Market Research Society*, 34 (3), 231-241.

Bloch, P. H. (1986). The product enthusiast: implications for marketing strategy. *Journal of Consumer Marketing*, 3(3), 51-62.

Bowden, J. L.-H. (2009). The process of customer engagement: a conceptual framework. *Journal of Marketing Theory and Practice*, 17(1), 63-74. doi: 10.2753/mtp1069-6679170105.

Brewer, M. (1991). The social self: on being the same and different at the same time. *Personality and Social Psychology Bulletin*, 17 (5), 475-482.

Bruhn, M., Schoenmueller, V., and Schäfer, D. B. (2012). Are social media replacing traditional media in terms of brand equity creation? *Management Research Review*, 35(9), 770-790.

Carroll, B. A., and Ahuvia, A., C. (2006). Some antecedents and outcomes of brand love. *Marketing Letters*, 17(2), 79-89.

Christodoulides, G. (2009). Branding in the post-internet era. *Marketing Theory*, 9(1), 141-144.

Christodoulides, G., de Chernatony, L., Furrer, O., and Abimbola, T. (2006). Conceptualizing and measuring the equity of online brands. *Journal of Marketing Management*, 22 (7/8), 799-825.

Chui, M. et al. (2012). The social economy: unlocking value and productivity through social technologies. Report by the McKinsey Global Institute, July 2012. http://www.mckinsey.com/insights/mgi/research/technology_and_innovation/the_social_economy.

Chung, E., Beverland, M., Farrelly, F., and Quester, P. (2008). Exploring consumer fanaticism: extraordinary devotion in the consumption context. *Advances in Consumer Research*, Vol. 35, pp. 333-340.

Cova, B., and Pace, S. (2006). Brand community of convenience products: new forms of customer empowerment – the case "my Nutella the community. *European Journal of Marketing*, 40 (9/10), 1087 – 1105.

Cova, B., and White, T. (2010). Counter-brand and alter-brand communities: the impact of Web 2.0 on tribal marketing approaches. *Journal of Marketing Management*, 26 (3/40), 256–270.

Dall'Olmo Riley, F., and deChernatony, L. (2000). The service brand as a relationship builder. *British Journal of Management*, 11 (20), 137-150.

deChernatony, L. (1993b). Categorizing brands: evolutionary processes underpinned by two key dimensions. *Journal of Marketing Management*, 9, 173-188.

Dholakia, U. M., and Algesheimer, R. (2011). Brand communities. In R. P. Bagozzi and A. A. Ruvio (Eds.), *Wiley International Encyclopedia of Marketing* (Vol. 3, pp. 9-17). Chichester, West Sussex: John Wiley and Sons Ltd.

Elliott, S. (2006). Letting consumers control marketing: priceless. *New York Times*, October 9, 2006, pp. C.8-C.8.

Flynn, L. R., Goldsmith, R. E., and Eastman, J. K. (1996). Opinion leaders and opinion seekers: two new measurement scales. *Journal of the Academy of Marketing Science*, 24(2), 137-147.

Fournier, S., and Yao, J. (1997). Reviving brand loyalty: a reconceptualization within the framework of consumer-brand relationships. *International Journal of Research in Marketing*, 14 (5), 451-472.

Goldsmith, R. E. (2006). Electronic word-of-mouth. In M. Khosrow-Pour (Ed.), *Encyclopedia of E-Commerce, E-Government and Mobile Commerce* (pp. 408-412). Hershey, PA: Idea Group Publishing.

Goldsmith, R. E. (1999). The personalized marketplace: beyond the 4Ps. *Marketing Intelligence and Planning*, 17(4), 178-185.

Goldsmith, R. E., and Horowitz, D. (2006) Measuring motivations for online opinion seeking. *Journal of Interactive Advertising*, 6(2). 3-14.

Greenwald, A. G., and Leavitt, C. (1984). Audience involvement in advertising: four levels. *Journal of Consumer Research*, 11(1), 581-592.

Guese, K. (2010). Relational norms in consumer-brand relationships: a comprehensive framework and an empirical test. 39th European Marketing Academy Conference (EMAC), 1-4 June, Copenhagen, Denmark.

Hamilton, K., and Hewer, P. (2010). Tribal mattering spaces: Social-networking sites, celebrity affiliations, and tribal innovations. *Journal of Marketing Management*, 26 (3/4), 271-289.

Hennig-Thurau, T., and Walsh, G. (2003). Electronic word of mouth: motives for and consequences of reading customer articulations on the internet. *International Journal of Electronic Commerce*, 8(2), pp. 54–74.

Heinrich, D., Albrecht, C-M. and Bauer, H. H. (2010). Love actually? Investigating consumers' brand love. *1st International Colloquium on the Consumer-Brand Relationship*, April 22-24, Orlando, Florida.

Hollebeek, L. (2011). Exploring customer brand engagement: definition and themes. *Journal of Strategic Marketing*, 19(7), 555-573.

Hirschman, E. C., and Holbrook, M. B. (1982). Hedonic consumption: emerging concepts, methods, and propositions. *Journal of Marketing*, 46(Summer), 92-101.

Houston, M. J., and Rothschild, M. L. (1978). Conceptual and methodological perspectives in involvement. 1978 Educators' Conference. S. C. Jain, ed., Chicago: American Marketing Association, pp. 184-187.

Huba, J. (2012). From word of mouth to customer evangelism. *Marketing News*, 46 (10), 2012, 46-46.

Keh, H. T., Pang. J., and Peng, S. (2007). Understanding and measuring brand love. In *Advertising and Consumer Psychology New Frontiers in Branding: Attitudes, Attachments, and Relationships*, Joseph R. Priester, Deborah J. MacInnis, and C. Whan Park, eds. Santa Monica, CA: Society for Consumer Psychology.

Keller, K. L. (2012). *Strategic brand management*, 4th edition. Upper Saddle River, NJ: Prentice Hall.

Laaksonen, P. (1994). *Consumer involvement: concepts and research*. London: Routledge.

Laaksonen, P. (1999). Involvement. In P. E. Earl and K. Simon (Eds.), *The Elgar Companion to Consumer Research and Economic Psychology* (pp. 341-347). Cheltenham, UK: Edward Elgar Publishing.

Malaer, L., Nyffenegger, B., Grohmann, B., and Krohmer, H. (2010). Characteristics of cult brands, 39th European Marketing Academy Conference (EMAC), 1-4 June, Copenhagen, Denmark.

McConnell, B., and Huba, J. (2003). *Creating customer evangelists: how loyal customers become a volunteer sales force*. Chicago: Dearborn Trade Pub.

McCracken, G. D. (1988). *Culture and consumption*. Bloomington, IN: Indiana University Press.

McGee-Cooper, A. (2005). Tribalism: culture wars at work. *The Journal for Quality and Participation*, 28 (1), 12-15.

Muniz, A., and O'Guinn, T. (2001). Brand community. *Journal of Consumer Research*, 27(March), 412-432.

Muniz, A., and Schau, H. J. (2005). Religiosity in the abandoned apple newton brand community. *Journal of Consumer Research*, 31(4), 737-747.

Muntinga, D. G., Moorman, M., and Smit, E. G. (2011). Introducing COBRAs exploring motivations for brand-related social media use. *International Journal of Advertising*, 30(1), 13-46.

Oracle (2011). Four effective service strategies that drive brand advocacy. 2011 White Paper, IT Business Edge.www.oracle.com/us/products/.../oracle-custadvocate-351029.pdf.

Ouwersloot, H., and Odekerken-Schröder, G. (2008). "Who's who in brand communities – and why? *European Journal of Marketing*, 42 (5/6), 571-585.

Peppers, D., and Rogers, M. (1993). *The one-to-one future: building relationships one customer at a time*. New York: Currency Doubleday.

Petruzzellis, L., Romanazzi, S., and Tassiello, V. (2011). Building relationships in financial services: paradigm in Mediterranean countries. *Journal of Brand Management*, 18 (4/5), 312-328.

Pongsakornrungsilp, S. (2010). Value co-creation process: reconciling s-d logic of marketing and consumer culture theory within the co-consuming group. University of Exeter. PhD Thesis.

Rust, R. T., Zeithaml, V. A., and Lemon, K. N. (2004). Customer-centered brand management. *Harvard Business Review*, 82, 110-118.

Saren, M., and Tzokas, N. (1998). The nature of the product in market relationships: a plury-signified product concept. *Journal of Marketing Management*, 14 (5), 445-464.

Schouten, J., and McAlexander, J. (2005). Subcultures of consumption: an ethnography of the new bikers. *Journal of Consumer Research*, 12 (June), 43-61.

Sullivan, E. A. (2009). Engage your target. *Marketing News*, 43(4), 20-20.

Swaminathan, V, Page, K. L., and Gürhan-Canli, Z. (2007). 'My' brand or 'our' brand: the effects of brand relationship dimensions and self-construal on brand evaluations. *Journal of Consumer Research*, 34 (August), 248-259.

Tsiotsou, R (2012). Developing a scale for measuring the personality of sport teams. *Journal of Services Marketing*, 26 (4), 238-252.

Tsiotsou, R., and Goldsmith, R. E. (2011). Exploring the formation process of brand love: a comparison between goods and services. 2011 Academy of Marketing Science World Marketing Congress (July 19-23). Reims, France, pp. 557-561.

Tsiotsou, R., and Veloutsou, C. (2011). The role of brand personality on brand relationships and tribal behavior: an integrative model. 40th European Marketing Academy Conference p. 1-8 (May 24-27, 2011), Slovenia.

Tzokas, N., and Saren, M. (1997). Building relationship platforms in consumer markets: a value chain approach. *Journal of Strategic Marketing*, 5 (2), 105-120.

Uncles, M. (2008). Know thy changing consumer. *Journal of Brand Management*, 15, 227-231.

Veloutsou, C. (2007). Identifying the dimensions of the product-brand and consumer relationship. *Journal of Marketing Management*, 23(1/2), 7-26.

Veloutsou C. (2009). Brands as relationship facilitators in consumer markets. *Marketing Theory*, 9(1), 127-130.

Veloutsou, C., and Tsiotsou, R. (2011). Examining the link between brand relationships and tribal behaviour: a structural model. 7th Thought Leaders International Conference in Brand Management, p. 1-8 (March 10-12, 2011), Lugano, Switzerland.

Wayland, R. E. and Cole, P. M. (1997): *Customer connections: New strategies for growth.* Boston: Harvard Business School Press.

Whang, Y. O., Allen, J., Sahoury, N., and Zhang, H. (2004). Falling in love with a product: the structure of a romantic consumer-product relationship. *Advances in Consumer Research,* B. E. Kahn and M. F. Luce (Eds.) Vol. 31. Provo, UT, Association for Consumer Research.

In: Psychology of Branding
Editor: W. Douglas Evans

ISBN: 978-1-62618-817-4
© 2013 Nova Science Publishers, Inc.

Chapter 5

A GENERAL BRAND ALLIANCE MODEL

Ronald E. Goldsmith[1] and Barbara A. Lafferty[2]
[1]Florida State University, Tallahassee, FL, US
[2]The University of South Florida, Tampa, FL, US

ABSTRACT

Creating brand alliances is a popular way for managers to create synergies with compatible partners for the benefit of both parties. These alliances can be with another brand, another company, a social group, a spokesperson, an event, or a cause. Alliances vary in length and in nature. They are created to influence a variety of outcomes, including successful new product introduction, enhanced corporate reputation, sales, and to encourage brand engagement among consumers. Although there are several types of brand alliances, researchers have viewed them as separate entities. This chapter proposes a general model of brand alliances that strives to identify the features these alliances have in common and to reveal how alliances work in a similar way to change consumer attitudes and purchase intentions. The authors also explore the psychological processes consumers go through in evaluating alliances and suggest implications for marketers and directions for future research.

INTRODUCTION[1]

Firms use many types of promotional strategies in an effort to build consumer engagement. Such engagement helps customers develop positive attitudes toward company brands, and ultimately encourage and increase the firm's sales. Among these promotional strategies is a family of related programs we term "alliances" between the brand and a partner(s). These alliances are unique in the promotion toolbox because they incorporate another party joining forces with a firm to help promote a brand to the consumer. Marketers

---

[1] This chapter is based on a Poster Session given at the Consumer Brand Relationship Colloquium, Orlando, Florida, March 17-19, 2011 and benefited from the contributions of Dr. Yimin Zhu of the Department of Marketing, School of Business, Sun Yat-Sen University and of Ms. Yvette Holmes, a doctoral student at Florida State University.

and advertisers have used such strategies for many years, but it seems they have made little effort to integrate and coordinate them into a single alliance model that would highlight their similar components. For instance, Belch and Belch (2012, p. 190) describe a model of meaning transfer from celebrity endorser to brand. Similarly, a model of the alliance between brands (Simonin & Ruth, 1998) and one between causes and brands have also been proposed (Lafferty, Goldsmith, & Hult, 2004).

Although researchers have developed individual models to describe and to explain specific instances of an alliance, integration across different types of alliances is lacking. Thus, the purpose of the present chapter is to present a general model of brand alliances that brings into focus their prominent common features. This model has some empirical support for specific alliances, but can be tested further to determine if it is robust for other types of brand alliances. In addition, it raises several issues for managers who seek to optimize the impact of the alliances they create with various partners and for potential partners or other stakeholders who wish to create alliances to benefit themselves and their constituencies. The model thus provides opportunities for theoretical development as well as empirical study.

The remainder of this chapter describes the concept of alliances in promotion strategy, lists several common types of alliances, and shows what they have in common. We present a model that purports to show how consumers evaluate and react to the various types of alliances that emphasizes their commonalities. We draw upon research across a variety of fields to show support for the model. The chapter concludes with suggestions for further theoretical and empirical development as well as managerial recommendations.

WHAT IS AN ALLIANCE?

In a general sense, an alliance is a partnership or joining of two or more parties into a joint effort to accomplish a shared goal. A relationship, according to the Merriam-Webster dictionary, is a connection, association, or involvement. Alliances are a type of formal relationship because they necessarily involve a legal or contractual bond. Based on descriptions given by Rao and Ruekert (1994) and Simonin and Ruth (1998), we propose that *alliances* or *partnerships* are marketing strategies in which firms develop either a short-term or a long-term formal relationship with a partner that associates or combines the brand with the partner in the consumer's mind. Partnerships vary widely in type and nature, but our underlying premise is that these relationships share may common strategic characteristics and that they function in a similar way so that a general brand alliance model (BAM) can describe them well. The partnerships included in the brand alliance model are:

1. co-branding (e.g., ingredient branding)
2. tie-ins with other brands (e.g., joint branding)
3. sponsorships
4. cause-related marketing, cause-brand alliances
5. social alliances (cause marketing)
6. spokespersons

Co-branding or *ingredient branding* is a strategy in which one brand is physically combined into a single product that consequently has multiple brand names (Chang, 2008; 2009). The new product can consist of two or more brands from the same company or from different companies. The co-brand benefits from the assets of the combined brands. Essentially, each brand contributes some of its brand equity to the creation. Brand equity is defined by Aaker (1996, pp. 7-8) as "*a set of assets (and liabilities) linked to a brand's name and symbol that adds to (or subtracts from) the value provided by a product or service to a firm and/or that firm's customers. The major asset categories are (1) brand name awareness, (2) brand loyalty, (3) perceived quality, and (4) brand association.*" In general, the partner brand offers unique attributes or benefits to the consumer in the joint brand that they cannot get from either brand alone. Breyer's ice cream with M&M candy or food products that contain *Nutra-Sweet* are examples where complementary food products utilize co-branding to share in the brand name recognition and equity of a partner.

Other co-branding examples include computers with *Intel* inside, electronics with *Dolby* noise reduction systems, or clothing made with *Lycra*. Commonly, managers use co-branding in brand extensions, line extensions, or with new product development. A unique type of co-branding can also be found in brand licensing, where a firm licenses its brand name, symbol, logo, or character to another firm to use on some of its products, effectively creating a co-branded product. Finally, mergers present a special type of co-brand alliance occurring when two firms merge (or one acquires the other) and both brand names are retained. Although co-branding is common in the U.S., its use in international marketing is growing (Ueltschy & Laroche, 2004).

Research shows that co-branding has positive influences on consumer attitudes and purchase intentions (Park et al., 1996). One study by Washburn, Till, and Priluck (2000) suggests that co-branding of potato chips and barbeque sauce (BBQ potato chips) is a win-win strategy for both partners regardless of whether either brand is perceived as having high or low brand equity prior to the partnership. While the low brand equity brand may benefit more, the high brand equity partner is not hurt by the co-branding partnership. Positive product trial seems to further enhance consumers' evaluations of the co-branded products. A more recent study, however, suggests that pairing a brand with strong equity with a brand of lesser equity might damage the stronger brand (Ueltschy & Laroche, 2004) and so managers must thoroughly test specific potential co-brand strategies to avoid hurting their brand's equity.

Tie-ins are a type of brand alliance in which the brand is not physically combined with another brand as it is with co-branding. A tie-in is a joint promotion of two or more products or services that can take a variety of forms. Loosely stated, tie-ins can be described as joint branding where "two or more brands or companies team up to increase pulling power" (Kotler, 2000, p. 602). This strategy can take the form of cross-promotions, which are advertisements or other activities such as coupons, refunds, and contests that are designed to help a company sell two different products or to help two companies sell their products or services together. For example, one company can run a contest where the prizes are contributed by the partner. Another cross promotion would be when two or more brands advertise together, as is the case when Nautilus Fitness Center promotes Brita reusable water bottles in their ads, and Brita likewise promotes Nautilus in theirs. These tie-ins can also be in the form of a sample bundled with a product. For example, in 2006 boxes of Post Great Grains cereal included a free trial package of Starbucks coffee as a value-added item for consumers. The tie-in promotion was intended to increase sales of both the cereal and the coffee.

One of the more familiar forms of a tie-in is when a company ties their product with a movie. *The Lorax,* a 2012 movie about one of Dr. Seuss's most enduring characters and a founding environmental hero, is an example. Universal Pictures linked more than 70 promotional tie-ins with the movie. Mazda, the Environmental Protection Agency, XFinity TV, IHOP, and Whole Foods are just a few of those who participated in this promotional tie-in. Whether the tie-in was Truffula chip pancakes at IHOP or a Hewlett-Packard printer, which promised to teach you how to "print like the Lorax," the idea of this alliance was to ultimately sell products and gain additional promotional exposure for the movie.

Sponsorships can be described as a corporation creating an association or connection with another party whereby the sponsoring company/brand becomes the "face" of the event (Rifon, Choi, Trimble, & Li, 2004). The sponsored event can be sports, social causes, concerts, the arts, or any other activity. With this type of alliance, the sponsor provides financial support in return for the right to display a brand name, logo, or advertising message and be identified as a sponsor of the event (Belch & Belch, 2012). This form of alliance also has rewards for both partners. The event receives financial support and promotional impressions from the sponsor's advertising. The sponsor, in turn, associates their brand with certain consumer lifestyles, interests, and activities. In general, consumers are more receptive to these promotional messages because they see the sponsors as making the event possible.

In the alliance literature, the Olympic Games are a widely studied, sponsorship event (Carrillat, Harris, & Lafferty, 2010; Crimmins & Horn, 1996; McDaniel, 1999; Miyazaki & Morgan, 2001). In fact, in the public-private partnership between the International Olympic Committee, the selected city, and various corporate sponsors, the latter have provided the primary financial support for the games since 1984 (Payne, 2007). Several companies including Coca-Cola, McDonald's, Visa, and Anheuser-Busch are recurrent corporate sponsors. Serving as an Olympic supporter since 1984, Budweiser has been named "the official beer sponsor" of more than a few Olympic Games. Sponsorships often come along with other marketing related benefits. For example, according to the Anheuser-Busch's company website, the sponsorship gave them "use of the U.S. Olympic Committee's USA five-ring logo in marketing activities," and Anheuser-Busch "became the exclusive malt-beverage advertiser for all Olympic Games telecasts in the United States" during that time. In line with sponsoring the 2012 Olympics, Budweiser continued to support its sponsorship with significant media buys on NBC and affiliated networks. In return, Budweiser received entitlement to a private facility that hosts members of the U.S. Olympic Committee, the U.S. Olympic team, other sponsors, and licensees among other benefits of being a sponsor. Shown to influence consumer recall, awareness, attitude, and purchase intentions, in general, a sponsorship utilizes the brand name of the sponsoring organization in its marketing efforts to leverage the associated brand recognition (e.g., Cornwell et al., 2006).

Cause-related marketing (also termed cause-brand alliances) is a marketing strategy whereby a company links its product/brand with a specific cause, and a portion of the proceeds from the sale of the product/brand are given to the cause satisfying organizational objectives for both partners (e.g., Belch & Belch, 2012, p. 594-596; Varadarajan & Menon, 1988, p. 60). Originally established as a short term sales promotion strategy and copyrighted by the American Express Company (Varadarajan & Menon, 1988), today, cause-related marketing (CRM) is often used as a long term strategy or cause-brand alliance designed to not only increase sales for the brand but to augment the firm's corporate social responsibility mission. Both partners benefit from this alliance in multiple ways. Firms that have aligned themselves with a cause can enhance their brand image ("how others and customers perceive the brand (Aaker, 1996, p. 69)) and the image or reputation of their firm. The alliance increases the perceived credibility of both partners, which translates into more positive consumer attitudes and increased purchase intentions (Goldsmith, Lafferty, & Newell, 2000a, 2000b; Lafferty, 2007; Lafferty & Goldsmith, 1999). The cause or non-profit benefits from the brand's advertising of the alliance, thereby increasing awareness of the cause (Andreasen, 1996). Plus, the non-profit receives valuable donations from the sale of the brand (Belch & Belch, 2012; Lafferty & Goldsmith, 2005; Lafferty et al., 2004).

While the brand has typically initiated the cause-related marketing campaign with the non-profit, Susan G. Koman for the Cure has recognized the potential of this strategy for fundraising and has created awareness for the organization's cause since 1983. In 2009 alone, CRM generated over $50 million in donations for Susan G. Koman For the Cure's breast cancer research and education while spending on CRM in general has increased more than 220 percent since 1998 reaching an estimated $1.5 billion in the U.S. and $25 billion worldwide (Belch & Belch, 2012). Cause-related marketing is such a widely used strategy that the Cause Marketing Forum (causemarketingforum.com) tracks new cause-related marketing campaigns weekly to update their list and acts as a clearinghouse for information to help both brands and partners develop campaigns. In addition, the future should see increasing use of the strategy. According to Cone Communications, a Boston based public relations and marketing agency, 83% of Americans wish more firms would use cause-related campaigns to support causes (see coneinc.com; Cone 2010 Cause Evolution Study).

CRM has even spread to the Internet (Husted & Whitehouse, 2002). Given the interactive nature of the Internet and the ability to offer many sales promotion tools online such as contests, sweepstakes, and coupons to name a few, providing consumers with the ability to participate in cause-related marketing campaigns through company websites makes perfect sense. Purchasing a specified product online with a portion of the proceeds going to a charity can extend the effectiveness of the campaign beyond purchases solely in retail locations. For example, the Reebok website offers a line of "Pink Ribbon" shoes and apparel where donations will be given to combat breast cancer. One of their Pink Ribbon product descriptions says: "Get your pink on with our Pink Ribbon Textured Jacket. As a proud sponsor of Avon breast cancer initiatives, we are doing our part, and by buying this jacket, you will be doing yours. Reebok will donate more than $500,000 this year to help combat breast cancer" (http://www.shop.reebok.com/us/).

A variation of the cause-related marketing strategy is called "affinity marketing." Early definitions of affinity marketing describe it as "a strategy used by vendors of goods and services to offer special incentives to association members in return for their endorsement" (Collins, 1987, pp. 122), and as "a unique exchange process, in which value-expressive products and services are marketed to reference groups with cohesiveness, common interests, and/or values, usually in return for the group's endorsement, as marketing leverage to its individual members of constituency" (Copulsky & Wolf, 1990, p. 16). Roy and Berger (2007) argue that the influence of affinity marketing comes from member connections to and identification with the organization.

The typical affinity marketing campaign is created by a credit card company offering a special "affinity" card to the members of an organization or association that gives a benefit to that organization when the card is used. Thus, like the other brand alliances, the brand and partner benefit from the consumer's purchase/use of the branded credit card, and association members benefit because the card displays their membership in an association that represents their values and self-image (Fock, Chan, &Yan, 2011; Mekonnen, Harris, & Laing, 2008).

Social alliances (Cause marketing) are partnerships between a company and a nonprofit that have moved beyond cause-related marketing. In a social alliance or cause marketing strategy, a mutually beneficial, generally long-term partnership is created that promotes the partnership and the fact that the firm is a regular donor to the cause (Berger et al., 2006, p. 129). In other words, social alliances are an outgrowth of cause-related marketing but with this strategy, contributions to the cause or non-profit are not tied to the purchase of the brand that forms the partnership. As cause-related marketing grew in popularity, companies saw the opportunity to be socially responsible by associating a brand with a cause and using that partnership to promote their donations.

Social alliances are also more strategic than tie-in promotions and often are intended to influence the morale of employees as well as influence consumers. One such social alliance was Clorox Fresh Step kitty litter and the ASPCA. Clorox created a promotional campaign about fighting feline homelessness and pledged to donate $250,000 to ASPCA annually. While Fresh Step was the brand that partnered with the ASPCA, purchases of the product were not necessary for the annual donation. Various promotional tools were used that resulted in more than 60 million media impressions benefiting the company, the cause, and the cats.

Today, companies decide if they want to do cause marketing, cause-related marketing, or even both. Haagen-Dazs utilized both strategies with their "Save the Honey Bees" initiative. With the purchase of their Honey Bee ice cream, proceeds were given to Penn State University and the University of California, Davis, two leading research facilities studying the decline of the honeybee. Haagen-Dazs also contributed additional funds to the universities that were not tied to the purchase of the ice cream.

Spokespersons are a widely-used form of brand alliance that takes many forms and is one of the oldest types of brand alliance. Its wide use, however, may have disguised the fact that it is an alliance much like the others we discuss. The general definition of a spokesperson is someone who is engaged to speak on behalf of another, such as the President's spokesperson or someone representing an organization at a meeting. In advertising, however, spokespersons are usually highly recognizable people appearing in ads who speak on behalf of the company and the brand, often on a long-term basis so that they come to represent the brand in the mind of many consumers. An early example of this partnership was Texaco sponsoring the radio broadcasts of several celebrities (Bob Hope, Jack Benny, Milton Berle) who in turn acted as the spokespersons for the brand. Scholars identify at least four types of spokespersons in ads: celebrities, CEOs, experts, and typical persons who might use the product. The latter can appear as genuine persons such as Jared for Subway, or as artificial, created "typical" spokespersons such as Progressive Insurance's salesperson, Flo. There can be other varieties such as spokesmodels (e.g., the St. Pauli Girl) and even icons (e.g., M&Ms candies or the Jolly Green Giant). Spokespersons are one of the most common types of alliances and one of the oldest. Companies enter into alliances with spokespersons who meet several criteria that are important to understating alliances in general.

For alliances to work, both partners should have several positive characteristics. In the case of spokespersons, these criteria are summarized as "credibility," which consists of measures of attractiveness, trustworthiness, expertise, and likability (Clow & Baack, 2007, p.

214). Thus, for alliances in general, consumer assessments of the characteristics of the partners (these are assessments of the attractiveness etc. of the partner) lead to an overall attitude toward the partner (positive or negative). In the case of the brand, several of the same characteristics are essential to the overall attitude. The company and/or its brand should be seen as credible, that is, trustworthy and an expert (Goldsmith et al., 2000a, 2000b; Lafferty, Goldsmith, & Newell, 2002; Newell & Goldsmith, 2001). In addition, perceptions of the company's eco-friendliness, good citizenship, and so forth influence consumers' attitudes toward the brand. These perceptions can be summed as the "reputation" of the company (Fombrum, 1996).

WHY ARE ALLIANCES SO PREVALENT?

We can think of at least four reasons why alliances are so common in the marketplace. First, consumers have become familiar with alliances in their many forms and have embraced this premise. Consumers understand the benefits of alliances such as sponsorships and cause-related marketing to the partners and to themselves and can thus appreciate them. Second, many alliances are created because both partners seek the benefits of the alliance for themselves. Brands see opportunities to reach new market segments or strengthen brand images in the minds of consumers. Alliances can boost profits for firms using them, improve corporate reputations, and build brand equity. Not-for-profit organizations seek cause-brand alliances as revenue streams. Potential spokespersons and their agents actively solicit opportunities to endorse products and consequently benefit from the lucrative contracts while events welcome the publicity and financial support that sponsors provide. Third, alliances are also prevalent because both partners realize that the new identity created by the alliance has positive, synergistic implications. Simply put, the whole should be greater than the sum of its parts. The alliance combines unique assets from each partner to create a new entity that can achieve several goals for both, including building awareness, encouraging trial, changing attitudes, generating sales and revenue, creating positive images, and inspiring employees to become increasingly productive. Finally, overall, alliances seem to work; they often accomplish the goals of the partners.

For-profit firms use alliances to stimulate short-term, spur-of-the moment sales by providing an extra incentive at the point of sale (that last little nudge in the brand's favor) to motivate the customer who is giving little thought to the purchase of a product. Alliances such as cause-related marketing and social alliances contribute to corporate social responsibility efforts, thus giving competitive advantage, enhancing brand image, and growing brand equity. In addition, brand alliances can encourage consumer engagement with the brand by facilitating the emotional bond some consumers forge with brands (Goldsmith, 2011). Brand engagement leads consumers to co-create the brand, to provide important feedback to the company, to spread positive word-of-mouth about the brand in addition to delivering long-term value to the company. Because brand engagement is so important to many marketers, they are eager to use tactics such as alliances that are successful in creating these bonds. Success breeds success, as firms and organizations increasingly want to ally with a partner in some form.

THE PROPOSED BRAND ALLIANCE MODEL

Figure 1 presents a general model of brand alliances. It is largely derived from Simonin and Ruth's (1998) model of brand-brand alliances and adapted into a general alliance model. The model has five antecedent constructs that directly and indirectly influence a consumer's attitude toward the alliance and consequently toward both the brand and the partner. We discuss these in order from left to right.

Pre-Attitude toward the Brand

Eagly and Chaiken (1993) define an attitude as a psychological tendency that is expressed by evaluating a particular entity with some degree of favor or disfavor. Brands serve as attitude objects. Exposure to them either indirectly through marketing communications or directly through usage enables people to evaluate the brand and formulate an attitude toward it. According to prior research, once favorable or unfavorable feelings about some person, object, or issue are formed, they are relatively stable and enduring (Fishbein & Azjen, 1975).

In the proposed BAM, pre-attitude toward the brand are those beliefs and feelings that form about the brand prior to the alliance. The term "pre-attitude" is simply the consumer attitude toward the brand prior to the alliance. It is used to distinguish it from the "post-attitude" toward the brand, the attitude after the alliance, which it is hoped reflects the effect of the alliance.

Brand attitudes are relatively stable and will endure over time unless new information coming from personal experience or external sources is integrated to alter the existing attitude. Without any new information, such as that provided by an alliance, pre-attitude toward the brand remains stable and is positively and highly related to post alliance exposure attitude toward the same brand (Lafferty et al., 2004; Simonin & Ruth, 1998). Examples of the types of thoughts and feelings that come into play here are the consumer's evaluations of the brand's sincerity, social responsibility, motives, perceived reliability, and credibility. Negative attitudes toward a brand can attenuate consumer response to the alliance and even lead to degraded attitudes toward the partner. On this account, partners are careful to select brands with which they form alliances in order to protect their own reputations.

Pre-attitude toward the brand predicts consumer behavior toward the brand (people buy the brands the like) and is a component of the concept of brand equity. In Keller's (2003) presentation of a model of Consumer-Based Brand Equity, brand attitudes are termed, "overall evaluations of the brand in terms of its quality and the satisfaction it generates" (Keller, 2003, p. 392) and are part of the consumer mindset, "which includes everything that exists in the minds of customers with respect to a brand: thoughts, feelings, experiences, images, perceptions, beliefs, attitudes, and so forth" (Keller, 2003, p. 392). Likewise, pre-attitudes toward the partner are the overall evaluations of the partner that exist prior to the alliance. These attitudes, comprising as they do part of the equity of both partners, are part of the equity of both partners and are key indicators of the success or failure of the alliance.

Brand-Consumer Congruence

Brand-consumer congruence is the fit or similarity between the consumer's self-image and the brand image (Dolich, 1969). Consumer self-concept researchers have long theorized that a brand image interacts with the consumer's self-concept or self-image to generate a subjective experience referred to as self-congruity. Positive self-congruity occurs when a positively valued self-image is matched with a positively valued brand image (Sirgy, 1982). For example, if a Lexus automobile has the brand image of sophistication and success and this image matches the consumer's self-image then positive self-congruity takes place. In this case, the theory predicts that the individual will respond favorably to the brand to maintain a desirable level of self-esteem (Sirgy, 1982, 1985). The self-congruity hypothesis can explain and predict different facets of consumer behavior such as product use, product ownership, brand attitude, purchase motivation, purchase intention, brand choice, brand adoption, store preference, and store loyalty (Claiborne & Sirgy, 1990; Sirgy, 1982, 1985).

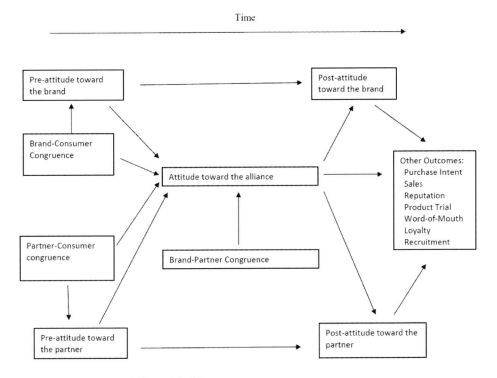

Figure 1. A General Brand Alliance Model.

Note that different authors use a variety of different terms to refer to the congruence between a brand or cause and the consumer. Various terms used include "compatibility," "fit," "relevance," "match," and "correspondence." There is no universally agreed upon term that all researchers share. They all seem to refer to similarities or complementarities shared by any of the partners. The American Heritage Dictionary of the English Language defines congruence with the synonyms "agreement," "harmony," "conformity," and "correspondence." Thus, we use the term "congruence" in this chapter to refer to all instances of the pairing between partners and between partners and consumers because congruence is a broad, general term that seems to sum up meaning common to all the other terms.

In the BAM, brand-consumer congruence is hypothesized to have a positive, direct effect on pre-attitude toward the brand. Pre-attitude toward the brand is more positive when there is greater congruity between the consumer's self-image and the brand image (Bhattacharya & Sen, 2003). By the same token, when congruence between consumer self-image and brand image is high, there is a direct, positive effect on attitude toward the alliance. This effect occurs because when the consumer sees the brand with which he or she identifies, the alliance should be viewed more positively than if the alliance contained a brand with whom the consumer does not identify. This effect is similar to the effect that brand equity has on ability to extend the brand (Aaker, 1996, p. 275).

Pre-Attitude toward the Partner

Pre-attitude toward the partner are those feelings that form about the partner prior to the alliance. Since the partner in a brand alliance represents another attitude object, attitudes toward the partner form in the same manner as attitudes form toward the brand (Fishbein & Ajzen, 1975). The partner can be another brand, a cause in a cause-brand alliance, a company, or a spokesperson (e.g., Lafferty et al., 2004; Scholder, Webb, & Mohr, 2006; Simonin & Ruth, 1998). An example of this pre-attitude is when firms test potential spokespersons with Q-scores for their ability to attract consumers and influence them to buy the endorsed brand (Belch & Belch, 2012, p. 190). The strength of the attitude is relatively stable and enduring unless new information is integrated that alters those feelings (Lafferty et al., 2004; Simonin & Ruth, 1998). The more positive the attitude toward the partner, the more positive the attitude toward the alliance and subsequently, the most positive the response to the alliance.

Partner-Consumer Congruence

Just as brand-consumer congruence may exist, there exists the potential for congruence between consumer self-image and the partner image whether this partner is a cause, spokesperson, company, or another brand. Broderick, Jogi, and Garry (2003) show that respondents believed that congruence must exist between the customer and the cause, and between the customer and the corporate donor. They argue that a consumer should be able to associate him or herself with the cause and company together. Chowdhury and Khare (2011) show that consumer self-schema, which is part of global self-concept, is the way a consumer views him or herself. Their study finds that the higher the match (fit, congruence) between the cause and the consumer's self-schema the more positive the preference for a cause-supporting brand, but that this effect is most pronounced when the brand is impression-relevant, meaning that using the brand enhances the consumer's social image. Vanhamme et al. (2011) also confirm that consumer identification (enhancing self-identity and promoting self-concept) with a cause influences consumer response to a CRM program, and that it does so by mediating the effect of the alliance on the socially responsible image of the firm. Overall, then, the weight of the evidence shows that when congruence between consumer self-image and partner image is high, consumer attitude toward the alliance should be more positive than when the congruence is low. Furthermore, given the similarity to brand-consumer congruence, partner-consumer congruence is hypothesized to have a positive, direct effect on pre-attitude toward the partner and on the alliance itself. Pre-attitude toward the partner and the alliance will be more positive when congruity is greater between the consumer self-image and the partner image than when congruity is weak.

Brand-Partner Congruence

The congruence between the brand and the partner can be a key factor influencing the success of an alliance (Bower, 2001). Brand-partner congruence appears to be the variable most often cited and researched in alliance studies, where it is often simply referred to as the "fit" of the alliance (e.g., Buil, de Chernatony, & Hem, 2009). A variety of studies show the importance of brand-partner congruence to the success of the alliance (e.g., Chowdhury & Khare, 2011; Rifon et al., 2004; Samu & Wymer, 2009; Trimble & Rifon, 2006). A few studies (Hamlin & Wilson, 2004; Hoek & Gendall, 2008; Nan & Heo, 2007), however, do not support this conclusion suggesting that important factors are moderating (see below) the relationship and further study is needed.

When are brands and partners congruent? Owing to the many definitions and operationalizations of congruence, this question has many answers. Gwinner (1997) argues that partners in event/sponsorship alliances can be congruent in two ways. *Image-based* congruence occurs to the extent that both partners have common characteristics in their images, perhaps derived from common values, interests, or goals. *Functional based* congruence predominates when the brand's product features or operation can be used by the participants in the partnership, as when runners can wear the brand of shoe that sponsors the race. Sometimes, congruence is not unequivocally conceptualized and is simply operationalized by some statement that the partners are compatible or via bi-polar adjective scales containing synonyms for compatibility.

Theories on cognitive consistency provide one rationale for this phenomenon (Eagly & Chaiken, 1993). People seem to prefer consistency between stimuli and cognitive states such as attitudes and intentions. Inconsistency can be felt as discomfort, and people will invest considerable cognitive energy in aligning their beliefs to avoid this discomfort. In the alliance context, consistency or congruence between the brand and the partner (often termed "fit") promotes positive responses to the alliance. Overall, the brand-partner alliance has to make sense to the consumer for its acceptance because a good match generally creates more positive outcomes than an incongruent match (Gwinner, 1997).

Attitude toward the Alliance

Cognitively, according to information integration theory, the alliance creates new information about the two partners (Anderson, 1981). Attitudes are formed and prior attitudes are modified when information about one partner is combined with information about the other in the alliance. The positive attributes of both partners should combine and create a more favorable impression as a result of the alliance. This effect, however, becomes increasingly problematic when consumers hold a mixture of positive and negative attitudes (e.g., Basil & Herr, 2006). What consumers think of the alliance is a good indicator of their intentions to react positively to it. As a consequence, in the proposed BAM, attitude toward the alliance is directly related to post attitude toward the brand and post attitude toward the partner.

Many studies of alliances incorporate some operationalization of attitude toward the alliance into their empirical assessment of the performance of the alliance (e.g., Simonin & Ruth, 1998).

Because positive attitudes are often proposed as precursors of specific behaviors (Ajzen, 2008), researchers who study alliances often point to attitude toward the alliance, or the positive cognitive and emotional evaluation of the alliance formed by consumers, as a key element in diagnosing and understanding how it is working. If consumers think the alliance is beneficial, they are more likely to respond behaviorally to it than if they do not like it. In the proposed BAM, attitude toward the alliance is directly and positively related to the outcome variables (sales, reputation, etc.).

Post-Attitude toward the Brand

Post-attitude toward the brand are the feelings and thoughts about the brand following the formation of an alliance. The intent of the alliance is to positively influence the pre-existing attitude toward the brand increasing favorable perceptions (Lafferty et al., 2004; Simonin & Ruth, 1998). This altered attitude is an important outcome of the alliance and an indicator of its success. Attitudes toward the brand and the partner after the alliance are intended by managers to be more positive than before the alliance and should contribute to the equity of both partners.

In the proposed BAM, post-attitude toward the brand is positively and highly related to the outcomes of the alliance. Studies on advertising effectiveness have shown the positive relationship between attitude toward the brand and purchase intentions (Heath & Gaeth, 1994; MacKenzie & Lutz, 1989).

The Dual Mediation Model, "which posits a direct effect of ad attitude on brand attitude as well as an indirect effect via brand cognitions" (Brown & Stayman, 1992, p. 46), shows a consistent pattern of attitude toward the brand influencing purchase intent. Furthermore, in the cause-related marketing literature, there is some indication that this relationship holds. Lafferty and Edmondson (2009) found that attitude toward the brand positively relates to purchase intentions regardless of whether the ad portrayed the brand or the cause.

Post-Attitude toward the Partner

Similarly, post-attitude toward the partner are the feelings and thoughts about the partner that exist following an alliance. It is the expectation that the alliance will enhance the attitude toward the partner as well as the attitude toward the brand in a symbiotic relationship. This enhanced attitude is a prime and essential outcome for the alliance. Research supports the achievement of this outcome in a cause-brand alliance (Lafferty et al., 2004) and a co-branding alliance (Simonin & Ruth, 1998).

In the proposed BAM, post-attitude toward the brand and toward the partner are positively and highly related to the other outcomes or consequences of the alliance. While the Dual Mediation Model looks at attitude toward the brand and its relationship to purchase intentions, the same findings should hold for attitude toward the partner given the fact that attitudes form in a similar fashion for other brands, causes, or companies. Supporting evidence is found in a study by Lafferty and Edmondson (2009), who conclude that attitude toward the cause positively relates to purchase intentions toward the partnering brand when the cause is the focal visual in the ad. In the Brand Alliance Model, the alliance has both indirect effects on several potential outcomes via the enhanced attitudes toward the brand the partner as well as a direct influence on several other outcomes.

Other Outcomes

In addition to the enhanced attitudes to both partners in the alliance, brand alliances have several other potential outcomes depending on the perspective of the brand or the partner, the type of alliance, and its strategic goal as specified by managers. Among the many goals of brand alliances, intention to purchase the brand is often a prominent dependent variable in academic studies of alliances (e.g., Hamlin & Wilson, 2004; Samu & Wymer, 2009), while selling more products stands out as a key managerial outcome (Thompson, 2006). Other typical outcomes for brands include product trial, enhanced corporate reputation, increased positive word-of-mouth for the brand, increased brand loyalty, and better recruitment of employees. Non-brand partners can seek similar outcomes, including awareness (publicity), revenue, donations, participation, memberships, and other benefits (Andreasen, 1996). Overall, alliance outcomes depend on the objectives of the partners or on the proposed dependent variables used by researchers in empirical studies.

HOW DO ALLIANCES WORK?

Both partners who establish alliances want to create synergy by combining the features of two entities. The reasoning is that positive attitudes and feelings toward the separate partners will transfer to the other partner and to the alliance itself, benefiting both partners. For example, a brand with a popular, positive image is sought after by potential partners in order to increase the partner's recognition and attract new donors, participants, or buyers. Popular celebrities are sought after by companies and nonprofits as spokespersons with expectation that attention will be attracted to their brand or cause and the charisma, popularity, and image of the spokesperson will transfer to them (Belch & Belch, 2012, pp. 190-194).

All the alliances seem to function psychologically in the same way. Consumers are confronted with two stimuli, a firm or brand and a partner, such as an event, a spokesperson, another brand, or a cause. How consumers feel, that is their preexisting attitudes towards these stimuli, are evoked to influence the consumers' attitude toward the alliance. A positive evaluation of the fit or appropriateness of the alliance is made and an attitude toward the alliance is formed. If positive, this attitude influences how the consumer responds to the alliance, forming a purchase intention, making a purchase, buying a ticket, etc. Moreover, the attitude toward the alliance also influences the consumer's attitudes toward the partners. The hope is that attitudes after the alliance (post-attitudes) are more positive than attitudes before the alliance (pre-attitudes). The psychology of *how* alliances work, however, is subject to multiple explanations. Among the different theories that researchers have proposed to account for the success or failure of alliances are a simple transfer hypothesis (Trimble & Rifon, 2006), balance theory (Basil & Herr, 2006), congruence or congruity theory (Cornwell & Maignan, 1998), schema theory (Chowdhury & Khare, 2011), attribution theory (Rifon et al., 2004), and information integration theory (Anderson, 1981).

The *transfer hypothesis* simply states that consumers transfer their thoughts and feelings from one alliance partner to the other without a great deal of conscious effort (Trimble & Rifon, 2006). Thus, the transfer hypothesis seems particularly applicable to low-involvement situations in which consumers do not have strongly felt attitudes toward either partner, but when presented with the alliance, transfer the image of the partners to each other creating a positive, weak response to the alliance. Intriguingly, consumers do not even have to be highly aware of a brand for a cause-related marketing program to work; awareness of the cause and its importance to the consumer may be sufficient to trigger a positive response (Baghi & Gabrielli, 2012).

Balance theory (Heider, 1946, 1958) is a consistency theory of attitude formation that proposes that people form evaluations of paired stimuli by comparing their feelings and thoughts about each stimulus to achieve a balanced set of attitudes. For example, a consumer viewing an ad featuring an admired spokesperson promoting a brand should achieve balance by forming a positive attitude toward that brand based not on intrinsic brand characteristics, but on the positive reaction to the spokesperson. Similarly, a negatively viewed spokesperson can degrade the promoted brand in the eyes of the consumer. Although this response can be largely unconscious in low-involvement situations, in high-involvement situations consumers devote more thought to the evaluation as they strive to avoid cognitive dissonance and achieve a balance in their attitudes. Basil and Herr (2006) invoke balance theory to explain why consumers exposed to cause related marketing programs develop positive attitudes toward such alliances, emphasizing the fit or congruence of the partners:

> Consumers are expected to judge as 'appropriate' alliances for which their pre-existing attitudes yield balance. Judgments of propriety represent the cognitive element in a CRM alliance attitude. Either a positive-positive or a negative-negative alliance should be judged 'appropriate.' ... An individual's attitude toward a CRM alliance should consist of some combination of his or her attitude toward the firm, the charity, and the pairing of these two, per Balance Theory (p. 393).

Congruence or congruity theory is proposed by several researchers to account for the operation of alliances. For example, Cornwell and Maignan argued in 1998 that sponsorship research badly needed to focus on explaining how sponsorships worked and pointed specifically to congruity theory as a prime avenue of this research.

Congruity theory holds that people seek to maintain and reestablish consistency among cognitive elements (Eagly & Chaiken, 1993). While balance theory can be seen as establishing a balance between one's attitudes toward the spokesperson and therefore, feeling similarly toward the brand, congruity theory proposes that the fit or similarity between the partners in a brand alliance, a cause-brand alliance, or sponsorship should make sense in order for the alliance to be effective (e.g., Lafferty et al., 2004; Simonin & Ruth, 1998). For example, the partnering of Crest toothpaste and Reach toothbrushes is a logical fit. Both products are used together, and it makes sense to develop a tie-in promotion with these two brands. In cause-related marketing, if Campbell soup partners with the American Red Cross, the fit also makes sense since the Red Cross is known for providing food for victims of natural disasters. In both cases, the logical fit enhances the likelihood of the alliance producing the desired results according to congruity theory. For the most part, the findings for fit as a relevant component in alliances are robust. While there are times with cause-related marketing when the fit is not a critical variable (Lafferty, 2009), selecting a good-fitting partner should ensure that the alliance will be an advantageous one.

If the fit is not logical, than creating a perception of fit can reduce cognitive inconsistency and increase the viability of the alliance. For example, Texaco, the official oil company sponsor of the 1992 summer Olympics equated the pursuit of excellence by athletes with the pursuit of excellence in the manufacturing of Texaco products (Crimmins & Horn, 1996).

Closely related to congruity theory in the information processing literature is *schema theory,* which suggests that consumers will process information more easily if the information fits well than if it does not fit well (Eagly & Chaiken, 1993). Consumers generally cluster likes with likes cognitively whether the likes are products, people, causes, or anything else. Therefore, when they are exposed to alliances, the information is processed more easily, recalled more easily, and tends to produce more favorable attitudes when the partners fit into the same cognitive schema and the relationship makes sense (Eagly & Chaiken, 1993).

Attribution theory can be used to explain what happens when people assess an alliance and find that the fit does not make sense (e.g., Rifon et al., 2004). This theory posits that consumers will cognitively infer a motive for the alliance (Rifon et al., 2004; Trimble & Rifon, 2006). If they feel that the partnership was formed for altruistic reasons, then motive attributions are formed and the outcome on attitudes and purchase behavior is positive. If, however, the consumers feel that the motives for the partnership are one-sided, or for purely monetary gains, or if the fit is illogical then the motive attributions can negatively affect the success of the alliance (Rifon et al., 2004). In an experiment conducted by Rifon et al. (2004), they found that a good fit between a company and the cause it sponsored generated attributions of altruism on the part of the brand partner and enhanced its credibility and attitudes toward the brand.

Information integration theory can be used to explain the processes that occur when new information arises from the formation of an alliance. According to information integration theory, attitudes are formed and modified as consumers receive and interpret information and then integrate this information with their pre-existing attitudes (Anderson, 1981). Therefore, in any alliance such as when a brand partners with another brand, or a cause, or sponsors an event, or employs a spokesperson, the existing information that the consumer has on each partner independently combines to form a new association in the consumer's mind creating new attitudes as a consequence of this new alliance (Lafferty et al., 2004; Simonin & Ruth, 1998).

The brand alliance model does not specify which if any of the forgoing theories most correctly explain the psychological mechanism through which the alliance influences consumer behavior. Fundamentally, all the alliances seem to function psychologically because of people's preference for cognitive consistency (Lafferty, 2009), although the strength of the consistency explanation also seems to vary with the level of consumer involvement evoked by the partners. Perhaps each formal theory makes a partial and valid description of how alliances work. Future research that distinguishes which ones are the most important in explaining alliances would be a major contribution to their study. The brand alliance model also proposes that several elements are involved in the overall function of a brand alliance, each of which contributes to the potential success or failure of its outcome. By examining each element, we can see some of the important factors that managers must take into account prior to initiating a brand alliance. Moreover, the BAM makes clear the theoretical linkages between the elements that deserve empirical research to uncover the mechanisms that make alliances work.

POTENTIAL MODERATORS

The BAM proposes that a set of attitudes toward the partners and toward the alliance are the key drivers of the outcomes of the alliance. These relationships, however, may not hold for all alliances or to the same degree depending on the situation. That is, how accurately the model describes how brand alliances function depends on contingent factors or moderators. These include product involvement (low vs. high), type of product (durable vs. package good), familiarity with the brand or with the cause, or the type and scope (local versus international) of the cause. Individual differences among consumers might also moderate the relationships in the model where consumers might differ in their interest in sponsorship partners, in participating in alliances in general, or in their willingness to respond to any social appeals. Although the influence of perceptions of the motivations of specific companies can be explicitly modeled and measured as part of the pre-attitude toward the brand, a global individual difference in socially responsible behavior may also influence model outcomes. Paying attention to potential moderators such as the ones above is especially important in the managerial use of alliances.

MANAGERIAL IMPLICATIONS

The BAM provides the theoretical foundation for a variety of managerial strategies. In addition, empirical research using the model suggests several general recommendations for managers seeking to use an alliance as part of their Integrated Marketing Communications strategy. First, partners should select their partners carefully to ensure that they will benefit from positive attitudes toward them. Allying with a negative or weak partner has the potential to actually harm the other partner. Moreover, partnerships should be created that fit together, that make sense to consumers, or are coherent. Fit enhances the outcomes of the alliance in most cases (e.g., Basil & Herr, 2006), so the alliance should be evaluated to affirm that consumers see the logic or sense of the alliance. Alliances may not be as effective in some contexts as they are in others. Managers should not be persuaded to enter into an alliance based on anecdotal accounts of their success, but should evaluate carefully if their brand, the partner, and the context are suited to an alliance or whether some contingency lessens the potential impact the alliance might have. Mangers should, of course, determine exactly what the desired outcome of the alliance will be and devise appropriate methods to measure these outcomes. Finally, alliances should be assessed for their ROI to provide guidance for managers who might desire future alliances. Like any other investment, they should pay for themselves and more.

A second managerial challenge is developing the right mix of alliances in the overall marketing plan. It may be that some alliances work better in some product fields than in others. Managers might learn that focusing on only a single or a few types of alliances is most effective, while it is conceivable that especially large firms might form all types of alliances simultaneously. Probably the best recommendation is for managers to develop whichever alliances they do in a consistent pattern with consistent themes that reinforce the brand's equity and do not conflict. Different alliances might have different short-term goals, but the overall goal should be a consistent brand image that builds brand equity and brand relationships with consumers.

Finally, alliances certainly "work" in the sense that the majority of the time they achieve their goals, or else why would the use of alliances, especially cause-related marketing programs, continue to grow? We can propose a downside to this scenario, however. As with any other strategy, the most advantage seems to accrue to the first movers. As other firms adopt the strategy, its effectiveness may decline as it becomes commonplace, or consumers might habituate to the strategy, in effect expecting it and failing to respond to the brand without an alliance. For example, price discounts, sales, coupons can be so frequently used that consumers come to expect them and refuse to buy without them. Managers should be prepared for the eventual "wearout" of the strategy (as advertisements wearout and need to be refreshed periodically; Belch & Belch, 2012, p. 206-209). On the other hand, long-term alliances may continue to be effective as the brand's partner continues to be important to consumers. One challenge to managing alliances is learning when to cease one, refresh one, or continue one.

RESEARCH IMPLICATIONS

A variety of studies across several fields support the validity of the BAM, yet much more is to be learned about this phenomenon. Research should particularly address the concept of fit, which at present is defined and operationalized in a bewildering variety of ways. Some agreement needs to be brought to this aspect of the model so that better comparisons can be made across studies by the use of identical or highly similar measures of this key construct. Researchers need to use a greater variety of outcome measures so that they can better describe the effects of alliances. Outcome measures need to become more concrete so mangers can better estimate the ROI for the strategy. Attention should be devoted to understanding both the short-term and long-term implications of alliances so that mangers can better develop their strategies. The search for additional moderators of the alliance model suggests many avenues of research, including cross-cultural studies and studies of varied possible alliance partners to assess the boundary conditions of the model.

Finally, the rise of social media, social networking, and the tendency for engaged consumers to take increasing control of brands through the activity of co-creation, suggest that in future, brand managers will have to consider their relationships or alliances with *brand communities*, groups of consumers who are drawn together through their involvement with a brand and who are increasingly influencing the brand's position and image in the marketplace (Dholakia & Algesheimer, 2011). Brand communities present managers with a variety of new challenges, including how much control over the brand manages must give up to these consumers and how best to respond to the opinions and concerns of these consumers. We suggest that forming alliances with brand communities that feature close communication and cooperation in branding decisions will be the primary corporate response so that a new type of alliance may need to be examined in the context of the BAM. The attitudes and behavior of consumers not in the brand community might be influenced by the activity of the brand community and its alliance with the brand so that brand managers will have to strategically manage their relationships with brand communities with this possible outcome in mind and initiate programs to enhance the brand's equity not only with the members of the brand community but also with those consumers outside it. This surmise suggests not only managerial implications but research implications as well.

CONCLUSION

In general, brand alliances take on a variety of forms, and the potentialities for their use seem to be growing. Thus, the topic of brand alliances is an important area of managerial concern and research interest. Unfortunately, researchers and managers have studied and managed alliances as separate and distinct topics, so the field has been marred by too many definitions of similar constructs and operationalizations as well as the absence of conceptual connections. It thus lacks the coherence of programmatic research. The present chapter proposes a general brand alliance model that could bring together the diversity of existing findings and suggest systematic studies of what remains to be learned. Thus, not only can the proposed BAM promote future research, but also the results of these studies could suggest valuable guidelines for managers seeking to use alliances to promote their brands.

REFERENCES

Aaker, D. A. (1996). *Building strong brands*. New York: The Free Press.

Ajzen, I. (2008). Consumer attitudes and behavior. In C. P. Haugtvedt, P. M. Herr & F. R. Kardes (Eds.), *Handbook of Consumer Psychology* (525-548). New York: Lawrence Erlbaum Associates.

Anderson, J. C. (1981). Integration theory applied to cognitive responses and attitudes. In R. E. Petty, T. M. Ostrom, & T. C. Brock (Eds.), *Cognitive Responses in Persuasion* (361-397), Hillsdale, NJ: Erlbaum.

Andreasen, A. R. (1996). Profits for nonprofits: find a corporate partner. *Harvard Business Review*, 74(6), 47-59.

Baghi, I. & Gabrielli, V. (2012). Co-branded cause-related marketing campaigns: the importance of linking two strong brands. *International Review on Public and Nonprofit Marketing*, 1-17.

Basil, D. Z. & Herr, P. M. (2006). Attitudinal balance and cause-related marketing: an empirical application of balance theory. *Journal of Consumer Psychology*, *16* (4), 391-403.

Belch, G. E. & Belch, M. A. (2012). *Advertising and promotion*. Boston, MA: McGraw-Hill.

Berger, I. E., Cunningham, P. H. & Drumwright, M. E. (2006). Identity, identification, and relationship through social alliances. *Journal of the Academy of Marketing Science*, *34* (2), 128-137.

Bhattacharya, C. B. & Sen, S. (2003). Consumer--company identification: a framework for understanding consumers' relationships with companies. *Journal of Marketing*, *67* (2), 76-88.

Bower, J. L. (2001). Not all M&As are alike - and that matters. *Harvard Business Review*, *79* (3), 92-101.

Broderick, A., Jogi, A. & Garry, T. (2003). Tickled pink: the personal meaning of cause related marketing for customers. *Journal of Marketing Management*, *19*, 583–610.

Brown, S. P. & Stayman, D. M. (1992). Antecedents and consequences of attitude towards the ad: a meta-analysis. *Journal of Consumer Research*, *19* (1), 34-51.

Buil, I., de Chernatony, L. & Hem, L. E. (2009). Brand extension strategies: perceived fit, brand type, and culture influences. *European Journal of Marketing*, *43* (11-12), 1300-1324.

Carrillat, F. A., Harris, E. & Lafferty, B. A. (2010). Fortuitous brand image transfer: investigating the side effect of multiple sponsorships. *Journal of Advertising*, *39* (2), 109-123.

Chang, W-L. (2008). A typology of co-branding strategy: position and classification. *The Journal of American Academy of Business*, *12* (2), 220-226.

Chang, W-L. (2009). Roadmap of co-branding positions and strategies. *The Journal of American Academy of Business*, *15* (1), 77-84.

Chowdhury, T. G. & Khare, A. (2011). Matching a cause with self-schema: The moderating effect on brand preferences. *Psychology & Marketing*, *28* (8), 825-842.

Claiborne, C. B. & Sirgy, M. J. (1990). Self-congruity as a model of attitude formation and change: conceptual review and guide for future research. *Developments in Marketing Science*. Vol. 13. Ed. B. J. Dunlap. Cullowhee, NC: Academy of Marketing Science, 1-7.

Clow, K. E. & Baack, D. (2007). *Integrated advertising, promotion, and marketing communications*. Upper Saddle River: New Jersey: Pearson Prentice-Hall.

Collins, C. P. (1987). Affinity Marketing -- It's Hot! *Association Management*, *39* (8), 122-122.

Copulsky, J. R. & Wolf, M. J. (1990). Relationship Marketing: Positioning for the Future. *The Journal of Business Strategy*, *11* (4), 16-20.

Cornwell, T. B., Humphreys, M. S., Maguire, A. M., Weeks, C. S. & Tellegen, C. L. (2006). Sponsorship-linked marketing: the role of articulation in memory. *Journal of Consumer Research*, *33* (3), 312-321.

Cornwell, T. B. & Maignan, I. (1998). An international review of sponsorship research. *Journal of Advertising*, *27* (1), 1–21

Crimmins, J. & Horn, M. (1996). Sponsorship: from management ego trip to marketing success. *Journal of Advertising Research*, *36* (4), 11-21.

Dholakia, U. M. & Algesheimer, R. (2011). Brand Communities. In R. P. Bagozzi & A. A. Ruvio (Eds.), *Wiley International Encyclopedia of Marketing* (Vol. 3, 9-17). Chichester, West Sussex: John Wiley & Sons Ltd.

Dolich, I. J. (1969). Congruence relationships between self images and product brands. *Journal of Marketing Research, 6* (1), 80-84.

Eagly, A. H. & Chaiken, S. (1993). *The psychology of attitude*. New York, Harcourt Brace Jovanovich, Inc.

Fishbein, M. & Ajzen, I. (1975). *Belief, attitude, intention and behavior: an introduction to theory and research*. Reading, MA: Addison-Wesley.

Fock, H., Chan, A. K. K. & Yan, D. (2011). Member-organization connection impacts in affinity marketing. *Journal of Business Research, 64* (7), 672-679.

Fombrum, C. J. (1996). *Reputation: realizing value from the corporate image*. Boston, MA: Harvard Business School Press.

Goldsmith, R. E. (2011). Brand engagement and brand loyalty. In A. Kapoor & C. Kulshrestha, eds., *Branding and Sustainable Competitive Advantage: Building Virtual Presence* (121-135), Hershey, PA: IGI Global.

Goldsmith, R. E., Lafferty, B. A. & Newell, S. J. (2000a). The impact of corporate credibility and celebrity credibility on consumer reaction to advertisements and brands. *Journal of Advertising, 29*(3), 43-54.

Goldsmith, R. E., Lafferty, B. A. & Newell, S. J. (2000b). The Influence of Corporate Credibility on Consumer Attitudes and Purchase Intent. *Corporate Reputation Review, 3*(4), 304-318.

Gwinner, K. (1997). A model of image creation and image transfer in event sponsorship. *International Marketing Review*, 14 (3), 145-158.

Hamlin, R. P. & Wilson, T. (2004). The impact of cause branding on consumer reactions to products: does product/cause 'fit' really matter? *Journal of Marketing Management, 20*(7/8), 663-681.

Heath, T. B. & Gaeth, G. J. (1994). Theory and method in the study of ad and brand attitudes: toward a systemic model. In E. M. Clark, T. C. Brock, & D. W. Stewart, eds., *Attention, Attitude, and Affect in Response to Advertising* (125-148), Hillsdale, NJ: Lawrence Erlbaum Associates.

Heider, F. (1946). Attitudes and cognitive organization. *Journal of Psychology, 21*, 107-112.

Heider, F. (1958). *The psychology of interpersonal relations*. New York: Wiley.

Husted, S. W. & Whitehouse Jr., F. R. (2002). Cause-related marketing via the World Wide Web: a relationship marketing strategy. *Journal of Nonprofit & Public Sector Marketing, 10* (1), 3-22.

Keller, K. L. (2003). *Strategic brand management*. Upper Saddle River, NJ: Prentice Hall.

Kotler, P. (2000). *Marketing management: the millennium edition*. Upper Saddle River, NJ: Prentice Hall.

Lafferty, B. A. (2009). Selecting the right cause partners for the right reasons: The role of importance and fit in cause-brand alliances. *Psychology & Marketing, 26* (4), 359-382.

Lafferty, B. A. (2007). The relevance of fit in a cause-brand alliance when consumers evaluate corporate credibility. *Journal of Business Research, 60* (5), 447-453.

Lafferty, B. A. & Edmondson, D. R. (2009). Portraying the cause instead of the brand in cause-related marketing ads: does it really matter? *Journal of Marketing Theory and Practice, 17* (2), 129-142.

Lafferty, B. A. & Goldsmith, R. E. (1999). Corporate credibility's role in consumers' attitudes and purchase intentions when a high versus a low credibility endorser is used in the ad. *Journal of Business Research, 44* (2), 109-116.

Lafferty, B. A. & Goldsmith, R. E. (2005). Cause-brand alliance: does the cause help the brand or does the brand help the cause? *Journal of Business Research, 58* (4), 423-429.

Lafferty, B. A., Goldsmith, R. E. & Hult, T. G. (2004). The impact of the alliance on the partners: a look at cause-brand alliances. *Psychology & Marketing, 21* (7), 511-533.

Lafferty, B. A., Goldsmith, R. E. & Newell, S. J. (2002). The dual credibility model: the influence of corporate and endorser credibility on attitudes and purchase intentions. *Journal of Marketing Theory & Practice,* 10 (3), 1-12.

MacKenzie, S. B. & Lutz, R. J. (1989). An empirical examination of the structural antecedents of attitude-toward-the-ad in an advertising pretesting context. *Journal of Marketing, 53* (2), 48-65.

McDaniel, S. R. (1999). An investigation of match-up effects in sport sponsorship advertising: the implications of consumer advertising schemas. *Psychology & Marketing, 16* (2), 163-184.

Mekonnen, A., Harris, F. & Laing, A. (2008). Linking products to a cause or affinity group: Does this really make them more attractive to consumers? *European Journal of Marketing, 42* (1/2), 135-153.

Miyazaki, A. D. & Morgan, A. G. (2001). Assessing market value of event sponsoring: coporate olympic sponsorhips. *Journal of Advertising Research, 41* (1), 9-15.

Newell, S. J. & Goldsmith, R. E. (2001). The development of a scale to measure perceived corporate credibility. *Journal of Business Research, 52* (3), 235-247.

Park, C. W., Jun, S. Y. & Shocker, A. D. (1996). Composite branding alliances: an investigation of extension and feedback effects. *Journal of Marketing Research, 33* (4), 453-466.

Payne, Michael (2007). A gold-medal partnership. *strategy+business, 46* (Spring), 55-67.

Rao, A. R. & Ruekert, R. W. (1994). Brand alliances as signals of product quality. *Sloan Management Review, 36* (1), 87-97.

Rifon, N. J., Choi, S. M., Trimble, C. S. & Li, H. (2004). Congruence effects in sponsorship: the mediating role of sponsor credibility and consumer attributions of sponsor motive. *Journal of Advertising, 33* (1), 29-42.

Roy, A. & Berger, P. D. (2007). Leveraging affiliations by marketing to and through associations. *Industrial Marketing Management, 36* (3), 270-284.

Samu, S. & Wymer, W. (2009). The effect of fit and dominance in cause marketing communications. *Journal of Business Research, 62* (4), 432-440.

Scholder P., Webb, D. J. & Mohr, L. A. (2006). Building corporate associations: consumer attributions for corporate socially responsible programs. *Journal of the Academy of Marketing Science, 34* (2), 147-157.

Simonin, B. L. & Ruth, J. A. (1998). Is a company known by the company it keeps? Assessing the spillover effects of brand alliances on consumer brand attitudes. *Journal of Marketing Research, 35* (1), 30-42.

Sirgy, M. J. (1982). Self-concept in consumer behavior: a critical review. *Journal of Consumer Research, 9* (3), 287-300.

Sirgy, M. J. (1985). Using self-congruity and ideal congruity to predict purchase motivation. *Journal of Business Research, 13* (3), 195-206.

Thompson, S. (2006). Raising awareness, doubling sales. *Advertising Age*, *77*(40), 4-4.

Trimble, C. S. & Rifon, N. J. (2006). Consumer perceptions of compatibility in cause-related marketing messages. *International Journal of Nonprofit and Voluntary Sector Marketing*, *11* (1), 29-47.

Ueltschy, L. C. & Laroche, M. (2004). Co-branding internationally: every wins? *Journal of Applied Business Research*, *20* (3), 91-102.

Vanhamme, J., Lindgreen, A., Reast, J. & Popering, N. (2011). To do well by doing good: improving corporate image through cause-related marketing. *Journal of Business Ethics*, 1-16.

Varadarajan R. P. & Menon, A. (1988). Cause-related marketing: a co-alignment of marketing strategy and corporate philanthropy. *Journal of Marketing*, *52* (3), 58-74.

Washburn, J. H., Till, B. D. & Priluck, R. (2000). Co-branding: brand equity and trial effects. *Journal of Consumer Marketing*, *17* (7), 591-604.

In: Psychology of Branding
Editor: W. Douglas Evans

ISBN: 978-1-62618-817-4
© 2013 Nova Science Publishers, Inc.

Chapter 6

RETAIL BRANDING ISSUES IN EMERGING COUNTRIES: RESEARCH INSIGHTS AND PRIORITIES

Mbaye Fall Diallo[*]

Univ Lille Nord de France-Skema Business School & LSMRC
(Lille School of Management Research Center), France

ABSTRACT

Retail brand products (also referred to as store brands, private labels, private label brands, own brands, etc.) are now offered by retailers in several emerging countries. They are increasingly investigated by researchers and draw a growing interest for managers. There are many incentives for retailers to create retail brand programs in emerging countries such as building store loyalty, increasing store traffic, enhancing negotiation strength with manufacturers and increasing retail margins. Simultaneously, emerging countries' consumers are willing to purchase retail brand products. With the retail internationalization of Western mass retailers in emerging countries, retail branding has a bright future in those countries. In this chapter, we propose to analyze retail brands and give more insights about them. We also integrate several concepts (store image, brand image, price and quality, perception of the retailer as local or international, etc.) to offer a better understanding of consumer behavior toward retail brands in the context of emerging countries. We put the emphasis on some important research areas (retail service quality, retail brand personality and innovation with retail brands) that should be further investigated in future studies.

Keywords: Retail brand, store image, service quality, brand personality, innovation, local/international

---

[*] Corresponding author: IMMD, 6 rue de l'Hôtel de ville BP59, 59051 Roubaix Cedex, France. mbayefall.diallo@univ-lille2.fr. Tel: 00 336 30 69 85 87.

1. INTRODUCTION

Retail brands (i.e. commercial retail product brands) experienced a phenomenal growth in various product categories in almost all countries. They were traditionally described as generic, no name product offerings that competed with manufacturer brands by means of a price-value proposition (Au-Yeung and Lu, 2009). However, today, they have significant improvement in terms of quality and image. They are for instance present in the fashion sector (e.g. H&M). For retailers, there are many incentives to create retail brand programs such as building store loyalty, increasing store traffic, enhancing negotiation strength with manufacturers, etc. (Baltas and Argouslidis, 2007). In Western Europe, retail brands' penetration exceeds 50% of sales by volume in Switzerland and more than 35% in markets such as the United Kingdom, Belgium and Germany (Lamey and colleagues, 2007). However, the increased globalization of economic activities has created opportunities for retailers in so-called emerging countries in general and especially in BRIC nations (Brazil, India, China and Russia). Furthermore, the competitive pressure in Western countries' retail sectors has led international retailers (Wal-Mart, Carrefour, etc.) to lay more focus on these markets. In such a context, it becomes paramount that retail scholars conduct more research on retail brands in emerging countries in the same way as some authors called for more marketing research in emerging countries in order to improve validity of findings in the marketing science (e.g., Burgess and Steenkamp, 2006). In fact, given their price/quality positioning, retail brands have an increasing strategic role in emerging countries (Diallo, 2009; Hernstein and Jaffe, 2007).

Consequently, the aim of this research is three-fold:

- To give more insights about retail brands in emerging countries by highlighting the main facts in various emerging markets (China, Brazil, Russia and South Africa).
- To investigate consumer behavior toward retail brands in emerging countries by emphasizing the main departures from developed markets' consumers.
- To propose a number of research priorities on retail branding in the context of emerging countries in the coming years.

This paper is organized as follows: first, we analyze retail brands in order to clarify their definition and to give insights about them in the context of emerging countries. Second, we lay the emphasis on consumer behavior toward retail brands in emerging countries. We focus on three types of factors: consumer-related factors, retailer-related factors and socio-demographic factors. Third, we set up a series of research priorities in three main areas in emerging countries: the relationship between retail service quality and retail brand purchase behavior, retail brand personality and innovation with retail brands. Finally, we conclude by offering a synthesis and a discussion of our research.

2. RETAIL BRANDS: DEFINITION AND INSIGHTS IN EMERGING COUNTRIES

2.1. Defining Retail Brands

There are several definitions of retail brands. However, they have limitations that should be noted, before proposing a more appropriate definition. Before defining retail brands, let us first clarify the notion of brand. There are several definitions of a brand. Indeed, given the diversity of approaches (economic, commercial, strategic, legal, etc.), branding is one of the most complex concepts in the marketing field. The American Marketing Association (AMA) defines a brand as a "name, term, sign, symbol or design, or a combination of them intended to identify the goods and services of one seller or group of sellers and to differentiate them from those of other sellers"[1]. In this sense, branding is not just about getting the target market to choose a product over the competition. It is about getting the prospects to see a product as the only one that provides a solution to a given problem or that satisfies a given need.

Based on previous research, Baltas (1997, p. 315) defined retail brands as "consumer products produced by, or on behalf of, retailers and sold under the retailers' own name or trade mark through their own outlets". However, this definition does not mention the role of retail brand as a differentiation tool for the retailer, neither the difference between store brands (retail brands with the retailer name) and private label brands or own brands (retail brands without the retailer name). Consequently, other authors have tried to bring more clarification in defining retail brands. For instance, Huang and Huddleston (2009) combined the brand definition of AMA and the definition of retail brands of Baltas (1997) to define premium retail brands as "as the consumer products, produced by or on behalf of retailers with high quality and priced close to national brands, that contribute to differentiating the retailer from its competitors" (p. 978).

In this research, we define retail brands as follows: *"A retail brand is a trademark made by a retailer or on his behalf, sold in its stores with or without his name and that can be associated with different branding strategies and with various price/quality positioning"*. This definition of retail brands seems to be more representative of the reality of these products in so far as it states that a retail brand is a trademark compared to manufacturer brands and service brands; there are various types of retail brands; there are different branding strategies for retail brands; and there is a given price-quality positioning of retail brands, which allows to include first-price retail brands, premium retail brands and hard discounter brands in the same definition.

2.2. Retail Brands Insights in Emerging Countries

According to Atsmon and colleagues (2012), as the rapid growth of emerging markets gives millions of consumers new spending power, those consumers are encountering a marketing environment swiftly evolving as its counterpart in developed countries. On most emerging markets, consumers have now retail brand ranges available on shelves. In fact,

---

[1] See: http://www.marketingpower.com/_layouts/dictionary.aspx?dletter=b.

international retailers are beginning to use retail brands as a part of their internationalization in emerging countries (Diallo, 2009). We focus our attention on four main emerging markets attractive for their retail market: China, Brazil, Russia and South Africa.

China

Over the past years, the Chinese retail industry maintained steady and rapid growth, which was driven by several factors such as the economic growth mode, increase in household income, development of technology, acceleration of urbanization and consumption upgrades. For instance, in 2010, the total number of stores owned by the Top 100 retailers in China grew at 9.7 percent over the previous year (Deloitte, 2011).

Following the development of the retail sector, retail brands are also getting increasing market shares in the Chinese market. China is a market where retail brands, from a very low base, could become a major force in years to come. Retail brands have already more than 20 years of history in this country, but for most of that time their presence and significance have been negligible. According to Nielsen[2], retail brands represent a very low consumer acceptance in China, with only one percent share within all Fast Moving Consumer Goods (FMCG) products and 0.3 percent share within the Personal Care segments in 2008. However, in the past three years, this situation has significantly changed. In fact, retail brand sales and product variety have begun to show very significant growth, and with that growth an increased significance in the total retail market.

According a report of Business Wire[3], at the current rate of development, retail brands are going to become very significant to retailers, suppliers and consumers in the coming years. For instance, Auchan is offering its entry-level 'Pouce' range in China, which it claims is 40% cheaper than the equivalent branded product. According to New Zealand Trade & Enterprise[4], in France there are 1,900 Pouce products, while in China there were 800 by the end of 2008, which represents a 60% increase over the year. China's local retailers are also heading into retail brands faster and sooner than predicted, and they will have a significant role to play in shaping the retail industry development. For example, Lianhua (China's largest supermarket retail chain operator) is at the forefront of development in the emerging retail brand sector, already having started its retail brand business in 1996. In this sense, Lianhua has turned to Daymon Worldwide, a US-based retail brand broker, to help it develop its retail brand business[5].

Brazil

The Brazilian retail market is today attractive for global retailers considering the country's large population and the relatively stable macroeconomic conditions that had emerged in recent years (De Angelo and colleagues, 2010). According to Alexander and De Lira e Silva (2002), the Brazilian retail food sector has undergone three phases of development: (1) the adoption of international best practices (e.g., self-service in 1953) which

---

[2] Source: http://blog.nielsen.com/nielsenwire/wp-content/uploads/2009/10/200909-PL-Report. pdf
[3] Source: http://www.businesswire.com/news/home/20110113005583/en/Research-Markets-Private- Label-China-2010-Market
[4] Source: http://www.prclive.com/pdf/uploads/Private%20labels%20in%20China%20-%20July %202010.pdf
[5] Source: http://www.marketresearch.com/Access-Asia-v213/Lianhua-Supermarket-Holdings-Company-Profile-2283407/

corresponds to the period before 1972, (2) the development of foreign direct investment from 1972 to the late 1990s and (3) the influx of European distributors in the late 1990s.

Retail brands accounted for a market share of 3.8% in Brazil in 2007 and this figure to reach a market share of 4.5% in 2011[6]. According to this magazine, the global financial crisis has led consumers to become more value-conscious. Therefore, Brazilian consumers have become more willing to try retail brand products at the expense of branded products in order to save on their grocery expenditure. Retailers continue to improve on the quality of their retail brand products and start marketing them between the leading and discounted brands (Newswire Today[2]). Retail brands are also offered by foreign retailers such as Carrefour and Casino, as well as Wal-Mart. Besides, non-food retailers such as C&A, Zara and H&M are also offering their retail brands. However, Brazil has very sophisticated home-grown retailers which also offer competitive retail brand ranges. For instance, the Group *Pao Açucar* had a great market share and competitive retail brand ranges before its take-over by the French group Casino.

Russia

The Russian modern retail sector is dominated by domestic retailers such as X5 Retail Group, Magnit and O'Key. The Russian market presents some contradictions (Deloitte, 2010). On the one hand, it is relatively characterized by the standards of emerging markets in terms of per capita income (around three times of that of China). Besides, some foreign retailers (e.g. Metro) have done well in Russia. On the other hand, Russia was seriously hit by the recent recession and the population is declining compared to other emerging markets, which gives less opportunity to develop retail brand offers in this market. Moreover, Russia does not seem to be willing to welcome foreign retailers (e.g., Wal-Mart and Carrefour exit from the Russian market).

According to Interbrand, Pyaterochka (of the X5 Retail Group) have so far the strongest retail brands in Russia. Despite the crisis, it continued its growth in new shops. It also increased its communication activities with the launch of a long-term and highly active communication campaign. According to The Moscow Times (2011), retail brands goods and services are a growing source of income for retail chains and have resulted in the emergence of specialized producers. Retail brand goods make up 10 to 15 percent of the total sales of retail chains depending on the type of store (The Moscow Times, 2011). However, the development of retail brand products did not live up to experts' optimistic expectations. The lack of manufacturers dedicated to producing high-quality retail brand products is a longstanding problem in Russia, even though there has been recent progress in this area (The Moscow Times, 2011).

South Africa

According to Euromonitor (2012), over the past years, the living costs of South Africans have drastically increased as food prices have significantly increased on almost every basic food commodity. At the same time cost for utilities (e.g., electricity or water) has more than doubled in some municipalities (Euromonitor, 2012). As a consequence, South Africans are experiencing the effects of the recession and are concentrating on essential grocery items. Nevertheless, with almost fifty million people, South Africa is a market of significant size. It

---

[6] Source: http://www.newswiretoday.com/news/108272/

is a relatively affluent market among emerging countries, comparable to Turkey in terms of per capita income (Deloitte, 2010). Until the recent announcement of Wal-Mart's possible acquisition in South Africa, no international retailers were present in the South African market (Deloitte, 2010).

South Africa's retail brand penetration rate is a mere 8%. According to Beneke (2010), two anomalies present themselves in terms of penetration of retail brands in South Africa. First, despite high retail concentration enjoyed by the major supermarket chains in South Africa, retail brands have not achieved the success of their global counterparts. Second, despite a much larger population of lower income consumers in South Africa, it is the higher Living Standards Measures (LSM) categories which appear to purchase these brands. South African consumers seeking to save some money in tough economic times are fuelling the current growth in retail brands, forcing retailers to rethink how they promote their retail brands[7]. There is also growing evidence which suggests that national brands are losing their hold on the consumer as compared to retail brands in this market.

3. CONSUMER BEHAVIOR TOWARDS RETAIL BRANDS IN EMERGING COUNTRIES

Atsmon, Kuentz and Seong (2012, p. 3) state that in general three factors in the consumer decision journey take on greater importance in emerging markets than in developed markets :

- The initial brand-consideration set is likely to be much smaller initially; consumers are less likely to switch later to a brand that was not in their initial set.
- Word of mouth plays a bigger role because of the higher mix of first-time buyers, a shorter history of familiarity with brands, a culture of societal validation, and a fragmented media landscape.
- The in-store experience influences a higher portion of consumers' final decisions; consumers rarely skip the hands-on in-store experience when making their decisions.

In the retail sector, the way in which brands influence consumer choice in emerging markets may be strengthened or weakened by several factors. We distinguish between three types of factors: retailer-related factors, consumer-related factors and socio-demographic factors.

3.1. Retailer-Related Factors

In general, the strategic importance and the potential role of retail brands for grocery retailers are evident in much of the literature. The key factors that motivate retailers in their retail brand development are numerous: generate higher margins, enhance store image and consumer loyalty, offer more options, increase the position and the performance of the retailer, etc. Several factors related to the retailer were investigated in previous research on

---

[7] Source: http://www.bizcommunity.com/Article/196/182/77935.html.

retail brands in emerging countries including retailer store image (e.g. Diallo, 2012) and retailer perception as local or international (e.g. Cheng and colleagues, 2007).

Store Image Perceptions

Store image is defined in the shopper's mind, partly by the functional qualities and partly by an aura of psychological attributes (Martineau, 1958). Store image develops from consumers' objective and subjective perceptions learned over time. Previous research in industrialized markets has established the relationship between store image perceptions and several constructs related or not to consumer behavior. According to the cue utilization theory, store image can be a determinant of product quality (Richardson and colleagues, 1994). Researchers have also investigated store image in the context of emerging countries. For example, Wu and colleagues (2011) found that store image directly affects the purchase intention of retail brands, but not retail brands image, in the Taiwanese market. However, Diallo (2012) stressed that retail managers must be aware that improving store image does not always lead directly to greater purchase intention, especially when perceived risk toward retail brand is taken into account. Consequently, store image improvement programs must be coupled with strategies of perceived risk reduction toward retail brands in the Brazilian market.

Retailer Perception As Local, International or Global

Previous research has investigated differences in emerging markets' consumer behavior towards local and foreign brands, particularly brands which can be considered to be international. In the context of retail brands, Lupton and colleagues (2010) demonstrated that US and Chinese consumers show statistically significant differences when addressing beliefs and perceptions concerning local and international retail brands. Parsons and colleagues (2012) found that retail brands benefited from being locally sourced and sold through a local store in terms of risk, quality, and value perceptions, whilst Cheng and colleagues (2007) found that Taiwanese consumers differentiate between international (foreign) retail brands and local retail brands in terms of brand personality and brand leadership. Chinese consumers tend to hold a more favorable brand image of foreign products compared to local ones, even when there is little brand awareness about the foreign product. International retail brands are generally perceived as being superior to local retail brands in terms of most perceptions (quality, leadership, personality) with the exception of price. Even though emerging markets' consumers are not familiar with foreign retail brands, they may be more prone to buy them compared to local brands because of their superior quality perceptions.

3.2. Consumer-Related Factors

Several consumer-related factors were associated with retail brand purchase behavior in previous research on emerging countries. These factors can be grouped in three categories: quality and price-related factors (e.g. Kara and colleagues, 2009), purchase-related factors and other various factors (e.g. Jin and Suh, 2005).

Quality and Price-Related Factors

Price and quality of retail brands have been extensively investigated in the context of developed countries. Retail brands have historically been affected by negative stereotypes, often characterized as low quality goods designed for low income consumers. For this reason, retail brands have held low market shares in some product categories such as shampoo and have traditionally been most successful in low value added product ranges. However, less attention has been given to price and quality of retail brands in emerging countries. According to Au-Yeung and Lu (2009), in the Taiwanese market, while low price is the key characteristic of retail brands, most of the retailers adopt multi-own label branding with an attempt to differentiate the positioning emphasis – either more price and/or quality driven – among their retail brands. In this emerging market, retail brands such as Wellcome's "First choice" and Tesco's "Finest" are positioned as more exclusive, quality driven. In contrast, retail brands such as No. 1 (Carrefour), Leader Price (Far-Eastern-Geant) and Value (Tesco) are price driven and assume key role in private labeling to retailers. Instead of focusing on price, Diallo (2012) investigated retail brand price-image and showed that it is a leading factor in retail brand choice for both local and international retailers.

Purchase-Related Factors

Purchase related factors comprise mainly retail brand purchase intention, retail brand choice and retail brand preference. Purchase intention refers to "the possibility that consumers will plan or be willing to purchase a certain product or service in the future" (Wu and colleagues, 2011, p. 32). It has been widely used in the literature as a predictor of subsequent purchase and the concept was found to be strongly correlated with actual behavior (Jin and Suh, 2005). In this respect, retail brand purchase intention should lead directly to retail brand choice. Sometimes, purchase intention has been used as a proxy for retail brand purchase, creating some confusion between the two variables. Jin and Suh (2005) attempted to integrate consumer perception factors into a solid research framework to understand better consumer retail brand purchase intention in South Korea in two product categories (food and household appliance). Their results showed that several factors including innovativeness, quality variability and value consciousness affect retail brand purchase intention.

Other Factors

Several other consumer-related factors were investigated in relation with retail brands in emerging countries. For instance, retail brand attitude was investigated in various emerging countries. Retail brand attitude is defined as a predisposition to respond in a favorable or unfavorable manner to retail brands due to product evaluation, purchase evaluations, and/or self-evaluations associated with private label grocery products (Burton and colleagues, 1998). Jin and Suh (2005) have empirically established the positive and direct influence of retail brand attitude on retail brand purchase behavior in the context of South Korea. Besides, Diallo (2012) showed that perceived risk toward retail brands has a negative influence on retail brand purchase behavior. Wu and colleagues (2011) found similar results in the Taiwanese market where retail brand perceived risk influences negatively price consciousness and purchase intention of retail brands. Finally, Beneke and colleagues (2012) examined empirically the perceived risks that may influence consumers' intention to purchase premium grocery retail brands in supermarkets in South Africa. They found that only functional and time risks actually have significant negative effects on purchase intention of premium retail brands in this market.

3.3. Socio-Demographic Factors

The relationship between retail brand purchase behavior and socio-demographic factors was less investigated in the context of emerging countries. Most of the existing research was undertaken on developed countries. In the Taiwanese market, Liu and Wang (2008) showed that psychological variables are weak mediators of the relationships between demographic variables and purchase attitudes. According to these authors, the direct effect of demographic variables on the two attitudes investigated (attitude toward retail brands and attitude towards promoted brands) seems weak in Taiwan. They also found indirect effects of socio-demographic variables weak. More recently, Diallo (2012) investigated the influence of demographic variables (income, gender and age) on retail brand purchase behavior in the Brazilian market. The results showed that when perceived risk toward retail brands is taken into account, household income has a negative influence on retail brand purchase intention, but not age and gender. This finding is in line with previous research reporting inconclusive results of the effect of socio-demographic variables on retail brand purchase behavior in developed countries.

4. RESEARCH PRIORITIES ON RETAIL BRANDING IN EMERGING COUNTRIES

Based on previous research, we identify several research priorities for researchers on retail brands in emerging countries. We focus on three main subjects: retail service quality, retail brand personality and retail brand innovation.

4.1. Retail Service Quality and Retail Brand Purchase Behavior

Service quality is conceptually defined as a global judgment or attitude related to the overall excellence or superiority of the service (Parasuraman and colleagues, 1988). A review of the literature in service marketing shows that service quality is one of the most discussed and debated concepts (Das and colleagues, 2010). It continues to arouse a tremendous interest for researchers as well as for practitioners. In fact, it has strategic consequences on financial performance, customer satisfaction, customer retention and loyalty, repeat purchasing behavior and so on. In the current competitive environment, delivery of high service quality has become essential for firms to achieve a differential advantage over their competitors and "has long been treated as the basic retailing strategy" (Siu and Cheung, 2001). Today, retailers are increasingly involved in emerging markets such as Brazil, Russia, India, China, etc. in order to be more consistent with the globalization of retailing operations. As they propose retail brand ranges in these markets, the influence of retail service quality on retail brand purchase behavior becomes a crucial issue which has not been investigated in the context of emerging countries. The expected contributions of such investigations are various. First, researchers can study the influence of retail service quality on retail brand perceived value and retail brand purchase intention in emerging markets. Second, the mediating effect of retail brand perceived risk should be taken into account in the analyses as little is known about the effect of this variable in emerging markets in contrast to Western countries. Third, authors should address the influence of retail service quality dimensions (e.g. physical aspects, reliability, personal interaction, problem solving and policy) on retail brand purchase behavior taking into account the presence of local and international retailers in emerging countries.

4.2. Retail Brand Personality

Personality refers to both a person's social reputation and his or her inner nature. Brand personality is commonly defined as a set of human characteristics associated to a brand. Brand personality mainly comes from three sources: the association consumers have with a brand; the image a company tries to create; and the product attributes (Lin, 2010). Therefore, like brand personality, retail brand personality and its impact on both other merchandise and overall store image across market segments are important issues, not widely investigated in existing research on emerging countries. In fact, consumers tend to buy products that are complementary to the perceptions they hold of themselves. The purchase of retail brands can therefore be a way for shoppers to express one or more aspects of their own persona (Whelan and Davies, 2006). Research on manufacturer brands showed that brand personality is an important issue in emerging countries. For instance, in the context of Taiwan, Lin (2010) found a significantly positive relationship between extroversion personality trait and excitement brand personality; a significantly positive relationship between agreeableness personality trait and excitement brand personality, sincerity brand personality and competence brand personality. Therefore, future research should address the effect of retail brand personality in emerging countries in order to show how it can affect consumer purchase behavior of retail brands and the retail store.

4.3. Innovation and Retail Brands

Innovating with retail brands may at first glance appear "iconoclastic" as innovation is the preferred area of manufacturer brands. However, successful retailers generally owe their success to innovation (e.g., Carrefour hypermarkets, Ikea furniture, H&M clothing trends, etc.). Similarly, denying to retail brand the right to innovate is to refuse to recognize the outstanding work done by some retail brands including Marks & Spencer, Migros and Ikea. Also, the French group Casino has recently attacked the monopoly of Nespresso coffee pods by launching a new pod compatible with Nespresso machines, but also 100% biodegradable and 25% cheaper. Investigating the Taiwanese market, Cheng and colleagues (2007) consider that innovative brands are recognized as being technologically ahead and can attract enough customers to buy into their brand concepts to make them sales leaders in Taiwan. Therefore, national brands usually have better capability to develop their products and simultaneously utilize their product design capability as a competitive weapon against retail brands.

However, according to these authors, through marketing communications, foreign retail brands should emphasize the quality and innovative designs of their product offers and show that they are good value for money. In this respect, Beneke and colleagues (2012) suggest that in addition to stimulating demand, supermarket chains should continue to invest in research and development of these products in South Africa so as to improve product quality through innovation. In the same way, Liu and Wang (2008) stated that since consumer lifestyle solutions, product quality, and innovation provide a necessary underpinning for a premium retail brand offering, retail brand products' communication and expressions should be developed in accordance with this underpinning.

CONCLUSION AND DISCUSSION

The aim of this paper was to analyze retail brand development in emerging countries, to investigate consumer behavior toward retail brands in these countries and to propose a number of research priorities on retail branding in the context of emerging markets. Retail brands are now present in many emerging countries and can have a strategic role in these markets as highlighted by Herstein and Jaffe (2007) and Diallo (2012). Several factors explain the growing interest for retail brands in emerging countries. For local retailers, retail brands are a means to modernize their retail offer and to compete more strongly against foreign actors. For international retailers, retail brands contribute to build their image and to attract more consumers. In the customer side, retail brands offer to emerging markets' consumers the opportunity to have access to products of good balance between quality and price. They are also an alternative to non-branded local products which are still mainly bought by low income consumers.

Comparing the four different countries investigated, we notice differences and similarities between these emerging countries in terms of retail brand development. The differences pertain to consumer behavior toward retail brand products. In the Chinese and Brazilian markets, consumers have a problem of confidence toward (local) retail brands while there is larger acceptance of these products in the South African market where retail brands are purchased by higher income consumer categories and in the Russian market where local retailers have a strong market position. As for the similarities, they relate to the market structure. In all these countries, retail brand market shares are very low compared to the situation in developed countries, but the growth rates are higher than those in industrialized countries. Emerging markets' consumers have also a wide acceptance of international retail brands which are perceived to have a good quality and sometimes close to national brands.

Our analysis shows also some departures between consumers in emerging markets and in industrialized countries in terms of perception and purchase behavior toward retail brands. For instance, for retailer-related factors, we emphasize that store image perceptions seem to be important for consumers in emerging countries (see Diallo, 2012) while price/quality-related constructs (e.g. price consciousness and value consciousness) were mainly associated to retail brand purchase in industrialized countries (see Burton and colleagues, 1998). Besides, while consumers in industrialized countries do not often care the retail origin, consumers in emerging markets highly take into account the retailer origin as local or international (Cheng and colleagues, 2007).

Based on this discussion, we proposed three main areas of research on retail brands in emerging countries:

- Investigating the effect of retail service quality on retail brands purchase behavior: as the retail sector is increasingly service-dominated, service quality becomes a critical issue. Consequently, retail researchers should focus more on the relationships between service quality and consumer behavior toward retail brands in emerging countries.
- Clarifying how retail brand personality affects retail brand purchase and store perceptions: researchers have already shown the importance of brand personality on consumer choice in developed countries. However, it is not clear how brand personality affects consumer behavior in emerging countries, especially in the retail sector.
- Focusing further on innovation to improve retail brand strength in emerging countries where retail brands are often viewed as true brands: innovation is considered as a prime mover of business. Therefore, investigating how retail brand innovation can help retailers to have more loyal consumers in emerging countries is a critical issue that needs to be addressed.

REFERENCES

Ailawadi, K. L. & Keller, L. K. (2004), "Understanding Retail Branding: Conceptual Insights and Research Priorities," *Journal of Retailing, 80* (4), 331-342.

Alexander, N. & de Lira e Silva, M. (2002), "Emerging Markets and the Internationalization of Retailing: The Brazilian Experience," *International Journal of Retail and Distribution Management, 30* (6), 300–314.

Atsmon, Y., Kuentz, J. -F. & Seong, J. (2012), "Building Brands in Emerging Markets", Report McInsey Quarly available here (on October, 15, 2012): http://www.asia.udp.cl/Informes/2012/brandsemergingmarkets.pdf

Au-Yeung, A. Y. S. & Lu, J. (2009), "Development of Retailers' Own Label Products in Taiwan," *Asia Pacific Journal of Marketing and Logistics, 21* (4), 540-554.

Baltas, G. (1997), "Determinants of Store Brand Choice: A Behavioral Analysis. *Journal of Product and Brand Management, 6* (5), 315–324.

Baltas, G. & Argouslidis, P. C. (2007), "Consumer Characteristics and Demand for Store Brand," *International Journal of Retail and Distribution Management, 3* (5), 328-341.

Beneke, J. (2010), "Consumer Perceptions of Private Label Brands within the Retail Grocery Sector of South Africa", *African Journal of Business Management, 4* (2), 203-220.

Beneke, J., Greene, A., Lok, I. & Mallett, K. (2012), "The Influence of Perceived Risk on Purchase Intent - the Case of Premium Grocery Private Label Brands in South Africa", *Journal of Product and Brand Management, 21* (1), 4–14.

Burgess, S. M. & Steenkamp J. B. E. M. (2006), "Marketing Renaissance: How Research in Emerging Markets Advances Marketing Science and Practice," *International Journal of Research in Marketing, 23* (4), 337-356.

Burton, S., Lichtenstein, D., Netemeyer, R. & Garretson, J. (1998), "A Scale for Measuring Attitude Toward Private Label Products and an Examination of its Psychological and Behavioral Correlates", *Journal of the Academy of Marketing Science, 26* (4), 293–306.

Cheng, J. M. S., Chen, L. S. L., Lin, J. Y. C. & Wang, E. S. T. (2007), "Do Consumers Perceive Differences Among National Brands, International Private Labels And Local Private Labels? The case of Taiwan", *Journal of Product* and *Brand Management, 16* (6), 368–376.

Das, A., Kumar, V. & Sahal, G. C. (2010), "Retail Service Quality in Context of CIS Countries", *International Journal of Quality and Reliability Management, 27* (6), 658-683.

De Angelo, C. F., Eunni R. V. & Fouto, N. M. M. D. (2010), "Determinants of FDI in Emerging Markets: Evidence from Brazil," *International Journal of Commerce and Management, 20* (3), 203-216.

Deloitte (2010). Emerging Retail Market Beyond China, Report Deloitte, available here (on October 15, 2012): http://www.deloitte.com/assets/ Dcom-Greece/Local%20Assets/ Documents/Attachments/gfsi/ hiddenheroes2010.pdf.

Deloitte (2011). "China Power of Retailing 2011", Report Deloitte, available here (on October 15, 2012): http://www.deloitte.com/assets/Dcom-China/ Local%20Assets/ Documents/Industries/Consumer%20business%20and%20transportation/cn_cbt_ChinaPo wersRetailing2011_181011.pdf.

Diallo, M. F. (2009). "Foreign Retailers' Private Label Brands' Strategy in Emerging Markets: Evidence from the Brazilian Retail Industry," *The Business Review,* Cambridge, *12* (1), 127-132.

Diallo, M. F. (2012). "Effects of Store Image and Store Brand Price-Image on Store Brand Purchase Intention: Application to an Emerging Market", *Journal of Retailing and Consumer Services, 19* (3), 360-367.

Euromonitor (2012). "Retailing in South Africa", Euromonitor Report, available here (on October 15, 2012): http://www.euromonitor.com/ retailing-in-south-africa/report.

Herstein, R. & Jaffe, E. D. (2007). "Launching Store Brands in Emerging Markets: Resistance Crumbles," *Journal of Business Strategy, 28* (5), 13-19.

Huang, Y. & Huddleston, P. (2009), "Retailer Premium Own-brands: Creating Customer Loyalty Through Own-brand Products Advantage," *International Journal of Retail and Distribution Management, 37* (11), 975-992.

Jin, B. & Suh, Y. G. (2005). "Integrating Effect of Consumer Perception Factors in Predicting Private Brand Purchase in a Korean Discount Store Context," *Journal of Consumer Marketing, 22* (2), 62-71.

Kara, A., Rojas-Méndez, J. I., Kucukemiroglu, O. & Harcar, T. (2009). "Consumer Preferences of Store Brands: Role of Prior Experiences and Value Consciousness," *Journal of Targeting, Measurement and Analysis for Marketing, 17* (2), 127-137.

Lamey, L., Deleersnyder, B., Dekimpe, M. G. & Steenkamp, J. B. E. M. (2007). "How Business Cycles Contribute to Private-Label Success: Evidence from the United States and Europe," *Journal of Marketing, 71* (1), 1-15.

Lin, L. Y. (2010). "The Relationship of Consumer Personality Trait, Brand Personality and Brand Loyalty: An Empirical Study of Toys and Video Games Buyers," *Journal of Product and Brand Management, 19* (1), 4 – 17.

Liu, T. C. & Wang, C. Y. (2008). "Factors Affecting Attitudes Toward Private Labels and Promoted Brands," *Journal of Marketing Management, 24* (3-4), 283-298.

Lupton, R. A., Rawlinson, D. A. & Braunstein, L. A. (2010). "Private Label Branding in China: What do US and Chinese Students Think?" *Journal of Consumer Marketing, 27* (2), 104–113.

Martineau, P. (1958). "The Personality of the Retail Store," *Harvard Business Review, 36* (January–February), 47– 55.

Parasuraman, A., Zeithaml, V. A. & Berry, L. L. (1988). "SERVQUAL: A Multiple-Item Scale for Measuring Consumer Perceptions of Service Quality," *Journal of Retailing, 64* (1), 12-40.

Parsons, A. G., Ballantine, P. W. & Wilkinson, H. (2012). "Country-of-Origin and Private-Label Merchandise", *Journal of Marketing Management, 28* (5-6), 594-608.

Richardson, P. S., Dick, A. S. & Jain, A. K. (1994). "Extrinsic and Intrinsic Cue Effects on Perceptions of Store Brand Quality," *Journal of Marketing, 58* (4), 28–36.

Siu, N. Y. M. & Cheung, J. T. H. (2001), "A Measure of Retail Service Quality," *Marketing Intelligence and Planning, 19* (2), 88- 96.

The Moscow Times (2011), Why Aren't Private Label Goods Catching On in Russia? The Moscow Times, 4752 (October), available on: http://www. themoscowtimes.com/ business/business_for_business/article/why-arent-private-label-goods-catching-on-in-russia/446201.html.

Whelan, S. & Davies, G. (2006), "Profiling Consumers of Own Brands and National Brands Using Human Personality," *Journal of Retailing and Consumer Services, 13* (6), 393– 402.

Wu, P. C. S., Yeh, G. Y. -Y. & Hsiao, C. -R. (2011), "The Effect of Store Image and Service Quality on Brand Image and Purchase Intention for Private Label Brands," *Australasian Marketing Journal, 19* (1), 30-39.

Chapter 7

BEHAVIORAL AND NEURAL INVESTIGATION OF BRAND NAMES

Mei-chun Cheung [1], Yvonne M. Han[2], Agnes S. Chan[3,4] and Sophia L. Sze[3,4]*

[1]Institute of Textiles and Clothing, The Hong Kong Polytechnic University,
Hung Hom, Kowloon, Hong Kong SAR
[2]Department of Special Education and Counselling,
The Hong Kong Institute of Education, Tai Po, New Territories, Hong Kong
[3]Department of Psychology, The Chinese University of Hong Kong,
Shatin, New Territories, Hong Kong SAR
[4]Integrative Neuropsychological Rehabilitation Center,
The Chinese University of Hong Kong, Shatin, New Territories, Hong Kong SAR

ABSTRACT

When a company takes its products into a foreign market, one of its important decisions is the choice of a suitable brand name. Many multinational companies from developed countries in the West often use their original English brand names. However, given that some consumers prefer brands in their own language, it is now common for companies to use both original English brand names and their corresponding Chinese translations, particularly if their products are marketed in China or other countries with a Chinese population. This chapter describes three experiments undertaken to examine the behavioral responses and neural mechanisms triggered by brand names to yield new insights into how such names are processed by consumers. The results of experiment 1 indicate that if people are familiar with and have knowledge of the brand name, they are able to identify and associate the brand with its respective English and Chinese names. Therefore, the use of both English and Chinese brand names for a product makes consumers familiar with the product. The EEG study conducted in experiment 2 reveals that brand names tend to be processed through semantic routes. Similar to proper names

---

* Corresponding author: Mei-chun Cheung, Ph.D. Institute of Textiles and Clothing The Hong Kong Polytechnic University Hung Hom, Kowloon, Hong Kong SAR Phone: 852-27666536 Fax: 852-27731432 Email: mei-chun.cheung@polyu.edu.hk.

and nonwords, they are represented in the lexical systems of both hemispheres. In addition, English and Chinese brand names are processed in similar ways at the semantic level, and the difference in EEG coherence patterns associated with English and Chinese brand names is likely to be due to the phonological and orthographic processing associated with English and Chinese, respectively. Experiment 3 used functional magnetic resonance imaging to investigate brain activation associated with brand names. The results show that English and Chinese brand name processing follow similar patterns of bilateral lateralization activation. Unlike English words or Chinese characters, brand names trigger activation in the limbic lobe. Therefore, as a special category of words, brand names activate distinct patterns of neural processing in areas of the brain associated with emotion and memory.

Keywords: Brand names, EEG, fMRI

INTRODUCTION

What constitutes a brand? A brand is a name, a term, a sign, a symbol, a design, a combination of the above, or any other feature that identifies the good or service and differentiates it from others (American Marketing Association, 1960; Keller, 2012). To facilitate identification and differentiation, brands consist of execution elements such as brand names, logos, symbols, characters, spokespeople, slogans, and packages (Keller, 2012). From the consumer perspective, these brand elements are aimed at enhancing consumers' awareness of a brand, enabling consumers to create a strong and distinct image for a brand, and/or eliciting positive and favorable judgments and emotional appeals towards a brand. Among these execution elements, brand names are one of the most important and commonly used extrinsic cues by which consumers evaluate products. Given that a good brand name can enhance the brand image, perception, awareness, attributes, and benefits of the product (Keller, Heckler, & Houston, 1998; Wanke, Herrmann, & Schaffner, 2007) and create brand personality (Klink & Athaide, 2012), it has a great influence on consumers' purchase decision processes, and is often regarded as one of a company's most fundamental and important assets.

With the growth of international marketing, it has become common for companies to use both original English names and their Chinese translations as brands, particularly if their products are marketed in countries with a Chinese population. Research indicates that English brand names can enhance the perceived global nature of products and are associated with the country of origin, which in turn is often associated with more favorable attributes and product quality (Steenkamp, Batra, & Alden, 2003). Because some consumers regard products with foreign brand names more favorably than those with local brand names (Leclerc, Schmitt, & Dube, 1994), they will recognize the original foreign brand name (such as its English brand name) more readily than its translated local brand name (such as its Chinese brand name). In contrast, some studies have suggested that consumers prefer brands in their own language (Harris, Garner-Earl, Spick, & Carroll, 1994; Gerritsen, Korzilius, Meurs, & Gusbers, 2000). For instance, Taiwanese consumers rated products with Chinese brand names higher on brand friendliness, brand trust, self-brand connections, and brand liking (Chang, 2008). At present, little branding research considers the transferability of original English brand names and their Chinese translations from the neuropsychological perspective. In view of studies suggesting the existence of cultural preferences towards brand names, this chapter focuses exclusively on the behavioral and neural investigation of brand names though other elements such as logos or symbols are central to branding and are worthy of investigation.

Brand name translation is considered one of the most important and complex marketing issues in international business. Some English brand names have been converted into Chinese brand names based on their phonological and/or semantic translations (Zhang & Schmitt, 2001, 2007). However, can giving products both English and Chinese names really increase brand knowledge or awareness among consumers? In addition, does the brain process their translated Chinese brand names in a similar way to brand names in the original language? In this chapter, we begin by describing an investigation of behavioral responses to English brand names and their Chinese translations to establish whether using names in both languages is a beneficial marketing strategy. Next, we present the findings of EEG and fMRI experiments designed to explore the neural mechanisms by which English brand names and their Chinese translations are processed. We conclude the chapter with a discussion of the marketing and neuropsychological implications of brand names.

EXPERIMENT ONE: BRAND NAME KNOWLEDGE

Brand knowledge represents the information stored in consumers' collective memory about a specific brand within a product category (Blackwell, Miniard, & Engel, 2006). Studies indicate that this fund of knowledge can affect product choice (Moorman, Diehl, Brinberg, & Kidwell, 2004) and decision making (Alba & Hutchinson, 1987; Liefeld, 2004; Sujan, 1985), and that better knowledge usually facilitates purchase intention (Wansink, Westgren, & Cheney, 2005). Consumers tend to purchase more familiar products, and having sufficient knowledge lowers their risk of purchasing poor quality or unsatisfactory products. Therefore, promoting brand knowledge among consumers is an essential task in marketing.

Free recall is one of the most commonly used knowledge and awareness testing tools employed in marketing research (Bettman, 1979; Krugman, 1986). In free recall tests, the subject has to recall from memory information about specific products and product categories. Because this test format requires that the person being assessed has good expressive language ability, it measures both the fund of knowledge and expressive verbal ability of the individual. However, empirical studies in neuropsychology indicate that free recall may not be an accurate representation or valid estimation technique, as it may underestimate the fund of knowledge of individuals with relatively poor expressive ability (Banich, 1998; Chan, Cheung, Sze, Leung, & Cheung, 2008; Rey, Levin, Rodas, Bowen, & Nedd, 1994). Therefore, Kaplan and her colleagues (1991, 2005) have highlighted the importance of using tests less dependent on expressive ability to gauge individuals' fund of knowledge, and the recognition format has been incorporated into some neuropsychological tests. Our previous study (Chan et al., 2008) suggested that the recognition format, which requires less expressive ability, is more sensitive in assessing the fund of verbal knowledge. Therefore, we have investigated the fund of brand knowledge using a free recall and recognition format to compare these two test formats in assessing brand knowledge and to investigate the interaction effects of language used and product categories on individuals' brand knowledge.

In this experiment, two test formats were used to assess the brand knowledge of the participants: free recall and recognition (Cheung & Chan, 2009). In the free recall trial, each participant was given one minute to recall names of fashion brands in English and Chinese from memory without prompting. In the recognition trial, a list of 48 names was printed on a page and given to the participant, who was asked to distinguish brand names from non-brand names. The list contained 24 fashion brand names, 12 brand names from the electronics and cars (E & C) categories, and 12 non-brand names that served as distracters, all of which were printed in black. The participants had to circle fashion brand names with a black pen and brand names from the E & C categories with a red pen. The recognition trial was conducted after the free recall trial to avoid a priming effect. Brands with both English and Chinese names that were formally used by the company were selected for recognition. Two lists, one having original English brand names and the other having their Chinese translations, were given to the participants in a counterbalanced sequence. These brands are commonly found in Hong Kong, and pilot screening was conducted to eliminate brands that could not be identified by young adults. Furthermore, to ensure that participants had basic knowledge of the brands, they had to read and match English and Chinese brand names after completing the assessment. All participants were able to read and match over 90% of the English and Chinese brand names correctly.

Table 1 reports the three English and Chinese fashion brand names the participants generated most frequently within one minute. Most of the English brand names the participants recalled were international brands, whereas the majority of Chinese fashion brand names they recalled were local Hong Kong brands. Therefore, the participants appeared more able to recall international brand names in English. Among Chinese brand names, local brands were more familiar than international brands. Figure 1 shows the number of English and Chinese fashion brand names the participants recalled and recognized. The results showed that the interaction effect between test format (free recall vs. recognition) and language (English vs. Chinese) was significant ($F(1, 39) = 70.91$, $p = 0.000$). In general, participants recalled (English: 16.03 ± 4.31; Chinese: 4.38 ± 3.41, $t(39) = 20.39$, $p = 0.000$) and recognized (English: 18.43 ± 2.85, Chinese: 12.35 ± 3.56, $t(39) = 14.423$, $p = 0.000$) more English fashion brand names than they did Chinese fashion brand names. Recognition performance was better than recall performance for English ($t(39) = -3.495$, $p = 0.001$) and Chinese ($t(39) = -15.691$, $p = 0.000$) brand names, and the difference was greater for Chinese brands. Among the 24 Chinese fashion brand names on the list, the participants recognized an average of 12 items, whereas they freely recalled an average of only 4 items.

Table 1. Three most popular brand names freely recalled within one minute (n = 40)

Brand names	Frequency count
English	
Louis Vuitton	29/40
Gucci	22/40
Armani	21/40
Chinese	
佐丹奴 (Giordano)	16/40
堡獅龍 (Bossini)	13/40
李寧 (Li Ning)	11/40

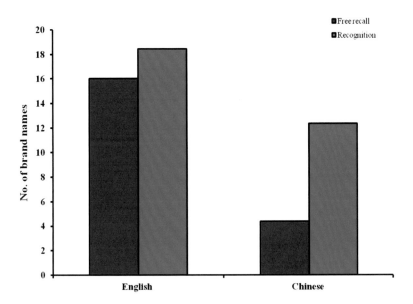

Figure 1. Total number of fashion brand names in English and Chinese freely recalled and recognized.

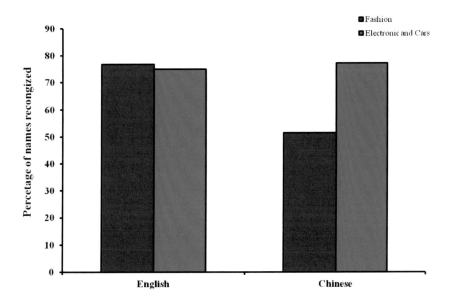

Figure 2. Percentage of brand names in English and Chinese correctly recognized for fashion and electronics and cars.

To test specific product categories, in addition to being asked whether they recognized fashion brand names, the participants were also asked whether they recognized English and Chinese brand names from the E & C categories. Given that the total number of fashion and E & C brand names was different (24 items for fashion and 12 items for E & C), the percentages of items recognized were used for comparison. Figure 2 shows the percentage of fashion and E & C brand names recognized in English and Chinese. The results demonstrated that the interaction effect between language used (English vs. Chinese) and product category (fashion vs. E & C) was significant ($F(1, 39) = 121.104$, $p = 0.000$). The participants recognized similar numbers of English and Chinese brand names from the E & C categories ($t(39) = -1.097$, $p = 2.79$). However, they recognized fewer Chinese brand names than they did English brand names from the fashion category ($t(39) = 14.423$, $p = 0.000$). Therefore, the language used for a brand name seems to have a differential effect on their recognition performance, depending on the product category. The participants were less familiar with Chinese brand names in the fashion category, but were similarly familiar with English and Chinese brand names from the E & C categories.

Double dissociation was found in the free recall and recognition performance of participants according to the language used across product categories. Specifically, their free recall of English fashion brand names was significantly correlated with their recognition of English brand names in the fashion and E & C product categories, respectively, (Fashion, $r(40) = 0.318$, $p = 0.045$; E & C, $r(40) = 0.358$, $p = 0.023$), but was not correlated with their recognition of Chinese brand names in either product category ($p > 0.05$). Similar correlation patterns were observed in the **participants'** free recall of Chinese fashion brand names and recognition of Chinese brand names in the fashion and E & C product categories, respectively, (Fashion, $r(40) = 0.477$, $p = 0.002$; E & C, $r(40) = 0.327$, $p = 0.040$), whereas no significant correlation was found between their free recall of Chinese brand names and their recognition of English brand names in either product category ($p > 0.05$). Therefore, individuals who freely recalled more Chinese brand names than their peers also performed significantly better in recognizing Chinese brand names.

This experiment investigated behavioral responses to English brand names and their Chinese translations. English and Chinese brand **names'** free recall was highly associated, suggesting that participants who were familiar with and had knowledge of a brand were able to identify and associate the brand with its English and Chinese names. Therefore, using English and Chinese brand names for a product enables consumers to become familiar with the product. In addition, the double dissociation we found between **participants'** free recall and recognition performance indicates that such familiarity can be transferred to other product categories. Participants who had better free recall performance in English fashion brand names were also better at recognizing English brand names in other product categories. A similar pattern of better performance was also found in Chinese brand names. The implication of such dissociation is that if a company introduces its products to a Chinese population, using Chinese brand names seems to make consumers more aware of Chinese brand names in other product categories. Therefore, using both English and Chinese names appears to be a marketing strategy that improves **consumers'** brand knowledge, which can also raise their awareness of brands in other product categories.

EXPERIMENT TWO: ELECTROPHYSIOLOGICAL INVESTIGATION OF BRAND NAMES

What are brand names? How are brand names processed in the brain? Are they processed in a similar way to proper names? Indeed, the literature provides a less detailed understanding of brand names as a category of proper nouns, and only a very small number of studies have investigated the neural substrates that process brand names (Crutch & Warrington, 2004; Gontijo, Rayman, Zhang, & Zaidel, 2002; Schaefer & Rotte, 2007; Schaefer, Berens, Heinze, & Rotte, 2006). Studies using lexical decision tasks (LDT, Gontijo & Zhang, 2007; Gontijo et al., 2002) have been conducted to compare brand names with common nouns and nonwords. Their findings suggest that the hemispheric lexical status of brand names is mixed, and that brand names behave like words in some ways and like nonwords in others. For instance, brand names are similar to nonwords in that they are less lateralized and stimulate greater right hemisphere involvement during processing than do common nouns. However, brand names share one feature with common nouns, in that they are processed more quickly and accurately than are nonwords in what is known as the lexicality effect. In addition, both common nouns and brand names exhibit length effects in the left visual field (Gontijo et al., 2002). Therefore, brand names seem to represent a special category of words and may be processed by distinct regions of the brain that do not deal with common nouns or nonwords. Several studies relating to language processing have examined EEG coherence patterns associated with different categories of words, such as concrete versus abstract words (Weiss & Rappelsberger, 1996, 1998), nouns versus verbs (Weiss & Rappelsberger, 1998), high imagery versus low imagery verbs (Weiss & Mueller, 2003), and sentence processing (Mueller, Weiss, & Rappelsberger, 1997; Weiss et al., 2002). Weiss and Mueller (2003) concluded in their review paper that the language processing of English words is generally accompanied by an increase in long-range coherence. Coherence in the theta, alpha and beta frequency bands plays important roles in the dynamic functional integration of brain structures involved in language processing. In particular, increased coherence in the theta frequency band tends to reflect non-specific components of language processing and is common for all word categories (Weiss & Mueller, 2003). Greater coherence in higher frequency bands (over 10 Hz) is associated with more complex linguistic sub-processes such as semantic or syntactic processing (Weiss & Rappelsberger, 1996; Weiss, Mueller, Schask, King, & Kutas, 2005). Coherence patterns in the higher frequency bands also differ between word categories (Weiss & Mueller, 2003; Weiss & Rappelsberger, 1996). For instance, in comparison with low imagery verbs, high imagery verbs are associated with increased intrahemispheric coherence in the beta frequency band (Weiss & Mueller, 2003). As brand names are known to be associated with brand attributes such as product quality, usage, image, and position, they are not regarded as a single entity but are considered to be complicated verbal stimuli embedded with phonemic, morphemic and semantic meaning (Lerman, 2007). Therefore, we proposed that reading brand names may evoke more imagery and have a greater association with the semantic network of other attributes than does reading concrete words or characters. It was hypothesized that in comparison with low imagery words, brand names tended to be a category of high imagery words demonstrating elevated intrahemispheric beta coherence.

One challenge faced by marketers is how to translate a brand name from a phonological into an orthographic system (Zhang & Schmitt, 2007). Some English brand names have been translated into Chinese brand names based on their phonological and/or semantic translations. It is questionable whether the brain processes translated Chinese brand names and brand names in the original language in similar ways. Therefore, another purpose of this experiment was to compare any differences in the EEG coherence patterns of English brand names and their translated Chinese brand names. Our previous study (Cheung, Chan, & Sze, 2009) suggested that due to the alphabetic and logographic systems associated with English words and Chinese characters, EEG coherence patterns in reading Chinese characters are different from those that occur in reading English words. In comparison with that observed during English reading, theta coherence during Chinese reading shows an increased intrahemispheric connection in the left hemisphere and interhemispheric connections over the temporal, central and parietal/occipital regions, which suggests that the interhemispheric cooperation between neuronal substrates in these regions is associated with Chinese reading. Therefore, it was speculated that if the neural processing of original English brand names and their Chinese translations varied due to the distinct phonological and orthographic systems of the two languages, increased theta coherence would be found in processing Chinese brand names. On the other hand, if this difference was more closely related to semantic processing, the coherence pattern in higher frequency bands (over 10 Hz), which is associated with more complex linguistic sub-processes such as semantic or syntactic processing (Mueller et al., 1997; Weiss & Rappelsberger, 1996; Weiss et al., 2005), would be different.

We employed EEG coherence as a measure to examine the electrophysiological correlates of processing brand names (Cheung, Chan, & Sze, 2010). The results suggested that in comparison with concrete English words, English brand names resulted in elevated short-range ($t(31)$ = 3.891, p = 0.000) and long-range ($t(31)$ = 3.002, p = 0.005) beta coherence in the left hemisphere, and higher short-range beta coherence in the right hemisphere ($t(31)$ = 2.892, p = 0.007) (Figure 3a). Translated Chinese brand names also demonstrated higher short-range and long-range beta coherence in both the left (short: $t(31)$ = 3.403, p = 0.002; long: $t(31)$ = 3.310, p = 0.002) and right (short: $t(31)$ = 3.104, p = 0.004; long: $t(31)$ = 3.168, p = 0.003) hemispheres (Figure 3b), in comparison with concrete Chinese characters. Therefore, English brand names and their Chinese translations generally prompted greater intrahemispheric beta coherence within both hemispheres than did concrete English words or concrete Chinese characters.

Given that increased coherence in higher frequency bands (over 10 Hz) is associated with more complex linguistic sub-processes such as semantic or syntactic processing (Weiss & Rappelsberger, 1996; Weiss, Mueller, Schask, King, & Kutas, 2005), the increased intrahemispheric beta coherence we observed in brand name reading suggests that brand names, whether English or Chinese, tend to be processed through the semantic route. The results of this experiment based on EEG coherence generally agree with those of a case involving a patient with a semantic refractory access disorder reported by Crutch and Warrington (2004), suggesting that brand names are grouped according to product type and are processed for their semantic meaning. In addition, beta coherence has been found to differ between word categories (Weiss & Mueller, 2003; Weiss & Rappelsberger, 1996). Specifically, high imagery words demonstrate higher intrahemispheric beta coherence than low imagery words. The specific pattern of increased intrahemispheric beta coherence observed in this experiment suggests that brand names are likely to be a category of high imagery words. Besides, the lateralization effect has also been investigated in different word categories. Right hemisphere involvement has been observed in some word categories such as proper names (Semenza, 1997) and nonwords (Gontijo, Rayman, Zhang, & Zaidel, 2002). Therefore, similar to the weaker lateralization observed in processing proper names (Semenza, 1997) and nonwords (Gontijo et al., 2002), brand name processing involves both the left and right hemispheres, the latter of which is more prominent in processing Chinese brand names. These findings provide further support for the proposition that brand names are represented in the lexical system of both hemispheres and share some of the linguistic features of proper names and nonwords.

Given that English and Chinese belong to different linguistic systems, that are phonological and logographic, respectively, Zhang and Schmitt (2004) proposed the language differential processing hypothesis whereby English words are more likely to be processed by phonemes, whereas Chinese characters are processed in a visual-semantic way. EEG coherence patterns in English brand names and their Chinese translations have been compared to investigate post-translation brand name transferability (Cheung et al., 2010). A Language (English versus Chinese) x Hemisphere (left versus right) x Range (short versus long) repeated measures ANOVA was also performed to compare intrahemispheric beta and theta coherence between English and Chinese brand names. The multivariate results did not show any significant difference between English and Chinese brand names. A further Language (English versus Chinese) x Location (frontal, temporal, central and parietal/occipital region) repeated measures ANOVA was conducted to compare interhemispheric beta coherence between English and Chinese brand names, and no significant difference was found. In contrast, a significant main effect of language ($F(1, 31) = 9.210$, $p = 0.005$) was found in the interhemispheric theta coherence between English and Chinese brand names. Chinese brand names generally had higher interhemispheric theta coherence than English brand names in the frontal ($t(31) = -3.088$, $p = 0.004$) and temporal ($t(31) = -3.146$, $p = 0.004$) cortical regions (Figure 4).

Our previous study (Cheung et al., 2009) suggested that due to the alphabetic and logographic systems associated with English words and Chinese characters, interhemispheric theta coherence was higher in Chinese reading than in English reading. Similar to the difference observed in EEG coherence patterns between English and Chinese reading, reading Chinese brand names resulted in higher interhemispheric coherence in the theta frequency band, particularly in the frontal and temporal cortical regions, than did reading English brand names. However, there was no significant difference in their intrahemispheric and interhemispheric EEG coherence patterns for the beta frequency band. Therefore, the difference in EEG coherence patterns between English and Chinese brand names is more related to the distinct phonological and orthographic processing associated with English words and Chinese characters, as shown in our previous study (Cheung et al., 2009). They are processed similarly on the semantic level. One may argue that there may have been differences among the participants in their familiarity with English and Chinese brand names, as recent fMRI studies have suggested differential brain activation patterns between familiar and unfamiliar brands (Schaefer & Rotte, 2007; Reimann, Castano, Zaichkowsky, & Bechara, 2012). To rule this out as a possible factor and ensure that the participants had knowledge of the translated Chinese brand names, they were asked to read them and match them with their original English brand names. The percentage of correct responses in the reading and matching tasks was over 90%. Therefore, increased interhemispheric theta coherence in the frontal and temporal regions associated with Chinese brand names does not seem to be related to the degree of familiarity. If we are familiar with a brand name, our brain will process the semantic meaning of the original brand name and its translation in a similar manner.

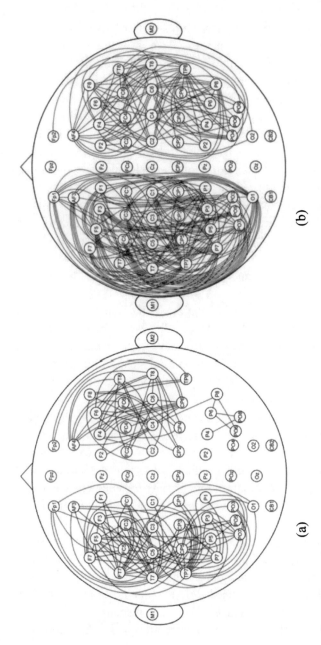

(a)

(b)

Figure 3. Increased intrahemispheric beta coherence for (a) English brand names (compared to English words); (b) Chinese brand names (compared to Chinese characters). Paired Wilcoxon tests were used as statistical filters, and the resulting error probabilities ($p < 0.01$) were mapped onto the topographic map as connecting lines between the electrodes involved.

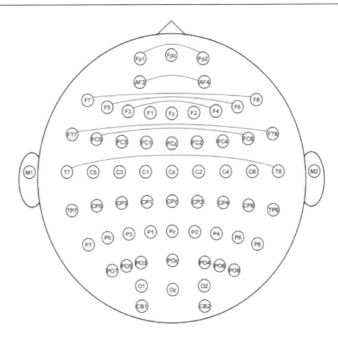

Figure 4. Chinese brand names had higher interhemispheric theta coherence than English brand names in the frontal and temporal cortical regions. Paired Wilcoxon tests were used as statistical filters, and the resulting error probabilities ($p < 0.01$) were mapped onto the topographic map as connecting lines between the electrodes involved.

EXPERIMENT THREE: NEURAL PROCESSING OF BRAND NAMES

Many studies have employed fMRI techniques to explore differences between word categories, such as between nouns and verbs (Berlingeri et al., 2008; Tyler, Bright, Fletcher, & Stamatakis, 2004), concrete and abstract nouns (Fiebach & Friederici, 2004; Kiehl et al., 1999), proper names and common nouns (Almor, Smith, Bonilha, Fridriksson, & Rorden, 2007), and different subgroups of words (Diaz & McCarthy, 2009). The advantage of conventional fMRI is that it can identify the cortical and subcortical brain regions in which activity is associated with the task. In this experiment, the neural mechanism by which brand names are processed was further examined by functional magnetic resonance imaging (fMRI) to establish the specific brain regions involved in processing original English brand names and their Chinese translations. Neuroimaging and lesion studies suggest that Chinese characters and English words are processed in distinct and overlapping regions of the brain (Chee et al., 2000; Tan, Feng, Fox, & Gao, 2001; Tan, Laird, Li, & Fox, 2005; Tan et al., 2000, 2001; Chen, Fu, Iversen, Smith, & Matthews, 2002; Cheung, Cheung, & Chan, 2004; Kuo et al., 2004; Dong et al., 2005; Cheung, Chan, Chan, & Lam, 2006). It has been shown that the neural processing of written English is largely dependent on the left hemisphere, and that the activated regions include the inferior frontal gyrus (BA 44, 45 and BA 9), the middle frontal gyrus (BA9), the precentral gyrus (BA6), and the fusiform gyrus (BA20 and BA 37) (Adcock, Wise, Oxbury, Oxbury, & Matthews, 2003; Tan, Laird, Li, & Fox, 2005; Bolger, Perfetti, & Schneider, 2005; Cheung et al., 2006). Although the left frontal and temporal regions activated when reading Chinese characters are similar (Tan et al., 2000; Dong et al.,

2005; Mo, Liu, Jin, & Yang, 2005), activation of specific regions in the right hemisphere, including the inferior (BA45) and middle frontal gyrus (BA9), the fusiform gyrus (BA20 and BA37), and the parahippocampal gyrus (BA36), has been observed in reading Chinese characters (Matthews et al., 2003; Dong et al., 2005; Cheung et al., 2006). Therefore, the brain activation pattern of Chinese processing involves both the left and right hemispheres, making it somewhat different from that of English processing, which is largely mediated by the left hemisphere. Moreover, it has been suggested that right hemisphere involvement plays a prominent role in the distinct orthographic processing of Chinese characters (Tan, Feng et al., 2001), such as in the mediation of spatial decoding and the analysis of Chinese characters (Dong et al., 2005).

In the fMRI experiment, 20 healthy normal subjects were recruited from The Hong Kong Polytechnic University. The data were collected by a 1.5T scanner using a standard head coil. Gradient echo-planar imaging sequencing was used with TR/TE/2000/40/90, a 64x64 matrix, FOV of 220mm and slice thickness of 5mm. Twenty horizontal slices were acquired to cover the whole brain, and 80 images per slice location were collected during four task-rest cycles (20s stimulation, 20s rest). During scanning, subjects were invited to read silently a total of 24 English words or 24 Chinese characters in four reading paradigms: concrete English words (such as orange, dog), concrete Chinese two-character words (such as 眼睛, 報紙), English brand names (such as Giordano, Puma), and their officially used translated Chinese brand names (such as 佐丹奴, 彪馬). Concrete words or characters that refer to living or non-living things that can be seen, heard, felt, smelled, or tasted were chosen, and were also relatively low in imagery. These stimuli were printed in black and were the same as those employed in our previous EEG studies (Cheung, Chan, & Sze, 2009, 2010).

The results of the fMRI experiment suggested that similar patterns of bilateral activation occurred in reading English and Chinese brand names (Table 2). The activated regions included the superior (BA 6, 9, and 10) and inferior (BA 9 and 47) frontal gyrus, the superior temporal gyrus (BA22) in the left hemisphere, and the middle frontal (BA10 and 46) and middle temporal (BA 20, 21, and 22) gyrus in the left and right hemispheres. Therefore, the neural processing of English brand names is somewhat different from that of English words, which is primarily associated with activation in the left hemisphere. In contrast, parts of the right hemisphere including the middle frontal and middle temporal gyrus tend to be more involved in reading English brand names, similar to the activation patterns that occur in reading Chinese brand names. These findings are consistent with those of previous studies using lexical decision tasks (LDT, Gontijo & Zhang, 2007; Gontijo et al., 2002) showing that brand names are similar to nonwords: they are less lateralized, and there is greater right hemisphere involvement during processing. The involvement of the right hemisphere in processing brand names implies that English brand names are not only processed by phonemes, but are embedded with the visual-spatial information associated with brand names. As a result, they tend to be processed in a visual-semantic way, similar to the processing of Chinese characters (Zhang & Schmitt, 2004; Tavassoli, 1999), and are represented in the lexical systems of both hemispheres.

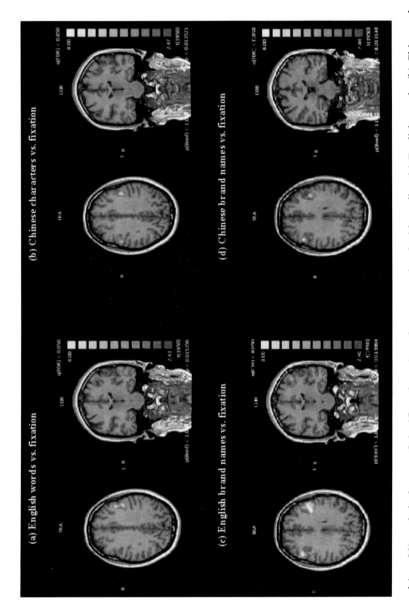

Figure 5. Group-averaged (n = 20) statistical maps of significantly activated areas associated with reading (a) English words; (b) Chinese characters; (c) English brand names; and (d) Chinese brand names as opposed to fixation. Activations are displayed at $p < 0.05$, FDR.

Table 2. Localization of activated regions in reading English and Chinese brand names, corresponding Brodmann areas (BA), no. of voxels and their *t*-values (n = 20)

Regions activated	BA	English vs. fixation			Chinese vs. fixation		
		Coordinate	t-value	No. of voxels	Coordinate	t-value	No. of voxels
Left Hemisphere							
Frontal							
Superior frontal gyrus	6				(-4, -5, +67)	6.36	1427
	9				(-10, +55, +24)	4.39	391
	10	(-10, 55, -3)	5.02	367	(-13, +52, -3)	4.05	309
Middle frontal gyrus	10	(-25, +55, +18)	3.53	116	(-41, +52, +9)	5.80	1488
Inferior frontal gyrus	9				(-43, +10, +24)	7.71	17461
	47	(-58, +25, -6)	4.66	1228	(-40, +16, -12)	3.27	171
Medial frontal gyrus	6	(-4, +4, +54)	5.90	7565	(-1, +34, +36)	3.48	232
Precentral gyrus	4	(-13, -23, +69)	3.66	283	(-37, -20, +58)	3.79	117
Temporal							
Superior temporal gyrus	22	(-52, +13, 0)	4.25	955	(-64, +1, 0)	6.08	703
Middle temporal gyrus	21				(-40, -5, -28)	4.16	679
	22				(-61, -48, +3)	3.91	680
Parahippocampal gyrus	34				(-25, +1, -12)	3.47	146
Occipital							
Lingual gyrus	17	(-13, -89, -3)	17.67	135340			
	18				(-28, -84, -9)	21.04	103593
Right Hemisphere							
Frontal							
Middle frontal gyrus	10	(+35, +46, +9)	5.80	3031			
	46				(+47, +22, +27)	7.77	15835
Precentral gyrus	6	(+41, -2, +33)	10.12	17936	(+47, -8, +39)	3.89	848
Temporal							
Middle temporal gyrus	20				(+62, -41, -12)	3.67	300
	22	(+47, -41, +3)	4.62	253	(+56, -32, +3)	3.39	184
Parahippocampal gyrus	28				(+23, -23, -6)	4.65	1193
	34	(+26, +4, -15)	3.74	107			

In addition, compared with reading English words or Chinese characters, brand name reading was found to stimulate functional activation in the limbic lobe (Figure 5), an observation not made in reading English words or Chinese characters. Given that the participants were familiar with the brand names, the involvement of the parahippocampal gyrus of the limbic lobe suggests that brand name processing evoked participants' recollections and emotions about the brands and their associated attributes. This finding has important implications for marketing and advertising, in that brand names are not simply words or characters, but can trigger consumers' recall of and emotions associated with the brands. Once brand familiarity is established, brand names can generate strong brand associations. This experiment further supports the notion that brand names are a special category of words that stimulate a pattern of neural processing distinct from that prompted by English words or Chinese characters.

CONCLUSION

This chapter summarizes three experiments undertaken as part of a behavioral and neural investigation of brand names. It makes a theoretical contribution to the neuropsychology of brand names and their Chinese translations, providing key implications for the understanding of how brand names are processed by the brain. The findings also make a practical contribution to the realm of international business by highlighting the importance of increasing consumers' familiarity with brand names and their translations during marketing and promotions. Using both English and Chinese brand names seems a beneficial marketing strategy to improve consumers' knowledge and promote their awareness of other product categories. Studies have indicated the benefits of using English and Chinese brand names (Chang, 2008, Steenkamp et al., 2003). Whereas English brand names can enhance the perceived globalness of products and are associated with the country of origin, which is in turn often associated with more favorable attributes and better product quality (Steenkamp et al., 2003), Chinese brand names have been rated higher on brand friendliness, brand trust, self-brand connections, and brand liking among a Chinese population (Chang, 2008). Products with both English and Chinese brand names may be associated with dual benefits if they are targeted at a Chinese population. Therefore, it is more effective for companies to have both English and Chinese brand names across international markets, especially those with Chinese populations, to maximize the memorability and likability of brands between cultures. The results of Experiment 1 also show that the participants were able to recognize the respective English and Chinese brand names for the E & C product categories. However, they recognized significantly fewer Chinese brand names than they did English brand names in the fashion product category. This may be related to the fact that the participants were less familiar with Chinese fashion brand names, resulting in their free recall and recognition of fewer such names. At the same time, this effect seems to have been product–specific, as the participants recognized similar numbers of English and their respective Chinese brand names in the E & C product categories. Therefore, when assessing brand knowledge, we should be careful in selecting product categories and languages as these two factors have differential effects on individuals' brand name knowledge being assessed.

The neural investigation of brand names revealed that English brand names and their Chinese translations are processed in similar ways at the semantic level, and that the difference in EEG coherence patterns associated with English and Chinese brand names is likely to be due to the phonological and orthographic processing associated with each of these languages. Our findings certainly provide support for the strategy of existing brands having Chinese translations, because phonological and semantic translations do not seem to affect the semantic processing of brand names. Given that consumers are able to process English brand names and their Chinese translations in a similar way on the semantic level once familiarity is established, one of the essential marketing strategy issues following brand name conversion is how to facilitate familiarity with translated brand names and their association with their original brands. Therefore, global marketing managers should formulate marketing strategies and promotional campaigns to guide their target customers toward English brand names and their Chinese translations and develop a semantic association between them. Moreover, the involvement of emotion and memory-related processing in brand name reading has significant implications for the existence of brand associations, especially in the emotional responses attached to brand names, which play a crucial role during hedonic consumption. These findings provide initial support for the proposition that brand names can themselves be sufficient to trigger the emotional appeal of a brand. Future research investigating emotional responses to brand names may aid our understanding of consumer preferences for certain brand names.

LIMITATIONS

Several limitations need to be addressed. First, these experiments focused exclusively on brand names as opposed to other brand execution elements such as logos, colors, symbols and packages. Second, they were conducted in experimental settings in which some parameters associated with brand names had to be controlled. The findings of our studies do not address the visual processing of some basic features associated with brand names. In practice, brand names are usually presented in specific colors, fonts and sizes, or are combined with symbols or slogans in the real market, and cultural preferences also influence some of these elements. For instance, blue, green and white share similar meanings and preferences across different countries, whereas black and red carry varying implications across different nationalities (Madden, Hewett, & Roth, 2000). Differences in color preferences and meanings may account for differences in consumers' perceptions of brand image or personality, and may be capable of evoking different emotional responses. Therefore, further research focusing on the interaction between brand names and other execution elements would be helpful. For example, neural processing may be compared between real brand names (combined with specific colors, fonts, or symbols) and brand names presented in a standard color or font. Moreover, the emotional appeal embodied in other execution elements should not be overlooked and warrants investigation.

Another limitation of these experiments is that brand names were only compared with concrete words in the experiments undertaken. Further comparison with other word categories such as proper names and nonwords would shed more light on the unique neural processing patterns associated with brand names. In addition, we compared the EEG coherence patterns of English brand names with those of their translated Chinese brand names with which the participants were familiar. However, because an fMRI investigation shows that brand name familiarity is associated with different patterns of brain activation (Schaefer & Rotte, 2007), it is not known whether unfamiliar or favorite brand names result in different EEG coherence patterns, as these findings may provide significant information on the neural processing involved in brand selection and decision making. In addition to language and product category, other factors such as marketing time, country of origin, usability in daily life, and the gender effect may influence brand name familiarity, and were not addressed in this chapter. It would be a worthwhile exercise to explore these potentially important factors in future research.

ACKNOWLEDGMENTS

Preparation of this chapter and the research discussed therein were supported by research grants from The Hong Kong Polytechnic University (4-ZZ64, A-PK13, A-PD1M, & A-PK67).

REFERENCES

Adcock, J. E., Wise, R. G., Oxbury, J. M., Oxbury, S. M. & Matthews, P. M. (2003). Quantitative fMRI assessment of the differences in lateralization of language-related brain activation in patients with temporal lobe epilepsy. *NeuroImage, 18*, 423-438.

Alba, J. W. & Hutchinson, J. W. (1987). Dimensions of consumer expertise. *Journal of Consumer Research, 13*, 411-454.

Almor, A., Smith, D. V., Bonilha, L., Fridriksson, J. & Rorden, C. (2007). What is in a *name*? Spatial brain *NeuroReport, 18*, 1215-1219.

American Marketing Association. (1960). *Marketing definitions: A glossary of marketing terms*. Chicago, IL: American Marketing Association.

Banich, M. T. (1998). *Neuropsychology: The neural bases of mental function*. New York: Houghton Mifflin.

Berlingeri, M., Crepaldi, D., Roberti, R., Scialfa, G., Luzzatti, C. & Paulesu, E. (2008). Nouns and verbs in the brain: grammatical class and task specific effects as revealed by fMRI. *Cognitive Neuropsychology, 25*, 528-558.

Bettman, J. R. (1979). Memory factors in consumer choice: a review. *Journal of Marketing, 43*, 37-53.

Blackwell, R. D., Miniard, P. W. & Engel, J. E. (2006). *Consumer behavior*. Mason, OH: Thomson South-Western.

Bolger, D. J., Perfetti, C. A. & Schneider, W. (2005). A cross-cultural effect on the brain revisited. *Human Brain Mapping, 25*, 92-104.

Chan, A. S., Cheung, M. C., Sze, S. L., Leung, W. W. & Cheung, R. W. Y. (2008). Measuring vocabulary by free expression and recognition tasks: implications for assessing children, adolescents, and young adults. *Journal of Clinical and Experimental Neuropsychology, 30*, 892-902.

Chang, C. (2008). The effectiveness of using a global look in an Asian market. *Journal of Advertising Research, 48*(2), 199-214.

Chee, M. W., Weekes, B., Lee, K. M., Soon, C. S., Schreiber, A., Hoon, J. J. & Chee, M. (2000). Overlap and dissociation of semantic processing of Chinese characters, English words, and pictures: evidence from fMRI. *NeuroImage, 12,* 392-403.

Chen, Y., Fu, S., Iversen, S. D., Smith, S. M. & Matthews, P. M. (2002). Testing for dual brain processing routes in reading: a direct contrast of Chinese character and Pinyin reading using fMRI. *Journal of Cognitive Neuroscience, 14,* 1088-1098.

Cheung, M. C. & Chan, A. S. (2008). Measures for brand knowledge: comparison of testing formats, languages and product categories. *Journal of Psychology in Chinese Societies, 9,* 153-167.

Cheung, M. C., Chan, A. S. & Sze, S. L. (2010). Electrophysiological correlates of brand names. *Neuroscience Letters, 485,* 178-182.

Cheung, M. C., Chan, A. S. & Sze, S. L. (2009). Increased theta coherence during Chinese reading. *International Journal of Psychophysiology, 74,* 132-138.

Cheung, M. C., Chan, A. S., Chan, Y. L. & Lam, J. M. K. (2006). Language lateralization of Chinese-English bilingual patients with epilepsy: a functional MRI study. *Neuropsychology, 20*(5), 589-597.

Cheung, R. W., Cheung, M. & Chan, A. S. (2004). Confrontation naming in Chinese patients with left, right or bilateral brain damage. *Journal of International Neuropsychological Society, 10,* 46-53.

Crutch, S. J. & Warrington, E. K. (2004). The semantic organization of proper nouns: the case of people and brand names. *Neuropsychologia, 42,* 584-596.

Diaz, M. T. & McCarthy, G. (2009). A comparison of brain *Brain Research, 1282,* 38-49.

Dong, Y., Nakamura, K., Okada, T., Hanakawa, T., Fukuyama, H., Mazziotta, J. C. & Shibasaki, H. (2005). Neural mechanisms underlying the processing of Chinese words: an fMRI study. *Neuroscience Research, 52,* 139-145.

Fiebach, C. J. & Friederici, A. D. (2004). Processing concrete words: fMRI evidence against a specific right-hemisphere involvement. *Neuropsychologia, 42,* 62–70.

Gerritsen, M., Korzilius, H., Meurs, F. & Gusbers, I. (2000). English in Dutch commercials: not understood and not appreciated. *Journal of Advertising Research, 40*(4), 17.

Gontijo, P. F. D. & Zhang, S. (2007). The mental representation of brand names: are brand names a class of themselves? In T. M. Lowrey (Ed.), *Psycholinguistic phenomena in marketing communication* (23-37). Mahwah, NJ: Lawrence Erlbaum Associates, Inc.

Gontijo, P. F. D., Rayman, J., Zhang, S. & Zaidel, E. (2002). How brand names are special: brands, words, and hemispheres. *Brain and Language, 82,* 327-343.

Harris, R. J., Garner-Earl, B., Sprick, S. J. & Carroll, C. (1994). Effects of foreign product names and country-of-origin attributions on advertisement evaluation. *Psychology and Marketing, 11*(2), 129-144.

Kaplan, E., Delis, D., Fein, D., Maerlender, A., Morris, R. & Kramer, J. (2005). *WISC-IV Integrated.* San Antonio, TX: The Psychological Corporation.

Kaplan, E., Fein, D., Morris, R. & Delis, D. (1991). *Wechsler Adult Intelligence Scales— Revised as a Neuropsychological Instrument (WAIS-R NI).* San Antonio, TX: The Psychological Corporation.

Keller, K. L. (2012). *Strategic brand management.* Upper Saddle River, NJ: Pearson Education, Inc.

Keller, K. L., Heckler, S. E. & Houston, M. J. (1998). The effects of brand name suggestiveness on advertising recall. *Journal of Marketing 62*(1), 48-57.

Kiehl, K. A., Liddle, P. F., Smith, A. M., Mendrek, A., Forster, B. B. & Hare, R. D. (1999). Neural pathways involved in the processing of concrete and abstract words. *Human Brain Mapping, 7*, 225-233.

Klink, R. R. & Athaide, G. A. (2012). Creating brand personality with brand names. *Marketing Letters, 23*, 109-117.

Kuo, W. J., Yeh, T. C., Lee, J. R., Chen, L. F., Lee, P. L., Chen, S. S., Ho, L. T., Hung, D. L., Tzeng, O. J. & Hsieh, J. C. (2004). Orthographic and phonological processing of Chinese characters: an fMRI study. *NeuroImage, 21*, 1721-1731.

Krugman, H. E. (1986). Low recall and high recognition of advertising. *Journal of Advertising Research, 26*, 79-86.

Leclerc, F., Schmitt, B. H. & Dube, L. (1994). Foreign branding and its effects on product perception and attitudes. *Journal of Marketing Research, 31*(2), 263-270.

Lerman, D. B. (2007). Phonology, morphology In T. M. Lowrey (Ed.), *Psycholinguistic phenomena in marketing communication* (79-99). Mahwah, NJ: Lawrence Erlbaum Associates, Inc.

Liefeld, J. P. (2004). Consumer knowledge and use of country-of-origin information at the point of purchase. *Journal of Consumer Behavior, 4*, 85-96.

Madden, T. J., Hewett, K. & Roth, M. S. (2000). Managing images in different cultures: A cross-national study of color meanings and preferences. *Journal of International Marketing, 8*(4), 90-107.

Matthews, P. M., Adcock, J., Chen, Y., Fu, S., Devlin, J. T., Rushworth, M. F. S., Smith, S., Beckmann, C. & Iversen, S. (2003). Towards understand language organization in the brain using fMRI. *Human Brain Mapping, 18*, 239-247.

Mo, L., Liu, H., Jin, H. & Yang, Y. (2005). Brain activation during semantic judgment of Chinese sentences: a functional MRI study. *Human Brain Mapping, 24*, 305-312.

Moorman, C., Diehl, K., Brinberg, D. & Kidwell, B. (2004). Subjective knowledge, search locations, and consumer choice. *Journal of Consumer Research, 31*, 673-680.

Mueller, H. M., Weiss, S. & Rappelsberger, P. (1997). EEG coherence analysis of auditory sentence processing. In H. Witte, U. Zwiener, B. Schack, & A. Doering (Eds.), *Quantitative and topological EEG and MEG analysis* (429-431). Jena: Universitaetsverlag.

Reimann, M., Castano, R., Zaichkowsky, J. & Bechara, A., (2012). Novel versus familiar brands: an analysis of neurophysiology, response latency and choice. *Marketing Letters, 23*, 745-759.

Rey, G. J., Levin, B. E., Rodas, R., Bowen, B. C. & Nedd, K. (1994). A longitudinal examination of crossed aphasia. *Archives of Neurology, 51*(1), 95-100.

Schaefer, M. & Rotte, M. (2007). Thinking on luxury or pragmatic brand products: brain response to different categories of culturally based brands. *Brain Research, 1165*, 98-104.

Schaefer, M., Berens, H., Heinze, H. & Rotte, M. (2006). Neural correlates of culturally familiar brands of car manufacturers. *NeuroImage, 31*, 861-865.

Semenza, C. (1997). Proper-name-specific-aphasias. In H. Glass, & A. Wingfield (Eds.), *Anomia neuroanatomical and cognitive correlates* (pp. 115-133). San Diego, CA: Academic Press.

Steenkamp, J. E., Batra, R. & Alden, D. (2003). How perceived globalness creates brand value. *Journal of International Business Studies, 34,* 53-65.

Sujan, M. (1985). Consumer knowledge: effects on evaluation strategies mediating consumer judgments. *Journal of Consumer Research, 12,* 31-46.

Tan, L. H., Feng, C., Fox, P. T. & Gao, J. (2001). An fMRI study with written Chinese. *NeuroReport, 12,* 83-88.

Tan, L. H., Laird, A. R., Li, K. & Fox, P. T. (2005). Neuroanatomical correlates of phonological processing of Chinese characters and alphabetic words: a meta-analysis. *Human Brain Mapping, 25,* 83-91.

Tan, L. H., Liu, H., Perfetti, C. A., Spinks, J. A., Fox, P. T. & Gao, J. (2001). The neural system underlying Chinese logograph reading. *NeuroImage, 13,* 836-846.

Tan, L. H., Spinks, J. A., Gao, J., Liu, H., Perfetti, C. A., Xiong, J., Stofer, K.A., Pu, Y., Liu, Y. & Fox, P. T. (2000). Brain activation in the processing of Chinese characters and words: a functional MRI study. *Human Brain Mapping, 10,* 16-27.

Tavassoli, N. T. (1999). Temporal and associative memory in Chinese and English. *Journal of Consumer Research, 26,* 170-181.

Tyler, L. K., Bright, P., Fletcher, P. & Stamatakis, E. A. (2004). Neural processing of nouns and verbs: the role of inflectional morphology. *Neuropsychologia, 42,* 512-523.

Wanke, M., Herrmann, A. & Schaffner, D. (2007). Brand name influence on brand perception. *Psychology and Marketing, 24*(1), 1-24.

Wansink, B., Westgren, R. E. & Cheney, M. M. (2005). Hierarchy of nutritional knowledge that relates to the consumption of a functional food. *Nutrition, 21,* 264-268.

Weiss, S. & Mueller, H. M. (2003). The contribution of EEG coherence to the investigation of language. *Brain and Language, 85,* 325-343.

Weiss, S. & Rappelsberger, P. (1996). EEG coherence within the 13-18 Hz band as a correlate of a distinct lexical organisation of concrete and abstract nouns in humans. *Neuroscience Letters, 209,* 17-20.

Weiss, S. & Rappelsberger, P. (1998). Left frontal EEG coherence reflects modality independent language processes. *Brain Topography, 11,* 33-42.

Weiss, S., Mueller, H. M., Schask, B., King, J. W. & Kutas, M. (2005). Increased neuronal communication accompanying sentence comprehension. *International Journal of Psychophysiology, 57,* 129-141.

Weiss, S., Mueller, H. M., King, J. W., Kutas, M., Schack, B. & Rappelsberger, P. (2002). Theta and beta synchronization reflect different processes during language comprehension. *International Journal of Psychophysiology, 45,* 45-46.

Zhang, S. & Schmitt, B. H. (2001). Creating local brands in multilingual international markets. *Journal of Marketing Research, 38,* 313-325.

Zhang, S. & Schmitt, B. H. (2004). Activating sound and meaning: the role of language proficiency in bilingual consumer environment. *Journal of Consumer Research, 31,* 220-229.

Zhang, S. & Schmitt, B. H. (2007). Phonology and semantics in international marketing: what brand name translations tell us about consumer cognition. In T. M. Lowrey (Ed.), *Psycholinguistic phenomena in marketing communication* (59-78). Mahwah, NJ: Lawrence Erlbaum Associates, Inc.

PART 2: SOCIAL AND HEALTH BRAND PSYCHOLOGY

In: Psychology of Branding
Editor: W. Douglas Evans

ISBN: 978-1-62618-817-4
© 2013 Nova Science Publishers, Inc.

Chapter 8

BRANDING SOCIAL AND HEALTH BEHAVIOR: AN EDUCATION AND RESEARCH AGENDA

W. Douglas Evans[*]

The George Washington University,
School of Public Health and Health Services, Washington, DC, US

ABSTRACT

Branding principles can be used to change social and health behavior. Social and health branding is a new theory of disease prevention that treats behaviors like products in that they are chosen based on costs and benefits, and thus can be branded. This chapter has three aims. First, it defines what social and health branding is, how it works, and the role and contributions of health brand research. Second, social and health branding represents a new theory of behavior change. It builds on existing theory, especially Social Cognitive Theory and the final version of the Theory of Planned Behavior. Third, this chapter provides an outline for a future education and research agenda for social and health branding. While branded social and health programs are now more prevalent than in the past, the field needs professional education and more experimental research and evidence on what works in social and health branding in order to continue its growth.

Keywords: Branding, health, social change, behavior change

INTRODUCTION

As illustrated in this volume, branding is a powerful strategy for building relationships between consumers and organizations, products and services. The psychological basis of branding lies in its ability to create an identity that consumers recognize, that stimulates neural mechanisms (Cheung, Han, Chan, et al., 2013), and creates mental representations of

[*]Corresponding author: W. Douglas Evans, Ph.D. Professor of Prevention and Community Health & Global Health. The George Washington University School of Public Health and Health Services 2175 K Street, NW, Suite 700Washington, DC 20037 202-994-3632 (office) 202-351-9546 (mobile)

the brand (brand associations) that lead to behavioral responses (Evans & Hastings, 2008). In the case of organizations, products and services those responses are brand loyalty and purchase behaviors.

In recent years, public health researchers have applied branding principles to the challenging task of changing social and health behavior. The basic idea is to treat behaviors like condom use or substance abuse like products – consumers perceive benefits and costs to both products and behaviors and on that basis decide whether to use or engage in them. Health branding is a new theory of disease prevention that posits building brand equity – positive associations on the part of the consumer with the branded product or behavior (i.e. a sense of identification with the product or behavior) – to promote healthy behaviors such as condom use and avoiding drug abuse (Evans, Holtz, & Snider, 2013). Health behavior can be branded using methods like those used successfully with products and services because each of these types of brands share common characteristics of promoting a beneficial exchange and relationship between consumer and object.

As commercial brands can frame and simplify product or service choices for consumers and highlight benefits in comparison to competing products and behaviors, so health branding can do the same thing for healthy behavioral choices. Competition is a central idea. All behavioral choices, whether healthy or unhealthy – are made in a marketplace of options that must be recognized by the marketer, whether she is selling soda, shoes, or programs to promote social good. For example, disease prevention and health promotion programs designed to prevent risk behaviors such as drug abuse and unsafe sex that create HIV/STI risks operate in competition with those very risky practices.

In this chapter, we will refer to 'prevention' as programs and interventions that are designed to prevent risk behaviors and associated morbidity and mortality and to 'health promotion' as programs and interventions that encourage healthy behaviors that reduce negative health outcomes. Branding of prevention and health promotion programs can serve to offer more attractive choices in the form of socially beneficial and healthy behaviors. Evans and Hastings (2008) used the term 'Public Health Branding' or simply 'health branding' to refer to such programs. Branded prevention and health promotion programs be more easily recognized by consumers, be seen as more appealing, and make it easier for consumers (i.e., participants) to make healthier choice. By easier, the idea is to make the benefits provided by healthier choices clearer and more distinct in comparison to unhealthy choices, thus reducing the cognitive, emotional, social, and other burdens for the consumer to make healthier choice.

Like products or services, *behaviors can be branded* as well. They have similar qualities. Just as products and services, and the organizations that offer them, have qualities and characteristics perceived by consumers, so too do behaviors. Like products and services, behaviors are essentially a set of benefits at a price point. To a large extent, one does a behavior because of how it benefits the individual and how much it costs in terms of time, effort, or other "currency" just as one decides to purchase and use a product or service for these same reasons. This is not to say that behaviors are not sometimes adopted for other reasons – altruism, or a sense of obligation, for example – but the point is that cost-benefit decision making in behavioral choice is just as prevalent as it is in product or service purchase choices. There are differences between behaviors, products and services that we will discuss later, but they share this essential core feature. As a result, behaviors can be branded.

Branding represents a new approach to social and health behavior change and a new research and programmatic agenda is emerging.

In this chapter, we will explore how socially beneficial and health promoting behaviors can be branded and the future of brand development and research in this arena. The chapter has three primary aims. First, we discuss what social and health branding is, how it works, and the role and contributions of health brand research. Comparisons between commercial and non-commercial branding are helpful here and the following explores several case examples, brand research, and evidence from the field.

Second, social and health branding represents a new theory of behavior change (Hecht & Lee, 2013; Evans, Holtz, & Snider, 2013). It builds on existing theory, especially Social Cognitive Theory (Bandura, 2004) and the final version of the Theory of Planned Behavior (Fishbein & Ajzen, 2010). In particular it creates a framework for the application of *social modeling* and the relationship between brand associations and beliefs targeted by behavior change communication and marketing campaigns, such as the belief that avoiding smoking is a way to express independence (Evans, Price, & Blahut, 2005) or that remaining drug free is a way to achieve social status and respect (Evans, Holtz, & Snider, 2013). We discuss examples of social and health brands and how they use theory.

Third, this chapter provides an outline for a future education and research agenda for social and health branding. There are a growing number of programs that apply branding principles. Chapters 9-12 in this volume illustrate such programs across a range of public health subject matter. While such programs are now more prevalent than in the past (Evans, Longfield, Shekhar, et al., 2011; Evans, Holtz, & Snider, 2013), the field needs professional education and more experimental research and evidence on what works in social and health branding in order to continue its growth.

2. BRANDING IN THE SOCIAL AND HEALTH SECTORS

Like commercial brands do with consumers and products, social and health brands build relationships between health behaviors and lifestyles made up of multiple behaviors (Gronroos, 1997; Evans & Hastings, 2008). Like commercial brands, they can be measured by the associations they form with health behaviors and lifestyles (Keller, 1999). Brands in both sectors can also apply to organizations, and upstream factors that promote organizational impact and well-being. Social and health branding – building positive associations with healthy behaviors and lifestyle choices – is a previously underutilized but growing strategy in social marketing (Lefebvre, 2011).

Brands and the role of brand research can be explained using the well-known concept of the 'brand onion' from commercial branding (Calkins, 2005). Brand development can be largely explained in terms of three basic nested concepts: 1) Positioning, 2) Personality, and 3) Execution. Positioning summarizes what the marketer wants consumers to know and feel about a product, service, or in social marketing a behavior and establishes an emotional point of difference (PoD) to distinguish the brand from competitors (Calkins, 2005). It serves as a shortcut for decision-making and helps to determine product or behavioral choice. These same concepts can be applied to social and health branding much as they are in organizational, product and service sector branding.

Brand personality is the expression of the PoD of the brand, the social and emotional features that distinguish the brand and its identity from others (Vu Ngoc, Mundy, Madan, et al, 2011). It can be expressed in adjectives such as 'fun,' 'sexy,' or 'serious,' like describing a person. For example, Marlboro cigarettes, a product that has been the target of much social marketing in tobacco control, is represented by the 'Marlboro man' persona: A rugged individual, a man's man, self-confident, able-to-get-the-job-done, the strong silent type (Evans & Hastings, 2008). At the same time, behaviors such as living a tobacco-free lifestyle have been branded in terms of the benefits they provide the consumer, much like products (Evans, Price, & Blahut, 2005). For example, in the Legacy for Health *truth* campaign, the psychological construct of *need for uniqueness* (i.e., a personality characteristic associated with self-orientation, aroused by the desire to be different from others, and positively associated with the need for autonomy and independence of opinion) was used as a basis to brand living tobacco-free as a way to establish autonomy and personal control for adolescents (Snyder & Fromkin, 1977).

Brand execution is how the brand is implemented in the real world. It is the images, colors, symbols, logo, tag lines, and other physical manifestations of the brand position and personality used to represent and market it to consumers. It's what the consumer experiences when s/he comes in contact with the brand and what shapes brand associations. Thus, like personality, it can be measured and evaluated – how did consumers experience the brand execution and what were their reactions?

The literature on social and health brand research is small but growing. In a systematic review, Evans and colleagues (2008) summarized recent public health brands and found that they span most modifiable behaviors. In particular, brands have been widely used and found effective in large-scale tobacco control (Farrelly, Davis, Haviland, et al., 2005) and physical activity (Huhman, Price, & Potter, 2008) campaigns. Notably, brands have not been shown effective in some behavior change campaigns such as drug use prevention (Slater, Kelly, Lawrence, et al., 2011). Brands have a global reach and have been used both for socially marketed product promotion (e.g., condoms) and to brand behaviors (e.g., condom use).

This chapter describes a framework for brand research as a tool for marketing to benefit consumers and society, or social marketing (Kotler & Lee, 2008), and sets out an education and research agenda for building capacity in social and health branding among prevention and health promotion scientists and practitioners. Brand research serves two functions, and occupies two places on the social marketing research continuum (Evans, Longfield, Shekhar, et al, 2011). First, it is about measuring and evaluating *determinants of brand choice.* Consumers choose to use a category of branded product or behavior (e.g., condoms as a *category* of product) and individual branded *products* within a category (e.g., *Durex* condoms in South Africa) due to market factors such as price, availability, and to the brand associations they form with the category or individual product. Brand research is concerned with identifying and analyzing those determinants of brand choice and informing brand managers to improve brand positioning and execution. Thus, it represents a kind of formative research.

Second, brand research is concerned with evaluating the outcomes of brand choice (Evans, 2010). Consumers who use the category of condoms, or individual condom products, are less likely to be exposed to HIV/STIs and to contract them compare to those who do not. What effect do brand choices and utilization of brands (categories or individual products) have on these individual health outcomes? Brand research, in its outcome evaluation function, is concerned with this question. In particular, it is concerned with 'brand equity' as a *mediator* of health outcomes. 'Brand equity' is the overarching construct that characterizes brands and brand identification among target audiences (Evans & Hastings, 2008) and is defined as "…a set of assets (and liabilities) linked to a brand's name and symbol that adds to (or subtracts from) the value provided by a product or service to a firm and/or that firm's customers…" (Aaker, 1996). This chapter examines brand research and its place in social marketing outcome evaluation.

Social and health brand research can and should occur at each level of the brand onion. First, formative research on what the audience values and how they think about a product, behavior, or category is crucial to establishing positioning. Social marketers need *audience insight* in order to build a solid brand positioning statement and develop subsequent strategy (French, Blair-Stevens, McVey, et al., 2010). Audience insight can also identify what kinds of personality traits might best convey the brand positioning and establish the value of the brand in the minds of consumers. In this way, we can segment consumers and identify determinants of consumer brand choice.

For example, in the American Legacy Foundation's well-known *truth* campaign, the key insight was that adolescents were attracted to smoking because it was viewed as a way to express independence, personal control, and rebellion against authority, as promoted in cigarette advertising (Allen, Vallone, Vargyas, et al., 2009). By developing a competing brand offering these same benefits through a distinctive personality and execution, designed by and for adolescents, *truth* was able to appeal to youth and take market share away from smoking as a behavior (Farrelly, Davis, Haviland, et al., 2005).

Or consider the PSI (www.psi.org) example of the Certeza water treatment product. Certeza is a product socially marketed to mothers in developing countries to treat and purify water for their children. Many such countries lack sufficient potable water, but mothers also have heavy time and work demands that make it difficult for them to take steps necessary to protect their children and families from water-borne contaminants and illnesses. Consider Maria, the archetypal consumer targeted by Certeza. For Maria, Certeza offers a solution based on the benefits it offers her within the range of water treatment options (PSI, 2010). Figure 1 illustrates how audience insight is used and how brand research can be applied.

Second, research on the effectiveness of a brand can identify whether its personality is perceived as intended. Do mothers like Maria perceive Certeza to be 'quick to use' and to 'have a pleasant taste.' Does she report that her family reacts as intended to her introducing the product in the home? Does she perceive it as a solution to her problems and a preferable alternative to boiling or bleaching?

Brand personality is projected through imagery, logos, colors, shapes, and other features used in brand execution. It can be measured through brand associations – personality traits such as being fun, serious, sexy, or cool – and through social norms, attitudes, and behaviors the target audience associates with the brand (Evans, Blitstein, & Hersey, 2008). To the extent that these associations represent social or functional benefits for the target audiences (e.g., a shortcut to water purification), they are more likely to promote the targeted behavior among audience members (e.g., buying and using Certeza). Brand research can measure these associations, the elements of brand promotions that produce them, and the extent to which they are correlated with engaging in target behaviors.

Brand executions – the advertising promotions that project the brand positioning and personality –build equity with the audience. As noted earlier, the consumer only experiences the brand execution, not the strategy behind it.

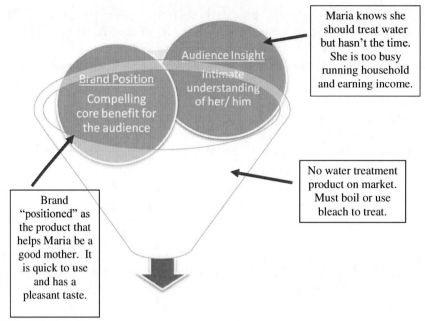

Source: PSI Marketing Department.

Figure 1. Certeza audience insight and brand positioning research.

Therefore, to the extent consumers are 1) aware of brand executions (i.e., actually exposed and capable of recalling exposure to executions), and 2) react positively to those executions, we expect that they will form the desired associations and build brand equity. There is a substantial body of research showing that message receptivity mediates the effects of exposure (Dillard, Shen, & Vail, 2007), and effective branding can improve receptivity (Evans & Hastings, 2008).

Consider the example of the Above the Influence (ATI) anti-drug brand. In November of 2005 the NYADMC introduced "Above the Influence" (ATI), a new brand and campaign approach that promotes the benefits of remaining drug free. The new ATI brand strategy is to represent being "Above the Influence" as the state of being directly opposite of "Under the Influence" of drugs and alcohol. ATI represents an ideal to which teens may aspire, one that celebrates being "better than" whatever negative influence is presented. It taps into the pride teens take in themselves when they resist influences such as peers, family, media, community or culture that make them less than what they are and what they know they can be (http://www.abovetheinfluence.com/).

The ATI message centers on drugs and the social context that leads to bad decisions (drug use). In this way, the ATI brand positions the competition – drugs – within the larger context of negative influences that bring teens down and limit their potential. A teen who is "Above the Influence" is smart enough to recognize the risks of negative influences, and both proud and capable enough to rise above them.

As in earlier efforts, the ATI campaign relies heavily on mass media, including radio, the Internet, magazines, and movie theaters. However, the rebranded ATI campaign uses an extensive social media strategy that promotes opportunities for engagement with the brand and positions ATI as a community for and by teens. The campaign has a Facebook page where teens can share experiences, a YouTube channel where they can view ads and post their own anti-drug videos, and the Website has a numerous features such as blogging where teens can express their opinions and their views on ATI and issues related to drugs and drug use in their own way, in their own voices. There is an interactive map where teens can share what influences them most and see what other teens are saying across the country. Additionally, the site prominently displays teen-generated artwork and has a dedicated section where teens can upload pictures directly from their mobile phone.

Prior to the ATI Campaign's expansion into the digital and social networking space, the campaign went off air and did not run from October 2009 to May 2010. The campaign re-launched in June 2010. During and after this time period, ATI evaluation studies have examined effects of the rebranded campaign on brand equity and campaign targeted outcomes. Evans and colleagues (2013) found that measured ATI brand equity scales were associated with higher odds positive ATI campaign attitudes and lower odds of negative normative beliefs about drug use. Based on factor analysis, these scale items were shown to form individual factors, confirming previous validation of the health brand equity scale (Evans, Price, and Blahut, 2005), which were then used in analysis. In particular, the ATI price premium factor (or willingness to invest time/effort in the campaign) and brand awareness (understanding what the campaign stands for) factors were associated with multiple positive outcomes, including a positive image of the campaign and less likelihood of believing that getting buzzed or high was the way to have fun with friends. As in previous studies that have demonstrated consistent associations between brand equity and improved prevention and health promotion attitudes (see Evans, Blitstein, Hersey, et al., 2008), results from this evaluation suggest but do not yet demonstrate a mediating effect of brand equity on improved attitudes.

3. SOCIAL AND HEALTH BRANDING AS A THEORY OF BEHAVIOR CHANGE

Social and health branding emerges from and represents an evolution in behavioral theory building on and integrates Social Cognitive Theory (SCT) and the Theory of Planned Behavior (TPB) (Bandura, 2004; Fishbein & Ajzen, 2010). It provides a way of conceptualizing and applying SCT's concept of modeling and a mechanism to explain the adoption of beliefs about the object being branded, drawing on TPB. In this way, social and health branding represents a synthesis and evolution of behavioral theory. It provides powerful explanatory mechanisms absent from either theory alone.

Branding provides a theoretical approach to prevention and health promotion interventions for situations in which members of at risk groups have internalized positive images of risk behaviors such as mixing substance use with sex and a negative image of healthy behaviors such as condom use (Evans, Holtz, & Snider, 2013). In effect, social and health brands can reverse the negative image of healthy alternative behaviors (e.g., making condom use hip and cool) and reverse the positive image of unhealthy behaviors (e.g., making using drugs seem not cool and dumb). Social and health branding theory argues that interventions should create (or if needed redefine) a brand image of risky behavior as less desirable and pro-social and healthy behaviors as widely accepted by high risk groups, such as young African Americans (see Hecht & Lee, 2013, Chapter 11 in this volume).

Many traditional intervention strategies are not well situated to overcome such challenges because they do not address the dual challenges of the brand images for risky and safe behaviors simultaneously. At the same time, branding offers the ability to address multiple, co-occuring risk factors at the same time by creating a brand identity that appeals to lifestyle factors (e.g., risk behavior such as consuming drugs or alcohol in a club followed by engaging in risky sex). While other theories and approaches tend to target individual risk factors, social and health brands target specific high risk groups with a combined risk profile by promoting benefits of alternative safer behavioral choices (e.g., always carrying a condom when going out, and not using drugs) that underlie the co-occurring conditions. Figure 2 illustrates this concept. As a result, brands represent a shortcut to making healthy choices as they can address multiple risk factors with one message, rather than many.

Overall, the significance of health branding lies first in the fact that it repositions healthy alternatives to risk behavior as having a positive image and being socially desirable. Social and health brands offer at risk populations with more positive behavioral alternatives (positive brand associations with healthy choices). Thus it is significant in that it has promise to overcome a seemingly intractable problem in prevention and health promotion research through advancement of existing behavioral theory.

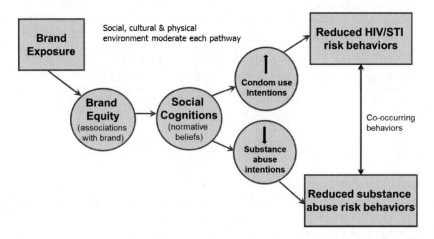

Figure 2. Conceptual model of branding effects on co-occurring risk behaviors.

With the social and health branding theory come new methods for developing interventions (Evans, Blitstein, & Hersey, 2008; Slater, Kelly, Lawrence, et al., 2011). HIV/STI and drug abuse prevention represent important domains in which to build available scientific resources for effective health branding. There are examples of effective branding of condom use and specific brands developed through social marketing programs aimed at increasing overall behavior change as opposed to maximizing product sales (Agha, 2003). Recent studies have also linked drug resistance branding to improved drug use attitudes and reduced drug use behavior (Hecht & Lee, 2008). But to date there is no scientifically validated methodology or product for use by HIV/STI or drug abuse prevention scientists and program developers to brand behavior change.

There is a growing body of evidence that brands can be effective tools to change health behavior (Evans, Blitstein, Hersey, et al., 2008; Evans, 2011). Evidence from recent research suggests brand equity mediates behavior change in multiple subject areas, including drug use, HIV/STI prevention, and nutrition and exercise (Lee, 2010; Evans, Blitstein, Hersey, et al., 2008). Uptake of health brands leads to greater adoption and maintenance of behaviors such as consistent condom use (Rideout, 2004). At the same time, health scientists are using some forms of marketing and branding in the development of health interventions. For example, the *keepin' it REAL (kiR)* drug resistance skills program has branded resisting drug use as normative and socially desirable for young adolescents (Hecht & Lee, 2008), creating an identity that young people aspire to be like and using tagline, logos, and imagery to build the brand identity (Lee, 2010).

Consider how ATI builds upon SCT and TPB and uses social and health brand theory to design and implement the ATI campaign. From SCT, the campaign posits that building self-efficacy to resist social and peer pressure to use drugs will build resistance skills. Additionally, role modeling by teens who have socially desirable characteristics (e.g., attractive, popular, successful) and are drug free will encourage emulation. This approach has been widely used in development of other behavioral and lifestyle branding (Evans & Hastings, 2008).

From TPB, the campaign envisions a sequence of drug-free attitudes, beliefs, perceived social norms, intentions, and ultimately behavior stemming from campaign exposure (Ajzen, 1991; http://www.abovetheinfluence.com/). Increased exposure will initiate a sequence of cognitive changes leading to perceptions that external norms (descriptive and subjective norms about drug use in the teens' environment) support remaining drug free (Hornik & Yanovitsky, 2003). Teens who adopt these attitudes and beliefs will be more likely to intend to remain drug free and ultimately avoid drug use. The ATI brand is designed to spur the behavior change process modeled on TPB.

From this basis in traditional behavioral theory, ATI follows health branding principles. ATI branding is based on the concept that drug non-use as a way for adolescents to express their autonomy and personal control, key elements of the need for uniqueness construct also used in the Legacy for Health *truth* campaign, as noted earlier. ATI aims to be a positive, motivational brand idea that is designed to be both aspirational and relevant. At its base, it is the state of being directly opposite of "Under the Influence" [of drugs and alcohol]. It also represents an aspirational ideal that celebrates being "better than" *whatever* negative influence is presented. It taps into the pride teens take in themselves when they resist influences (peer influence, media influence, cultural influence) that make them less than what they are and what they know they can be. ATI positions negative influence as the competition, the enemy, and being Above the Influence as the positive choice, the hero. It seeks to empower teens by respecting and supporting them to choose in favor of themselves, for themselves. This stands in contrast to the Anti-Drug branding that came before, which focused on rejection of a substance (Hornik, Jacobsohn, Orwin, et al., 2008). Above the Influence is "pro-me."

The communication strategy behind ATI centers on drugs and the social/societal context that leads to bad decisions (drug use). In this way, the ATI brand theme positions drugs (the competition) within the larger, highly relevant context of negative influences that bring teens down and limit their potential. A teen who is Above the Influence is smart enough to recognize the risks of negative influences, and is able to rise above.

4. SETTING AN EDUCATION AND RESEARCH AGENDA

Branding is among the most successful behavior change strategies ever devised, yet research on social and health brands has evolved recently and is only now gaining traction in public health (Evans, 2011). For example, branding as a health behavior change strategy has not been the subject of any substantial program of research funded by the National Institutes of Health (NIH). As discussed in this chapter, recent research demonstrates that prevention and health promotion behaviors such as tobacco use prevention (e.g. the well-known *truth* tobacco use prevention brand), exercise, and condom use can be branded and that branding promotes behavior change (Evans, Price, & Blahut, 2005; Huhman, Potter, Nolan, et al., 2008; Agha, 2003). At a 2011 NIH-sponsored workshop, discussion focused on how branding can be better integrated into HIV/STI, drug abuse and other prevention programs, and identified the central need for training and resources for the scientific community (Evans, 2011).

Despite growing evidence showing benefits of branding discussed earlier, there has been limited diffusion of successful branding approaches in the prevention and health promotion fields. Little has been done to train the healthcare workforce and scientific community to effectively use branding in program development and translational research. HIV/STI programs and researchers need a training program to build branding knowledge, skills and aptitude (KSA) and resources to support their branding efforts for behavior change.

With the enormous public health burden of HIV/STIs, and other risk behaviors such as substance abuse, effective behavior change strategies are essential. NIH has made major investments in programs to prevent these risk behavior (Fauci, 2008), but translation of effective initiatives into sustained programs with effective delivery and distribution has proven challenging (Global Health HIV Prevention Working Group, 2008). One reason for this problem is that programs are not adequately marketed, recognized, and appealing to targeted populations who could benefit from them.

This void needs to be filled by developing and testing a health branding research and education program. There are two main elements that need to be addressed. First, experimental brand research needs to be sponsored and conducted to build the evidence base and establish the effectiveness of branding in multiple subject matter domains using rigorous methods. Second, educational tools need to be developed, tested, and disseminated to increase KSA in the public health and scientific workforce.

One example of how these needs can be addressed is a recent project aimed at designing a user-friendly, step-by-step training guide with integrated tools for development of branded prevention programs and services based on branding principles leveraging behavioral and scientific evidence along with validated metrics and evaluation tools to measure the effectiveness of branded program (Evans, 2013). This project, called the *Behavioral Brand Builder (B3)*, was sponsored by the National Institute on Drug Abuse (NIDA) under a grant from the Small Business Innovation Research (SBIR) program (NIH grant number 1 R43 DA034531-01). B3 focused on HIV/STI to demonstrate feasibility of a self-guided, online educational tool that would effectively lead practitioners and researchers through the brand development process. The aims of this project were to: 1) Develop a prototype, web-based Rich Internet Application (RIA) training program and resource toolkit using user-centered design (UCD); 2) Conduct usability testing of B3 with 20 participants in initial pilot on HIV/STI prevention; and 3) Conduct a market analysis for the B^3 in HIV/STI prevention.

The hypotheses underlying the B3 project were that such a product would be perceived as user-friendly, needed and would be positively received. It would effectively guide practitioners and researchers in development of HIV/STI prevention brands. Further, there would be a market for such a branding educational tool among HIV/STI prevention scientists and practitioners. It would form a starting point for a long-term agenda to educate and train the prevention workforce in the use of branding principles to improve program effectiveness.

Researchers hypothesized further that successful design and testing of an initial prototype of the B3 product would lead to a larger, nationwide test and implementation study to add functionality to measure the impact of branding using B^3 with other health behavior interventions including multiple prevention and health promotion intervention domains, across the range of chronic and infectious disease interventions. The *impact* of successfully completing this work would be to increase branding KSA for researchers in the field of behavioral health interventions, increased return on NIH and other public and private sector investment for translational research, and ultimately improved uptake and effectiveness of health behavior adoption for prevention and health promotion practices through branding.

As noted at an NIH Health Branding workshop in 2011 (Evans, 2011), health researchers typically have little or no training in branding applications, and lack the knowledge and skills to make informed decisions about resources to access, partners to work with, and how to develop effective health brands. Beyond degree programs in business and marketing, which are typically prohibitive for them in terms of cost and time, there are no existing resources to help researchers and practitioners build the KSA needed for brand development and integration into intervention design and research. In contrast, many health researchers and practitioners lack these skills and would benefit from a low-cost, easy-to-use product to increase their KSA in health branding.

Thus the time is right for products such as B3 to fill the gap in the capabilities of prevention health promotion professionals. Prevention programs and intervention studies seek to motivate behavior change, such as increasing rates of consistent condom use among at-risk populations. Branding and marketing skills are missing ingredients in the public health toolbox. The research and practice community needs these skills and tools to replicate successful branded programs and measure branding efforts.

Specifically, the B3 aimed to advance prevention science by improving KSA for health branding with researchers as they learn about health branding, providing an integrated resource toolkit for researchers to apply translational research in the field of effective health branding in behavioral science for disease prevention, and providing a reliable and valid instrument based on the previously validated health brand equity scale to monitor and measure branding for behavioral research (Evans, Price, & Blahut, 2005; Evans, Holtz, & Snider, 2011).

Figure 3 summarizes the step-by-step, self-guided, web-based training in branding. It follows a process that begins by identifying behavior change objectives, developing a brand to convey the compelling core benefit of the behavior change, designing and executing the brand, and researching brand development and metrics for evaluation of outcomes, including measures of brand associations contained in the validated brand equity scale. The training includes tutorial with questions, exercises, illustrative examples, and concrete suggestions for decision making and taking action at each step as depicted in Figure 3. As part of the comprehensive software, an integrated resource toolkit offers trainees the distinctive benefit of wizards to apply the branding knowledge to deliver output (e.g. prototype of the brand) with additional resources including literature, information about services and vendors to assist with branding and marketing creative work (e.g., graphics and visuals), and relevant tools. Finally, B3 solution offers a diagnostic assessment of brand equity characteristics of the branded output. This diagnostic is a checklist to ensure the branded product or program has effectively applied branding methodologies. The product is designed for users at varying levels of branding experience with modular components that allows building of KSA from different starting levels of branding knowledge. By building KSA in health branding, the B3 product will enable HIV/STI prevention practitioners and scientists to brand their interventions and ultimately improve prevention and health promotion program outcomes.

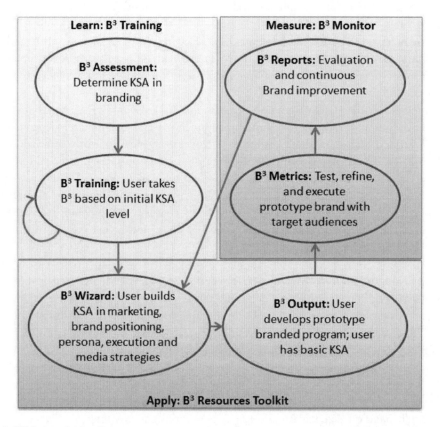

Figure 3. KSA Acquisition Process.

In the research arena, we see that social and health branding theory serves as a bridge between traditional behavior changes strategies and a new theory of behavior change. Based on evidence from multiple domains of health research in infectious and chronic diseases, there is evidence that social and health brands are effective as mechanisms of behavior change and product use. Risky behaviors including drug abuse and unsafe sex are especially difficult to change, and branding has the potential to improve uptake of prevention behaviors

(Noar, 2008). However, more research is needed in order to establish the full potential of branding for prevention and health promotion.

One of the reasons that branding has only recently begun to be adopted in public health has been the difficulty in specifying the effects of branding strategies. While demonstrating the promise of branding as a public health strategy, most of this work relies on quasi-experimental designs and has yet to explain the causal processes through which brands manifest their effects.

Evidence from recent health research suggests that brand equity mediates behavior change in multiple subject areas, including drug use, HIV/STI prevention, and nutrition and exercise (Evans, Blitstein, Hersey, et al., 2008). Uptake of health brands leads to greater adoption and maintenance of behaviors such as consistent condom use. At the same time, health scientists are using some forms of marketing and branding in the development of health interventions. For example, the *keepin' it REAL (kiR)* drug resistance skills program has branded resisting drug use as normative and socially desirable for young adolescents, creating an identity that young people aspire to be like and using tagline, logos, and imagery to build the brand identity.

There is also evidence that health branding operates as a mediator of behavior change through the brand equity construct. Figure 2, earlier in this chapter, presents one version of this model. Multiple preliminary studies provide observational and quasi-experimental evidence for the mediating role of brand equity (associations with the brand) as a summary measure of health message attitudes/beliefs (Huhman, Price, Potter, 2008; Evans, Price, & Blahut, 2005).

But while branding appears to impact health behaviors, the evidence is not strong. For many, branding is simply the use of a logo. Studies need to investigate the added value of *strategic branding* as defined in this volume – the creation of a strategic brand positioning and personality aimed at specific behavior changes. The effects of fully articulated social and health brands need to be identified and the difference between strategic branding and simply naming a program or creating a logo (what might be called *minimal branding*) documented in controlled studies. Studies need to be explicitly designed to distinguish between outcomes of the full branding and the added value to social and health branding in achieving prevention and health promotion outcomes.

At the NIH workshop on Health Branding mentioned earlier, discussion focused on the need for more experimental research to isolate the effects of health branding compared to unbranded messages and to specify the causal processes (Evans, 2011). Research sponsors such as NIH and other public and private agencies should support experimental studies to evaluate the added value of branding in promoting positive prevention and health promotion outcomes in comparison to minimally branded and non-branded strategies.

CONCLUSION

Social and health branding grows out of commercial branding, but differs in terms of its objectives and outcomes. By creating an identity for social behaviors, and healthy behavioral choices, it has tremendous potential to improve and public health and society as a whole.

Social and health programs aimed at behavior change should adopt branding principles wherever possible and apply them in program design and implementation.

This field is growing rapidly. As noted in this chapter, there are increasing numbers of branded programs and prevention and health promotion scientists and practitioners are beginning to recognize the benefits of branding as a strategy. Major funders such as NIH recognize the importance of this field as well, and are beginning to invest in the research and practice of branding social and health behavior. There is reason to expect this growth to continue as the number of complexity of social and health issues demanding attention grows, and the existence of inter-related and co-occurring conditions calls for innovative strategies to address them.

It represents an evolution in behavioral theory. Social and health branding grows out of traditional behavioral theory, and specifically out of SCT and TPB. The increasing complexity and intertwined nature of social and health issues, which are magnified by social changes such as the growing role of information technology in human life, demand that behavioral theory evolve and grow. Health branding represents one aspect of this evolution.

There is pressing need to disseminate and translate this practice in the workforce of scientists and practitioners that conduct social and health behavior change programs. As the evidence base in social and health branding grows, so too does the application of what works in the field need to expand and grow. The education and research agenda described in this chapter represents a first step in that long-term process.

REFERENCES

Aaker, D. (1996). *Building strong brands*. New York, NY: Simon & Schuster Inc.

Agha, S. (2003). The Impact of a Mass Media Campaign on Personal Risk Perception, Perceived Self-Efficacy and on Other Behavioral Predictors. *Aids Care*, *15*(6), 749-762.

Ajzen, I. (1991). The theory of planned behaviour. *Organisational Behaviour and Human Decision Processes*, *50*,179–211.

Allen, J.A., Vallone, D. & Vargyas, E. et al. (2009). The truth® Campaign: Using Countermarketing to Reduce Youth Smoking. In Healey, B. J. & Zimmerman Jr., R.S., *The New World of World of Health Promotion: New Program Development, Implementation, and Evaluation*. Sudbury, MA: Jones and Bartlett Publishers.

Bandura, A. (2004). Health promotion by social cognitive means. *Health Education & Behavior*, 31(2), 143-164.

Calkins, T. (2005). The Challenge of Branding. In Tybout and Calkins (Eds.), *Kellogg on Branding*. New York: John Wiley and Sons, Inc., 1-10.

Cheung, M., Han, Y. M. & Chan, A. S. et al. (2013). Behavioral and Neural Investigation of Brand Names. In Evans, W.D. (Ed.), *Psychology of Branding*. Hauppage, NY: Nova Science Publishers.

Dillard, J. P., Shen, L. & Vail, R. G. (2007). Does Perceived Message Effectiveness Cause Persuasion or Vice Versa? 17 Consistent Answers. *Human Communication Research*, *33*(4), 467-488.

Evans, W. D. (2013). Systematic Review of Public Health Branding: Growth of an Emerging Field. Presented at the 34th Annual Society for Behavioral Medicine Annual Meeting, San Francisco, CA.

Evans, W. D., Holtz, K. & Snider, J. (In press). Effects of the Above the Influence Brand on Adolescent Drug Use Prevention Beliefs. *Journal of Health Communication.*

Evans, W. D., Longfield, K. & Shekhar, N. et al. (2012). Social Marketing and Condom Promotion in Madagascar: A Case Study in Brand Equity Research. In *Handbook of Global Health Communication,* R. Obregon, and S. Waisboard (Eds.). New York: Wiley.

Evans, W. D. & Hastings, G. (Eds.) (2008). *Public Health Branding: Applying Marketing for Social Change.* Oxford University Press. London, United Kingdom.

Evans, W. D., Blitstein J. & Hersey, J. (2008). Evaluation of Public Health Brands: Design, Measurement, and Analysis. In *Public Health Branding: Applying Marketing for Social Change,* Evans, W.D. & Hastings, G. (Eds.). London: Oxford University Press.

Evans, W. D., Blitstein, J. & Hersey, J. et al. (2008). Systematic Review of Public Health Branding. *Journal of Health Communication, 13*(8), 351-360.

Evans, W. D., Price, S. & Blahut, S. (2005). Evaluating the truth® Brand. *Journal of Health Communication, 10*(2), 181-192.

Farrelly, M. C., Davis, K. C. & Haviland, M. L. et al. (2005). Evidence of a Dose-Response Relationship Between 'truth' Antismoking Ads and Youth Smoking. *American Journal of Public Health, 95*(3), 425-431.

Fauci, A. S. (2008). Testimony before the Committee on Oversight and Government Reform, U.S. House of Representatives. Retrieved from http://www.hhs.gov/asl/testify/2008/09/t20080916f.html on December 13, 2012.

Fishbein, M. & Ajzen, I. (2010). Predicting and changing behavior: *The reasoned action approach.* New York, NY: Psychology Press.

Global HIV Prevention Working Group. (2008). Behavior Change and HIV Prevention: (Re)Considerations for the 21st Century. Retrieved from http://www.globalhivprevention.org/pdfs/PWG_behavior%20report_FINAL.pdf on December 13, 2012.

Grönroos, C. (1997). Value-Driven Relational Marketing: From Products to Resources and Competencies. *Journal of Marketing Management, 13,* 407–419.

Hecht, M. L. & Lee, J. K. (2013). Brand Alliance of D.A.R.E. and *keepin' it REAL:* A Case Study in Brand Dissemination. In Evans, W.D. (Ed.), *Psychology of Branding.* Hauppage, NY: Nova Science Publishers.

Hecht, M. L. & Lee, J. K. (2008). Branding through cultural grounding: The keepin' it REAL curriculum. In W. D. Evans & G. Hastings (Eds.), *Public health branding: Applying marketing for social change.* Oxford: Oxford University Press.

Hornik, R. & Yanovitsky, I. (2003). Using Theory to Design Evaluations of Communication Campaigns: The Case of the National Youth Anti-Drug Media Campaign. *Communication Theory, 13*(2), 204-224.

Hornik, R., Jacobsohn, L. & Orwin, R. et al. (2008). Effects of the National Youth Anti-Drug Media Campaign on youths. *American Journal of Public Health, 98*(12), 2229–2236.

Huhman, M. E., Potter, L. D. & Nolin, M. J. et al. (2010). The Influence of the VERB Campaign on Children's Physical Activity in 2002 to 2006. *American Journal of Public Health, 100*(4), 638-45.

Huhman, M., Price, S. & Potter, L. (2008). Branding Play for Children: VERB It's What You Do. In *Public Health Branding: Applying Marketing for Social Change*, Evans, W.D. & Hastings, G. (Eds.). London: Oxford University Press.

Kotler, P. & Lee, N. (2008). *Social Marketing: Influencing Behaviors for Good,* Thousand Oaks, CA: Sage, 3rd edition.

Lee, J. K. (2010). The Role of Branding in the keepin' it REAL Substance Use Prevention Curriculum. Dissertation in partial fulfillment of doctoral degree requirements at the Pennsylvania State University. Retrieved from http://cas.la.psu.edu/graduate/graduate-spotlight/jeong-kyu-lee on December 14, 2012.

Lefebvre, R. C. (2011). Social models for social marketing. In G. Hastings, K. Angus, & C. Bryant (Ed.), *The SAGE Handbook of Social Marketing*. Thousand Oaks, CA: Sage Publications, Ltd.

Noar, S. M. (2008). Behavioral interventions to reduce HIV-related sexual risk behavior: Review and synthesis of meta-analytic evidence. *AIDS and Behavior*, *3*, 335–353.

Rideout, V. (2004). Assessing Public Education Programming on HIV/AIDS: A National Survey of African Americans. Report to the Henry J. Kaiser Family Foundation. Retrieved from http://www.kff.org/entmedia/ loader.cfm?url=/commonspot/security/getfile.cfm&PageID=47732 on December 13, 2011.

Slater, M. D., Kelly, K. J. & Lawrence, F. R. et al. (2011). Assessing Media Campaigns Linking Marijuana Non-Use With Autonomy and Aspirations: "Be Under Your Own Influence" and ONDCP's "Above the Influence," *Prevention Science*, DOI 10.1007/s11121-010-0194-1.

Snyder, C. R. & Fromkin, H. L. (1977). Abnormality as a positive characteristic: The development and validation of a scale measuring need for uniqueness. *Journal of Abnormal Psychology*, *89*, 518-527.

In: Psychology of Branding
Editor: W. Douglas Evans

ISBN: 978-1-62618-817-4
© 2013 Nova Science Publishers, Inc.

Chapter 9

IMPLICATIONS OF BRAND COMPETITION FOR SOCIAL MARKETING

Alec Ulasevich
Ipsos Public Affairs, Paris, France

ABSTRACT

When purchasing goods or services, consumers are often faced with many choices among brands in product categories. Branding should thus be seen in terms of competition. Development of a brand involves positioning that brand so that it has a competitive advantage over the others. It follows that models of consumer decision making must account for this competitive context. Consumer choice depends on the more favorable assessment of one brand over the others in a consideration set, as well the role of market factors such as price and availability of the products in comparisons to the others. This chapter proposes an extension of the consumer choice models into the subject area of health behavior. The central argument is that like purchasing decisions the commercial space, adopting health behaviors also occurs in a competitive context. Unlike the more typical conceptualization of competition in social marketing that considers the impact of attractiveness of unhealthy behavior on uptake of the promoted healthy behaviors (e.g., lure of sedentary activities as barriers to physical activity), it is also argued that competition occurs between different means of achieving a same health outcome. For example, physical activity may compete with dieting as means of losing weight. Similarly, various ineffective "immune boosting" strategies may compete with annual influenza vaccination as a way to prevent flu. More broadly, evidence also suggests that competition may be between behaviors corresponding to different health outcomes such as reducing cholesterol intake, drinking in moderation and getting enough sleep. When it is considered in a competitive context, adoption of a behavior is influenced by a) the comparison of that behavior with other salient behaviors in the consideration set in terms of attitudinal and social dimensions as well as b) "market" factors such as availability of resources and opportunities to engage in behavior and psychological price that may favor some behaviors over the others. c) Characteristics of the decision space. It is also argued that motivation factors such as health orientation, as well as acquired commitment to maintain a behavior, may mitigate the influence of marketing factors. The conceptualization of health behavior as a consumer choice is contrasted with other models of health behavior adopted by social marketers that do not consider the competitive context.

INTRODUCTION

Brands compete for obvious reasons. Unless one lives in the strictest of command economies where the only brand of, let's say, toothpaste, is the "Dear Leader's Clean Healthy Teeth," a typical consumer is faced with a myriad of choices in the toothpaste aisle alone. Whereas the competition between brands is typically conceptualized as competition between similar products or services (for example, toothpaste, cars, laundry detergent or fast food restaurants) brands in different product categories may also compete (Johnson, 1984). For our hapless proletariat, this may be a cross-category choice between buying the toothpaste or "Dear Leader's Tightie-Whitie Laundry Soap." A more likely example in the consumer society is a choice between larger expenditures: a new computer or a television set or a new appliance versus a vacation. Weinberg and Ritchie (1999) referred to the competition between brands with in a product a category as brand competition and the competition across product categories as product competition. Regardless of whether the brands compete with in or across product categories, the survival of a brand in a free economy depends on consumers choosing it over other brands. It follows that understanding the competition between brands is of the utmost practical and existential importance for businesses (Weitz, 1985).

In the commercial sector, competition arises because there are usually several products or services that achieve a similar function, need, goal or desire. Where alternative brands typically differ is in how they promise to achieve a function. For example, whereas all laundry detergents clean clothes, one brand may promise to fight hard to get rid of tough stains, another brand may promise to protect the fabric from the effects of multiple washes, and yet another brand may stress its value by promising a solid performance for a reasonable price. The choice between brands still achieves the same basic function (clean clothes), but the choice of brand X may yield advantages not available if one chooses Brand Y or Brand Z.

The way competition is conceptualized in the public sector (and health promotion in particular) is different from the commercial sector scenario described above. Let us forget for now that social marketing focuses on behavior whereas commercial marketing is concerned with consumer products and services. The key difference is the understanding of what the alternatives are in a competitive situation. Grier and Bryant (2005) highlight this difference by noting that in social marketing the competition is between recommended behaviors and services on one hand and non-recommended behavioral alternatives on the other. The non-recommended alternatives are conceptualized as the "bad guys." For instance, video games, television and internet lure people to their couches as we are trying to get them to be more physically active. Grier and Bryant note, as in the commercial sector, we need to understand what personal advantages those alternatives may offer. However, unlike the commercial sector, those alternatives do not satisfy the same needs, desires or functions. Rather, the alternatives to the promoted behavior lead to the opposite consequences than engaging in the promoted behavior. If we sit on a couch playing video games rather being active we gain weight rather than losing it, our cardio-vascular health suffers and we are more likely to get diabetes. Thus, in social marketing, competition is most often conceptualized in terms of the behaviors that stand in the way of the individuals adopting the promoted behaviors (Hasting, 2003).

Only in rare circumstances do we refer to competition among ourselves. For instance, Wayman, Beal, Thackeray, and McCormack-Brown, (2007) note competition among Federal agencies for audience attention tackling a similar issue and Yancey, Fielding, McCarthy, and Breslow (2007) point out rivalries between health advocates. The discussion of competition between social marketing programs is most often framed in terms of resource allocation, overlap between messages, and even in-fighting between advocates.

This chapter proposes that there is also competition between health behaviors that is similar to the competition in the commercial sector. Competition may exist when individuals perceive several behaviors as relevant to the same health outcome. For example, we may choose exercise over dieting in order to lose weight. The competition may also exist between behaviors corresponding to different health goals or recommendations: an example of this would be a situation in which we are asked to quit smoking, maintain weight, reduce alcohol consumption, and get enough sleep, but cannot or are unwilling to comply with all these health recommendations. Obviously, social marketing or any other health promotion programs do not intend the audience to comply with one legitimate health recommendation at the expense of another. Rather, this chapter will argue that audiences may show preferences for some behaviors over the others as they are trying to achieve a specific health outcome or be healthy in general.

A CLOSER LOOK AT COMPETITION IN COMMERCIAL SECTOR AND CONSUMER CHOICE

Before we proceed with the argument that there is a competition among health behaviors, a review of some of the tenets of competition in the commercial space is warranted. The purpose of this review is not to be exhaustive. A single chapter with the narrow focus to argue that health behaviors compete against each other cannot possibly capture the scope of the relevant literature. Rather, the intent here is to introduce conceptual blocks that will allow us to build an understanding of health behavior in terms of consumer choice.

Consideration Set

As was noted in the Introduction, brands may compete with the same product category or across product categories. The brands that compete directly against each other comprise a competitive set. In the marketing science definition the term, the competitive set may be defined as set of brands within a product category that target a similar consumer segment. For example, toothpaste featuring a cartoon character is likely to be competing against other toothpastes targeting children. On the other hand, a brand of whitening toothpaste that promises teeth so white that they trigger an almost Pavlovian response from a potential mate is competing against other toothpaste brands that may target single women, 18 to 34 years of age, living in the urban areas. Across product categories, competitive set may be defined in terms of other classification criteria, such as things to spend disposal income on, or holiday gifts.

On the individual consumer level, the competitive set is conceptualized as the decision or consideration set (Alba & Chattopadhyay, 1985). Decision set is composed brands actually considered in a purchasing decision. The consideration set may be a smaller subset of a formally defined competitive set, comprised of the brands an individual is aware of and excluding those he or she never heard of or those that do not come to mind. Like cross product competitive sets, the consideration set may not be constrained by a product category (Zeithaml, 1988). As such, consideration sets may resemble categories organized around conceptually related features (see Ahn & Medin, 1992; Medin, Wattenmaker, & Hampson, 1987) rather than defined by the product category. The distinction between brand and product competition as defined by Weinberg and Ritchie (1999) may not be important if we look at the brands that are considered on level of individual's cognition.

The bottom line is that in order to be selected, the brand must be included in the consideration set and those brands that have an advantage of often being included in the individuals' consideration sets have the overall advantage in the competitive context. Some factors that determine whether or not a brand will be considered should be obvious such as those that affect the retrieval of the brand from memory; for example the strength of association between the brand and product category (Nedungadi, 1990). In other words, when we think of a product category, only a subset of brands most strongly associated with it comes to mind. Similarly, promotional activities such advertising may keep a brand salient in the consumer's minds and therefore increase the likelihood that the consumer will consider it. In-store displays and other placement strategies such as shelf location play a similar function: they serve as prompts that increase the salience of the brand at the time of the purchasing decision. These marketing strategies assure that the brand is considered.

BRAND EQUITY

Since the focus of this chapter is consumer behavior, the conceptualization of brand equity most pertinent to this discussion is what Keller (1993) termed customer-based brand equity. Keller distinguishes the customer-based brand equity from the more financial-based definitions of the concept in terms of added value to stock prices or corporate assets. Keller also incorporates added value into his definition of customer-based equity, but in the differential effects of brand knowledge on the consumer response to the marketing of the brand." (p 8). The essence of Keller's definition is that brand equity is the difference in consumer response to a branded product versus identical unbranded product. For example, the more positive evaluation of a branded product than unbranded would be indicative of higher brand equity.

Other conceptualizations of brand equity are more evaluative of the brand itself. Lassar, Mittal and Sharma (1995) define customer-based brand equity in terms of greater consumers' confidence in brand in comparison to the competitors. Hofmeyr, Goodall, Bongers, and Holtzman, (2008) define attitudinal brand equity as the measure of the consumer's desire to engage with a product. Erdem, Swait, Broniarczyk, et al. (1999) conceptualize brand equity as a utility function based on brand attributes.

Foremost, the brand equity depends on consumer awareness of the brand. (Aacker, 1996, Keller, 2003). Awareness is the salience of the brand in the consumer's mind. In view of the previous discussion of the consideration set, the importance of the brand awareness is clear: salient brands are more likely to be considered in consumer choices. In fact, we can consider awareness as the pre-requisite for any other decision making. However, awareness in itself can be heuristic in consumer choice especially among low involved consumers making decisions about common products (Hoyer & Brown, 1990, Macdonald & Sharp, 2000). In other words, if the consumers are not particularly invested in the decision, they choose a familiar brand without really considering the merits of the alternatives. Paradoxically, in these cases, brand awareness negates the need for any further decision making.

The brand equity also depends on what we think, feel and know about the brand. Keller initially referred to these characteristics of the brands as brand image (Keller, 1993), although he later seemingly abandoned the term and mentioned product attributes, perceptions of benefits, and so forth as distinct dimensions of brand equity (see Keller, 2003) Broadly defined these aspects of the brand are what most authors refer to as brand attributes. As suggested by Keller (2003), these may be characteristics pertinent to products' performance, such as the taste or a nutritional content of a frozen dinner, or more intangible aspects of the brand such our identification with the brand and the positive affect we may have toward it because of some personal connection or aspirations. Brand attributes could also be the "personality of the brand." (Aacker, 1997) For example, we may see a particular brand as "hip" and "innovative," or as not particularly fashionable but reliable friend.

Brand attributes may be considered in several ways. From the perspective of individual cognition, brand attributes can be conceptualized as components of our mental representation of a brand. Brand attributes are what is invoked when we think about the brand. In fact, this representation may define what brand is.

From the measurement perspective, brand attributes may comprise the overall measure of brand equity or brand strength. For example, Lassar, Mittal and Sharma's (1995) measure of brand equity is essentially an average of the individual ratings on several brand attributes. Basing their on the multi-attribute utility approach, Erdem, Swait, Broniarczyk, et al (1999) consider individual perceptions of brand attributes as well as probabilities that it would be considered in the consumer choice to derive a utility function that defined brand equity. Hofmeyr, Goodall, Bongers and Holtzam (2008) use a global measure of brand equity, but look at the ratings on the relevant brand attributes to understand what drives the equity measure for different brands. In their work, the rating of brand attributes serve as a diagnostic function to explain why some brands performed better than others.

CONSUMER CHOICE IN THE COMPETITIVE CONTEXT

From the consumer choice perspective, higher brand equity typically translates into greater probability of purchase. We tend to choose the brands we hold in high esteem and are more willing to pay a premium price for them. Hofmeyr, Goodall, Bongers and Holtzam (2008) argue that the predictors of consumer behavior are attitudinal brand equity and market factors. As defined above, attitudinal brand equity is the measure of consumers' engagement with the brand. Market factors as defined as by Hofmeyr, Goodall, Bongers and Holzman are contextual factors such as product availability and affordability. Affordability is the price. Product availability has to do with product distribution. The logic is simple: although it is important to think highly of the brand, the brand equity in itself it is not enough. Even if we are enamored with a particular brand and are willing to pay more for it, we will not buy it if the price is too high. Similarly, if we cannot easily find the favored brand on the store shelves we may choose another brand that is available, even we if do not like it as much as the preferred brand.

It is not necessary to consider competition from other brands in order to calculate a measure of brand equity. In fact 10 out of 11 measures of brand equity reviewed by by Hofmeyr, Goodall, Bonger and Holzman did not. There are two problems, however, with the conceptualization of brand equity independent of the competitor brands. First, as argued by Hofmeyr, Goodall, Bongers and Holtzman, calculations of brand equity that do not consider competitive brands lead to weaker prediction models than those that measure brand attributes in relationship to the competing brands. The issue may be that of measurement. Brand attributes measured in isolation from competitors are rated more positively than in comparison to competitors (Posavac, Kardes, Sanbonmatsu, & Fitzsimons, 2005). Thus, measures of brand equity in isolation from competitors may overestimate positive sentiment, leading to inaccurate predictions.

Another issue is that models that consider brand equity in isolation from other brands do not capture the psychology of consumer choice. In a competitive context, a consumer does not just decide whether to buy or not buy a brand, rather a consumer choses one brand among the alternatives. As noted by Aacker (1996) brand equity measures must differentiate the brands in order to explain consumer behavior. What really matters in the competitive context is not just that we like Brand X, but that we like Brand X more than it's the competitors.

Not considering the competitive set was also the central criticism of the application of traditional psychological models of attitude-behavior relationships (e.g., Fishbein, 1967) to consumer psychology made by Bass and Talarzyk (1972). Fishbein's model looks at the relationship between attitudes and behavior as the as a sum of attribute ratings weighted by the personal importance of the attribute. For example, some consumers may consider the "cavity protection" of a toothpaste brand to be a more important attribute than the "fresh breath" it leaves in one's mouth. In that case, the ratings given to brand on "cavity protection" would be given more weight than the ratings on the "fresh breath" attribute and thus would contribute more to the overall preference. However, only one behavior is considered in the outcome. The solution offered by Bass and Talarzyk was to measure individuals' preferences for several brands in a product category and then look at the rank order based on those preferences as the predictor of choice. Rank ordering is less sensitive to small differences between the overall sentiments and captures the order of preference among several alternatives. The preference itself was defined in term of Fishbein's model described above. Bass and Talalarzyk's findings were that the rank orders of the brand preferences were better predictors of the purchase intent that the preference ratings for individual brands. The model that considers the sentiment toward only one brand cannot provide any insight into whether a consumer intends to purchase that brand or a similarly rated competitor. Similarly, Hofmeyr, Goodall, Bongers and Holzman (2008) proposed a measure of attitudinal equity based on the brand's rank in the consideration set.

The literature on consumer decision making like that on brand equity emphasizes the comparisons between brands in a consideration set. In short, consumers choose between alternative brands based on their evaluation of competing brands' attributes (Bettman, Johnson, & Payne, 1991) What attributes consumers consider in a competitive context and how those attributes affect brand equity or consumer choice has been the subject of much research in the marketing literature. It is not the purpose of this chapter to exhaustively summarize this body of research and to enumerate all the nuanced effects studied. However, in more general terms, we do know that some attributes may be more important than others in the decision making process depending on consumers' goals and the number of attributes considered is influenced by the consumers' involvement in the decision task.

For example, unique features of products may be more important than common features (Chernev, 1996; Dhar & Sherman, 1996). Whereas all toothpastes fight cavities, the fact that brand X is the only one that keeps your breath fresh for twenty hours may be an important consideration. These findings fit nicely with the point that differentiation between brands is the key aspect of brand equity made by Aaker (1996). Brand positioning as a marketing technique may emphasize the superiority of the brand's unique features in comparison to the competitors or in fact create a new product subcategory for a brand by distinguishing the brand from the competitors in terms of the unique features (Sujan & Bettman, 1989).

Consumer goals also play a role. Consumers looking for satisfaction may focus on more vivid characteristics of the product, whereas those who seek to make a good choice may focus on the characteristics that are more easily contrasted (Shiv & Huber, 2000). Similarly, individuals may who want to avoid disappointment may focus on the reliability of the product whereas those looking for satisfaction are more likely to consider performance (Chernev, 2004).

Consumer involvement also plays an important role in the choice process. (see Petty, Cacioppo and Schuman, 1983). Low involvement consumers do not allocate substantial cognitive resources to decisions and may make decisions based on few features or employ simple heuristics. As was noted earlier, some consumers rely solely on brand awareness in making a decision and do not seek additional information about the competitors. Consumer decisions may be based simply on affective reaction to the brand (Slovic, Finucane, Peters & MacGregor, 2002). Individuals less engaged in the purchase may end their cognitive calculus once one of the alternatives reaches some threshold for being acceptable and ignore possible additional information. This is a classic example Satisficing Heuristic described by Simon (1955). Additionally, the low involved consumer may rely on the information readily available to them, basing their decisions on brand attributes they remember from readily available sources of information such as advertising or world of mouth (Bettman, 1979; Beihal & Charkavarti, 1983). The more involved consumer will seek additional information about the product before making a decision. Those are people who are more likely to seek unbiased reviews and peruse features of different brands.

BRAND LOYALTY

The final building block in understanding the competition between brands is brand loyalty. Brand loyalty is defined as consumers commitment to the brand based on positive experiences with the brand and resulting strong positive attitudes toward it (Chaudhuri & Holbrook, 2001; Lassar, Mittal, Sharma, 1995, Oliver, 1999,). Creating brand loyalty is the "holy grail" of branding efforts. In the context of typical branding pyramid models (e.g., Dyson, Farr, & Hollis, 1996), the apex of the pyramid is defined by a high degree of engagement with the brand which translated into consumer loyalty or "bonding."

Loyal consumers buy the brand consistently, less likely to switch and may serve advocates for the brand, recommending it to their friends (Aacker, 1991). They are more forgiving of the brand's missteps. The importance of brand loyalty in the discussion that will follow is that brand loyalty also mitigates the influence of marketing factors. A loyal consumer is less sensitive to price increases, and is thus willing to pay even higher premiums for the brand they like. Loyal consumers are also less likely to be swayed by discounts offered by competitors (Aacker, 1996, Jacoby & Chestnut, 1978). A loyal consumers is also committed to the brand to the extent that she is likely to postpone a purchase if her favorite brand is temporary unavailable on the store shelves rather than buy a brand that is available.

BRAND COMPETITION BETWEEN HEALTH BEHAVIORS

As was discussed earlier in the chapter, the competition between health behaviors is most often conceptualized as the competition between the promoted behavior and behavioral alternatives that stand in the way of adopted the promoted behavior. The main difference between the competition as described in the social marketing literature and competition as conceptualized in the commercial sector is that the alternative behaviors in social marketing literature lead to different outcomes than the promoted behavior. In the commercial sector, the competing brands satisfy the identical needs or desires but claim to do so differently, better or more cheaply. As will be clear, however, the form of competition seen in commercial sector may also exist in the context of health behaviors.

The clearest example of competition in the health promotion domain is when the behavior is essential to the use of a product. For example, Harvey (1994) briefly mentions the effect of competition from other methods of birth control on the distribution of condoms in several developing markets. This issue is most analogous to commercial competition because we are dealing with actual products in a competitive set. For example, if the competitive set is "birth control," condoms are but one of the products that prevent conception available to the consumer. Another emergent issue indicative of similar type of competition is the recent approval of PrEP for prevention of HIV, due to the commercial availability of Truvada® PreP is already a preferred alternative to condoms among certain populations (Mansergh, 2010; CDC, 2011), despite its only partial effectiveness (Buchbinder, 2011; Grant 2010). Again, we are seeing a product (PreP) competing with another product (condoms) in the same product category: HIV prevention.

In most cases, however, social marketers promote behaviors and not products, and thus the evidence of competition is thus more subtle. For now, let us consider condom use in terms of behavior. Risk reduction strategies such as strategic sexual positioning based on HIV status, withdrawal before ejaculation, and "negotiated safety" (an agreement between non-monogamous primary partners to use condoms with casual partners) (Suarez, 2001; Van de Ven, Mao, Fogarty, et al, 2005) have been used by Men who have Sex with Men (MSM) as alternatives to condom use. These strategies suggest competition between health behaviors.

All the aforementioned behavioral strategies serve the same goal, namely the prevention of HIV infection, and are employed in lieu of consistent condom use.

We can also consider findings from the focus groups conducted for the development of the USDA *Eat Smart Play Hard* campaign (Zawislanki & Ulasevich, 2003). Like many campaigns targeting obesity, the *Eat Smart Play Hard* campaign is intended to co-promote nutrition (the Eat Smart part) and physical activity (the Play Hard part) among school children. However, the findings showed that children as well as their parents expressed a consensus that one can eat pretty much anything one wants as long as one exercises. The children themselves expressed a somewhat negative stereotype of children who "eat healthy," suggesting preference for physical activity over nutrition. Similarly, Hesketh, Waters, Salmon, and Williams (2005) found that children thought that even a small amount of physical activity would counteract the negative effects of bad nutrition.

This qualitative research thus suggests that whereas both physical activity and nutrition are clearly seen as ways to achieve the same health outcome (in this case obesity prevention), the audience shows a preference for physical activity over nutrition, at least among school age children. The notion that children may prefer physical activity over nutrition provides a plausible explanation of the findings that showed that the programs promoting both nutrition and physical activity among school age children succeeded only in increasing physical activity but not nutrition (Shilts, Townsend, & Horowitz, 2002).

The results of the analysis of data for adult populations provide additional evidence that there may be competition between nutrition and physical activity. For instance, Mokdad, Bowman, Ford, Vinicor, Marks, and Koplan,(2001) report that the majority of adults trying to maintain or lose weight were dieting (73%) whereas a smaller percentage (59%) reported increasing physical activity. Only 17% of adults trying to maintain or lose weight tried to both limit caloric intake and to increase physical activity. The relationship between healthy eating and exercise among college students has been described as modest by Johnson, Nichols, Salis, Calfas, & Hovel, (1998). The authors reported that 54% of college women and 40% of college men both exercise and diet to lose or maintain weight. Other research obtained similar numbers (about 60% for women and about 41% for men) for college and high school students (Lowry, Galuska, Fulton, Wechsler, Kann, & Collins, 2000; Lowry, Galuska, Fulton, Wechsler, & Kann, 2002).

The competitive set may also include behaviors that the audience *believes* are effective, even though the beliefs may not be rooted in empirical evidence or reality. For example, seasonal flu vaccinations may be competing with other health behaviors that audiences think are sufficient substitutes for an annual shot. Even among health care workers, beliefs in the effectiveness of actions such as exercise and good nutrition, thought to boost wellbeing and the health of the immune system, were cited as reasons for not accepting a seasonal flu vaccination (Manuel, Henry, Hockin, & Naus, 2002; Steiner, Vermeulen, Mullahy, & Hayney, 2002). Beliefs in the effectiveness of "healthy living" and social isolation were also stated as reasons for not accepting influenza vaccination among the elderly (Telford & Rogers, 2003).

The evidence of competition between behaviors corresponding to different health goals is similar to that for competition between behaviors related to a very specific outcome. In fact, there is little correlation between health behaviors that may correspond to different health goals and there are variations in the patterns of adherence to various health recommendations. For instance, Srebnik & Brenner (2003) found no correlation between the using sunscreen use, smoking and alcohol consumption and Langlie (1979) found no or very weak association between a variety of health behaviors including regular dental and physician visits, smoking, and so forth. Berrigan, Dodd, Troiano, Krebs-Smith, and Barbash (2003) identified 32 patterns of adherence to recommendations regarding physical activity, tobacco use, alcohol consumption, fruit and vegetable consumption, and dietary fat intake, with only 5.9 percent of the sample adhering to all recommendations and 4.9% adhering to none. Kronenfeld, et al., 1988 noted that alcohol consumption, smoking, management of stress, diet, maintenance of proper weight, and exercise failed to form a single "health" factor, thus further suggesting differential adoption of these behaviors among adults.

THEORETICAL FRAMEWORK FOR UNDERSTANDING BRAND COMPETITION BETWEEN HEALTH BEHAVIORS

In sum, the evidence suggests that individuals pick and choose among health recommendations related to various health outcomes as well as behaviors related to specific health outcomes, showing preference for some behaviors over others. The fundamental theoretical question is this: how do we decide which recommendations to follow or which behaviors to adopt in order to achieve a health goal or perhaps more generally to be healthy? This question requires us to answer a second series of questions: what constitutes a consideration set for health and is the consideration set constrained by a specific health goal or is it unconstrained thus including all health behaviors under consideration. A key additional question iscwhy are there some who choose more behaviors than others to achieve a specific health outcome (e.g., they both diet and exercise to maintain or lose weight) or choose a greater number of behaviors corresponding to different health goals?

To begin answering these questions, we should look first at the models of health behavior currently adopted by social marketers. For instance, ecological models advocate multilevel analyses of health behavior but typically emphasize social and environmental determinants of health behavior and stress actions on a population wide basis (McLeroy, Bibeau, Steckler, & Glanz, 1988; Stokols, 1996). The structural and policy intervention is seen as giving advantage to the promoted behavior over the unhealthy alternative. Competition between healthy behaviors that lead to the similar outcomes does not exist in this theoretical framework: if we saturate the same community with healthy eating options and opportunities for exercise, people should adopt both approaches. Sallis, Bauman, & Pratt, (1998) however note that evaluations of environmental and policy interventions to promote physical activity produced only limited success. This outcome could be because availability does not necessarily generate demand or because the population chose other means of achieving their goals.

Attitudinal-based models such as Health Belief Model (Becker, 1974) or Theory of Planned Behavior (Ajzen, 1991) or the more recent Integrated Model offered by Fishbein and Cappella (2006) also predict adoption of behaviors without considering a possibility of a competitive set. For example, an explanation of vaccination behavior made in terms of the Health Belief Model , stresses the individual assessment of the severity of flu, effectiveness of the vaccine and belief in the likelihood of adverse reaction to the vaccine (Frank, Henderson, & McMurray, 1985; Poland, 2010; Chapman & Coups, 1999; Setbon & Raudez, 2010).

Fishbein and Cappella (2006) predicted intentions to quit smoking based on a set of normative and attitudinal factors. The outcome is binary: behavior is either adopted or not. For example, Fishbein and Cappella differentiated between those intending to quit smoking and those who did not.

The criticism of similar approaches in the commercial sector was noted earlier in this chapter. Following those arguments, the low predictability (explaining about 20% of variance in predicting various behaviors) of these attitude based models (Nejad, Wertheim, & Greenwood, 2005; McClenahan, Shevlin, Adamson, Bennett, & O'Neill, 2007) may be attributed to not analyzing the attitudes of individuals toward promoted behavior in the context of their attitudes toward alternative behaviors that lead to the same outcome. For instance, dieters may consider the consequence of being overweight as severe as those who exercise and are subject to similar social norms regarding the ideal body image. However, if the model predicts dieting, the acceptance of an alternative behavior (in this case exercising) is considered a null result, the same as if the individuals continued with the unhealthy lifestyle of eating fatty foods.

The issue of measuring brand attributes in isolation from the competitors noted previously may also play a role. In the public sector, this may explain why individuals have more positive attitudes toward condom use when responding to a condom only message than when responding to hierarchical messages that mention other prevention options, such as the female condom (Miller, Murphy, Clark, Hamburger & Moore, 2004). The presence of other prevention options in fact sets up a competitive context that affects the perception of condom use through contrast with other prevention options.

With its roots in the commercial sector, namely the work of Kahneman (2003) the now popular "Nudge" (Thaler.& Sunstein, 2008) behavioral economic approach to behavior change at least implicitly acknowledges of competition. The behavioral economics postulate that at least some decisions are made almost unconsciously based on simple heuristics influenced by the characteristics of the decision space. Therefore as the characteristics of the decision space may favor one brand over another, the characteristics of the decision space may favor one behavior over another.

Thus, unlike the ecological models that rely on regulatory action and public policy initiatives, behavioral economic strategies rely on subtle changes in the decision environment to encourage certain behaviors over the alternatives. For example, offering healthy sides as the first option (thus in fact making students beg for greasy French fries) serves as a nudge toward healthier meal choices in school cafeterias (Just & Wansink, 2009). Similarly, placing healthier snacks instead of candy by the check-out stations redirects impulsive purchasing toward healthier alternatives. In the commercial sector, attractive packaging draws our attention to a particular brand and nudges us to buy it rather than its competitor. Similarly, an effort to make staircases more prominent and attractive than building elevators has been suggested as a nudge to increase physical activity (Marteau, 2011).

In the examples above, the competition has been framed almost exclusively in terms of the promoted behavior versus its contrary alternative (e.g., one that leads to a different outcome). However, there is nothing in the theoretical foundation of the behavioral economics to preclude strategies that aim to give advantage to one behavior over the others in a competitive set. In fact the decision space characteristics favoring one behavior over another may be an important determinant of whether an individual engages in it. For example, this author recently went to a retail outlet that prominently features "immune" boosting supplements at it entrance, whereas the clinic offering flu shots was toward the back and clearly marked. The decision space at this location clearly favored the supplements.

It is not a long stretch to translate the marketing science's consumer choice framework to social marketing and decisions regarding health behaviors. Brand image after all is comprised of everything we associate with a particular brand; the brand image of behavior is therefore everything we know or associate with a particular behavior. In other words, regardless of whether there were efforts to "brand" a behavior as in Truth or Verb campaigns, any behavior is cognitively represented by set of attitudes, affects, perceived benefits and so forth. In fact, factors identified in literature as influencing the adoption of health behaviors: including self-efficacy, perception of method efficacy, social norms as well as subjective beliefs like self-identification with one behavior over another fit well under the rubric of brand attributes. As suggested above, children may more closely identify with someone who is physically active then with someone who eats healthy. Some prefer the social environment of a gym versus the solitary efforts to diet. We can have our individual beliefs regarding what is more effective in maintaining weight based on our experience — some of us tried to diet and failed and others could not maintain an exercise regimen.

These beliefs may be influenced by various marketing efforts. For example, diet plans that promise weight loss without a drop of sweat and exercise equipment manufacturers that promote their products as easy means of achieving incredible physique without ever mentioning nutrition are each promoting their unique attributes of both their brand and weight control behavior. We listen to our friends for advice, and search for information on the web. Naïve theories (e.g., beliefs that supplements may prevent infection by 'boosting" the immune systems) may also play a role in our perceived knowledge of health behaviors and outcomes (Leisler, 2003).

Our the choice of healthy behavior will thus depend in part, on the extent we think that one behavior is better than the alternative in terms of attributes such as effectiveness, our ability to engage in it, the extent to which it fits our perception of ourselves, and our preferences. In turn, our perceptions of behavior are based on a variety of experiential, informational and inferential influences. The same factors influencing the choice between brands in the commercial space may influence the choice between the health behaviors. For example, individuals who "want a beach body by spring" may be more likely to focus on how fast an exercise regimen or a diet will help them achieve the results, whereas those who want to be certain that they will lose and maintain weight in the long term will more concerned with the success rates and ease of compliance.

In the context of the consumer choice model, the factors identified as contextual barriers to behavior by the ecological models easily fall within the framework of the marketing factors. For instance, lack of nutritious selections in school cafeterias or parental food choices are typically used to explain why children do not adopt healthier eating habits. In a sense, this is a measure of availability and distribution, but in these cases it is also dictated by school policy decisions and parental shopping habits. Similarly, as illustrated by the initial 2009 H1N1 vaccine shortage, regardless of one's motivation to get vaccinated, the flu vaccine shortage might have lead some individuals who otherwise wanted to receive the vaccine to adopt different prevention or even "immune boosting" strategies which were readily available.

Another aspect of marketing factors — affordability or price — is well established in the social marketing literature. In its most common definition, the price is the financial, emotional, psychological, or time related cost of the behavior (Lefebvre & Flora, 1988) In other words, price can be conceptualized as a barrier which requires some amount of effort and resources to overcome. Person specific factors such lack of free time, lack of financial resources or psychological factors such as extent of addiction, or loss of peer approval or fear of sexual partner's rejection increase the cost of behaviors. Lack of availability (e.g., shortage of vaccine or lack of healthy choices in a cafeteria) also drives up the price by increasing the amount of effort needed to actualize the behavior, for instance making individuals spend hours in line for a vaccine or make an effort to bring your own lunch to work.

Within this framework, some unhealthy behaviors affect the price of the healthy behaviors because of the psychological cost of giving up the bad ones. In this sense, the unhealthy behaviors are barriers to healthy choices rather than competitors. For example, a committed foodie may not follow dietary recommendation because of the personal cost associated with giving up certain food choices. If she is still concerned about her weight, however, the same individual may be likely to engage in physical activity because unlike the diet changes, the "cost" of physical activity is not affected by giving up food choices.

Since decisions regarding health behavior occur in the context of a consideration set, understanding what comprises a competitive set is important for both theoretical and methodological considerations. As was noted before, the competitive set is typically defined by brands directly competing within a market segment. The simple analogy in the health context may be particular health outcomes or goals. For example, the competitive set defined by methods of weight loss may include exercise, healthy diet, current fad diets and diet pills. Similarly, as was discussed previously, the competitive set defined by HIV prevention includes condom use; various risk reduction behaviors and now PrEP.

In social marketing a broader understanding of a competitive set may be warranted. One reason is that specific health behaviors do not always map with just one health outcome. Physical activity for example, not only helps to lose weight, but also has known cardio vascular benefits, reduces stress, and according to some, can ward off the flu. According to some, nutrition offers a plethora of benefits, some real and some dubious. It follows that the choice of a particular behavior may not only be influenced by its relationship to the health outcome we may be promoting, but also by its relationship to other health outcomes. Competition may exist on both the behavior and outcome levels simultaneously.

One approach to explaining competition between health behaviors that address the same health outcome but also each contribute to (and may be undertaken to achieve) different health outcomes is to expand the competitive set from being constrained by a specific goal to one constrained by the more general goal of achieving health. The competitive set thus simply becomes a consideration set comprised of all salient health behaviors. These may include behaviors corresponding to specific health outcomes (e.g., physical activity and diet related to weight loss) as well as behaviors that represent other health goals (e.g., having more energy, reducing stress, and quitting smoking). The constraining factor may be awareness of specific health recommendation and/or limitations on cognitive processing capacity. For example, at any given time, the most heavily publicized health recommendation may be the most salient in an individual's awareness, but there must be a finite number of them that the individual can keep in their consciousness simultaneously.

As suggested in the beginning of this chapter, the process of comparison between behaviors that do not correspond to the same health outcome could be similar to behaviors that the same health outcome. Based on the arguments by Sing, Hansen and Gupta (2005) that there are common attributes that enter into judgments of brands across product categories, we can assume that there are certain attributes that matter across health outcomes. For example, let us assume that both "moderating drinking and "quitting smoking" may be in an individuals' consideration set after a visit to a physician. The choice between "moderating drinking" and "quitting smoking" may still depend on attributes of behavior such as self-efficacy, a common attribute considered for both behaviors. Similarly, the decision may also be based on the perceived severity of and susceptibility to consequences of not following each recommendation. The psychological costs of giving up that "after the meal" cigarette may be compared to giving up being part of the group which values heavy drinking.

A way to account for multiple relationships between behaviors and goals is to postulate that the characteristics of the health goals associated with behaviors also comprise the attributes of specific behaviors. For example, in order to lose weight, an individual may choose to exercise rather than to diet because he also believes that exercise may relieve stress which he sees as another major health concern. Conversely, the same individual may not consider the relationship between better nutrition and colorectal health as something particularly relevant to him. A more involved calculus may consider the perceived utility as one of the attributes comprising the attitudinal equity of each behavior. The utility may be based on the number of health benefits associated with each behavior as well as the perceived importance of each of the benefits. The perceived utility of a behavior associated with several health outcomes may be higher than for a behavior associated with fewer benefits, and would therefore have a competitive advantage. On the other hand, a behavior associated with a few outcomes that an individual considers to be very important and relevant may win over another behavior associated with more numerous but less vital outcomes.

Still, as was mentioned previously, it is not the goal of any health promotion efforts to promote a behavior at the expense of discouraging any other legitimate health behavior. Ideally we want people both to exercise and eat healthy, as well as to quit smoking and get regular mammography and colonoscopy screenings. Thus an important question remains: why are there some people who adopt more health behaviors or try to follow more health recommendations than others?

The answer to this question could be based on the availability of concrete resources necessary to perform behaviors, such as time and money. However, availability of a particular resource (e.g., time for physical activity) may be contingent on how an individual allocates his or her available time: there is no guarantee that non-committed time would necessarily be allocated to physical activity. Instead, the explanation may lie in the individual differences in health motivation or orientation. Individuals with higher levels of health orientation are more likely to engage in preventive and health behaviors and more of them (Moorman & Matulich, 1993) as well as seek information about health related issues (Dutta-Bergman, 2004). Motivation may be seen as one of the factor that mitigates the influences of the market barriers. Metaphorically, it can be seen as "health currency." If market barriers essentially increase the price of behavior, those with more motivation will be able to "afford" more expensive behaviors and more of them. For example, if the limited time for exercise makes physical activity more "expensive," an individual will higher degree of motivation will be more likely to find time to exercise than someone with a lower of motivation. Of course, one's motivation does not discount the influence of attitudinal equity: if one does not think that the behavior that requires more effort is better than the alternatives, one will not adopt it.

As in the commercial sector, we should also consider the influence of commitment or loyalty as mitigating the influence of the market factors. As noted earlier in the chapter, individuals who are committed to the brand are less affected by price increases or brand shortages.. Even an individual who may not be "health orientated" overall, but who initially decides to follow an exercise regimen, can over time develop a strong commitment to exercise. The degree of commitment to exercise may mitigate the changes in a person's situation that influence her ability to continue with the exercise regimen. For example, committed individuals will be likely to find time to exercise when work schedules changes or will be willing to drive longer if the nearby gym closes.

CONCLUSION AND IMPLICATIONS

Based on this discussion, health behavior can be best understood as a "contextualized brand." Even without formal branding efforts, any behavior is cognitively represented as a set associated attributes reflecting our knowledge, affects, social norms, and attitudes. These attributes are shaped by our experiences, information gathered from a variety of sources, as well as our inferences based on naïve theories. Health behavior is contextualized foremost because it exists in a competitive context defined not just by the unhealthy alternatives, but also behaviors that we think achieve the same health outcomes or other health goals. This behavior also exists in the context of market factors defined not only by social policy, regulations, and other influences that affect our opportunities to engage in behavior, but also the monetary, and more importantly, psychological cost of the behavior. This behavior is also contextualized by the decision space: The subtle cues in our environment that may nudge us toward one behavior or another.

Understanding behavior as a contextualized brand integrates the three approaches to health promotion and behavior change: Social marketing, ecological models, and behavioral economics. Contextualized brand is essentially a decision making approach to the adoption of health behavior, where the decision to engage in behavior is influenced by: (a) Our perception of the behavior on different dimensions in comparison to other behaviors in the consideration set, (b) consideration of the market factors that may favor one behavior over the others, and (c) characteristics of the decision space that give some behaviors advantages over others. The final context is an individual making a decision. As was argued in this chapter, both the individual's health orientation and their commitment to behavior mitigate the influence of market factors.

However, the distinctions between social marketing, ecological models, and behavioral economics are false in the first place. As in the parable of three blind men and the elephant, the behavioral economic approaches, the communication approaches, and ecological approaches are looking at the same thing without seeing the big picture. It is all social marketing: Applying commercial marketing techniques to promote pro-social (in this case pro-health) behavior.

The problem is that social marketing came to be viewed as "social promotion," or even more narrowly as "social advertising." The formulation of social marketing as "social advertising" was not the original intent. Lefebvre and other early pioneers of Social Marketing (LeFebvre & Flora, 1988) cited the four P(s) of marketing as the foundation of the approach: Price, Promotion, Product, and Place. Advertising and communications are but one of the tools available to marketers that fall under Promotion. Behavioral economics, with its emphasis on environmental cues and simple heuristics, suggests another set of marketing tools that best falls under Placement. However, marketers were concerned with packaging that drew attention, or shelf placement that made a brand salient to the consumers at the time of the purchasing decision long before the Nudge. Factors identified by the ecological models influence both Place and Price: For instance, policy and regulations make behaviors more accessible and lower their price, both financially and in terms of required effort. The simple truth is that if we consider engaging in a behavior as a consequence of a consumer choice influenced by our attitudes and experiences, as well as contextual market factors and the characteristics of the decision space, all approaches based on communications, ecological models, and behavioral economics are potentially viable and necessary.

Which marketing strategies will be most effective depends on both the competitive set and the potential influence of brand equity, market factors, or decision space cues on the choice to engage in the behavior. For example, some competitors may promise to achieve the same goals as the health behavior, but the alleged benefits are based on empirically unfounded conclusions and dubious information, or are simply inferred by people relying on naïve theories. The examples used previously were "immune boosting" strategies to ward off the flu competing with the flu vaccination. The communications strategy may be straightforward: Attack the competition by finding out why individuals choose ineffective and potentially dangerous behaviors or products to prevent the flu as opposed to getting vaccinated. However, this strategy may not be necessary if the target audience already prefers the flu vaccine over competitors. Issues preventing vaccination may be vaccine availability or convenience of obtaining the flu shot. If the issue is the convenience of getting a flu shot, encouraging work place vaccination and perhaps offering incentives to employees for getting vaccinated may be a better strategy than a communication effort.

There is, however, a dilemma posed when we are faced with competition between beneficial health behaviors. Nutritional strategies and physical activity are often promoted separately to reduce obesity. For instance, the Verb campaign never mentioned nutrition by design (Cavill & Maibach, 2008). The NFL's Play60 initiative does have a nutrition component, Fuel up, for Play60 sponsored by the Dairy Council and the USDA, but it is not mentioned on the program's splash page (National Football Association, 2012). It is doubtful that those promoting physical activity as a way to fight obesity want to do so at the expense of encouraging better nutrition. Rather, the intent should be to reduce competition between health behaviors by developing co-branding strategies.

Successful co-branding strategies depend on understanding the competition between nutritional strategies and physical activities as opposed to just looking at determinants of and barriers to each behavior separately. For example, knowing that tweens saw "eating right" as not necessary if one is physically active, that they considered kids who watched what they ate to be "geeky," and that athleticism was valued, the Eat Smart Play Hard campaign partially reversed the theme to Play Hard Eat Smart. Good nutrition was promoted as a necessary ingredient to athletic success. Thus the campaign attacked two notions that differentiated physical activity and nutrition in the mind of the audience: (1) No you cannot eat "whatever you want," if you aspire to much admired physical prowess, and (2) admired successful athletes, not just "geeky" kids, care about what they eat. But there is nothing to preclude adding a nudge or two into the marketing mix, especially if the decision space in school cafeterias does not favor healthy choices. And if the school cafeterias do not offer healthy alternatives and kids have no place to play outside or practice sports, the effect of even the most brilliant co-branding strategy may be nil.

REFERENCES

Aacker, D. A. (1991). *Managing Brand Equity*. New York, NY: The Free Press.

Aacker, D. A. (1996). Measuring brand equity across products and markets. *California Management Review, 36*(3), 102-120.

Aacker, J. L. (1997). Dimensions of brand personality. *Journal of Marketing Research, 34* (3), 347-356.

Abbas, U. L., Hood, G., Wetzel, A. W. & Mellors, J. W. (2011). Factors influencing the emergence and spread of HIV drug resistance arising from rollout of antiretroviral pre-exposure prophylaxis (PrEP). *PLoS Med, 6*(4), e18165.

Ahn, W. & Medin, D. L. (1992). A two-stage model of category construction. *Cognitive Science, 16*, 81–121

Alba, J. W. & Chattopadhyay, A. (1985). Effects of context and part-category cues on recall of competing Brands. *Journal of Marketing Research, 22* (August), 340-349.

Ajzen, I. (1991). The theory of planned behavior. *Organizational Behavior and Human Decision Processes, 50*, 179-211.

Bass, F. M. & Talarzyk, W. W. (1972). An attitude model for the study of brand preference. *Journal of Marketing Research, 9*(1), 93-96.

Becker, M. H. (1974). The Health Belief Model and personal health behavior. *Health Education Monographs, 2*, 324–473.

Berrigan, D., Dodd, K., Troiano, R., Krebs-Smith, S. & Barbash, R. (2003). Patterns of health behavior in U.S. adults. *Preventive Medicine, 36*(5), 615-623.

Bettman, J. R. (1979). Memory factors in consumer choice: A review. *Journal of Marketing, 43*, 37-53.

Buchbinder, S. P. & Liu, A. (2011). Pre-exposure prophylaxis and the promise of combination prevention approaches. *AIDS and Behavior, 15*, S72-S79.

Cavill, N. & Maibach, E. W. (2008). VERB[tm] Demonstrating a viable national option of promoting physical activity among our children. *American Journal of Preventive Medicine, 34*(6), s173-s174

Centers for Disease Control and Prevention (2011a). Pre-Exposure Prophylaxis (PrEP) for HIV Prevention: Promoting Safe and Effective Use in the United States. Atlanta, GA: US Department of Health and Human Services. Retrieved from http://www.cdc.gov/hiv/prep/pdf/ PrEP_TrialsFactSheet.pdf.

Chaunduri, A. & Holbrook, M. B. (2001). The chain effects form brand trust and brand affect to brand performance: The role of brand loyalty. *Journal of Marketing, 65*, 81-93.

Chapman, G. & Coups, E. (1999). Predictors of influenza acceptance among healthy adults. *Preventive Medicine, 29*(4), 249-262.

Chernev, A. (1997). The effects of common features on brand choice: moderating role of attribute importance. *Journal of Consumer Research, 23*, 304-311

Chernev, A. (2004). Goal-attribute compatibility in consumer choice. *Journal of Consumer Psychology*, *14*(1&2), 141-150.

Dhar, R. & Sherman, S. J. (1996). The effect of common and unique features in consumer choice. *Journal of Consumer Research*, *23*,193-203

Dutta-Bergman, M. (2004). Primary sources of health information: Comparisons in the domain of health attitudes, health cognitions, and health behaviors. *Health Communication*, *16*(3), 273-288.

Dyson, P., Farr, A. & Hollis, N. S. (1996). Understanding, measuring and using brand equity. *Journal of Advertising Research*, *36*(6), 9 -21.

Frank, J., Henderson, M. & McMurray, L. (1985). Influenza vaccination in the elderly: I Determinants of acceptance. *Canadian Medical Association Journal*, *132*(4), 371-375.

Fishbein, M. (1967). *A consideration of beliefs and their rule in attitude measurement*. M. Fishbein, ed. Readings in Attitude Theory and Measurement. New York: John Wiley and Sons.

Fishbein, M. & Cappella, J. N. (2006). The role of theory in developing effective health communications. *Journal of Communication*, *56*, s1-s17.

Grant, R. M. (2010a). Antiretroviral agents used by HIV-uninfected persons for prevention: pre- and postexposure prophylaxis. *Clinical Infectious Diseases*, *50*(Suppl 3), S96-S101.

Grant, R. M., Lama, J. R., Anderson, P. L. & Glidden, D. V. (2010b). Pre-exposure chemoprophylaxis for HIV prevention in men who have sex with men. *New England Journal of Medicine*, *363*, 2587-2599.

Greir, S. & Bryant, C. A. (2005). Social marketing in public health. *Annual Review of Public Health*, *26*, 319-339.

Harvey, P. (1994). *The impact of condom prices on sales in social marketing program*. Studies in Family Planning, *25*(1), 52-58.

Hasting, G. (2003). Competition in social marketing. *Public Health Quarterly*, *9*(3), 6-10.

Hesketh, K., Waters, J. G., Salmon, L. & Williams, J. (2005). Healthy eating, activity and obesity prevention: A qualitative study of parent and child perception in Australia. *Heatlh Promotion International*, *20*(1), 19-26.

Hofmeyr, J., Goodall, V., Bongers, M. & Holtzman, P. (2008). A new meassure of brand attitudinal equity based on the Zipf distribution. *International Journal of Marketing*, *50*, 181-202.

Hoyer, W. D. & Brown, S. P. (1990). Effects of brand awareness on choice for a common repeat-purchased product. *Journal of Consumer Research*, *17*, 141-148.

Jacoby, J. & Chestnut, R. (1978). *Brand Loyalty Measures and Management*, New York: John Wiley and Sons.

Johnson, M. D. (1984). Modeling choice strategies for noncomparable alternatives. *Journal of Consumer Research*, *11*, 741-753.

Johnson, M., Nichols, J., Salis, J., Calfas, K. & Hovel, M. (1998). Interrelationships between physical activity and other helath behaviors among universtiy women and men. *Preventive Medicine*, *27*, 536-544.

Just, D. R. & Wansink, B. (2009) Smarter lunchrooms: Using behavior economics to improve meal selection. *Choices*, *24* (3).

Kahneman, D. (2003). A perspective on judgment and choice. *American Psychologist*, *58*, 697-720.

Kronenfeld, J., Goodyear, N., Pate, R., Blair, A., Howe, H. & Parker, G. et al. (1988). The interrelationship among preventive health habits. *Health Education Research*, *3*(3), 317-323.

Keller, K. L. (1993) Conceptualizing, measuring, and managing customer-based brand equity. *Journal of Marketing*, *57*, 1-22.

Keller, K. L. (2003). Brand synthesis: The multidimensionality of brand knowledge. *Journal of Consumer Research*, *29*, 595-600.

Langlie, J. (1979). Interrelationships among preventive health behaviors: A test of competing hypotheses. *Public Health Reports*, *94*(3), 216-225.

Leibowitz, A. A., Parker, K. B. & Rotheram-Borus, M. J. (2011). A US policy perspective on oral preexposure prophylaxis for HIV. *American Journal of Public Health*, *101*, 982-985.

Lefebvre, G. R. & Flora, J. (1988). Social marketing and public health intervention. *Health Education and Behavior*, *15*(3), 299-315.

Leisler, D. (2003). Support for non-conventional medicine: Cognitive and socio-cultural coherence. *Sociology and Health and Illness*, *25*, 457-480.

Lowry, R., Galuska, D., Fulton, J., Wechsler, H. & Kann, L. (2002). Weight management goals and practices among U.S. high school students: Association with physical activity, diet and smoking. *Journal of Adolescent Health*, *31*(2), 133-144.

Lowry, R., Galuska, D., Fulton, J., Wechsler, H., Kann, L. & Collins, J. (2000). Physical activity, food choice, and weight management goals and practices among U.S. college students. *American Journal of Preventive Medicine*, *18*(1), 18-27.

Mansergh, G., Koblin, B. A., Colfax, C. N., McKirnan, D. J., Flores, S. A. & Hudson, S. M. (2010). Preefficacy Use and Sharing of Antiretroviral Medications to Prevent Sexually-Transmitted HIV Infection Among US Men Who Have Sex With Men. *Journal of Acquired Immune Deficiency Syndromes*, *55*(2), e14-16.

Manuel, D., Henry, B., Hockin, J. & Naus, M. (2002). Health behavior associated with influenza vaccination among healthcare workers in long-term-care faclities. *Infection Control Hospital Epidemiology*, *23*, 609-614.

Marteau, T. (2011). Judging nudging: can nudging improve population health. *British Medical Journal*, *342*, 263-265.

McClenahan, C., Shevlin, M., Adamson, G., Bennett, C. & O'Neill, B. (2007). Testicular self-examination: a test of the health belief model and the theory of planned behaviour. *Health Education Research*, *22*(2), 272-284.

McLeroy, K., Bibeau, D., Steckler, A. & Glanz, K. (1988). An ecological perspective on health promotion programs. *Health Education and Behavior*, *15*(4), 351-377.

Medin, D. L., Wattenmaker, W. D. & Hampson, S. E. (1987). Family resemblance, conceptual cohesiveness, and category construction. *Cognitive Psychology*, *19*, 242–279

Myers, G. M. & Mayer, K. H. (2011). Oral preexposure anti-HIV prophylaxis for high-risk US populations: current considerations in light of new findings. *AIDS Patient Care and STDs*, *25*(2), 63-71.

Miller, C. L., Murphy, S. T., Clark, L. F. Hamburger, M. & Moore, J. (2004). Hierarchical messages for introducing multiple HIV prevention options: Promise and pitfalls. *AIDS Education and Prevention*, *16*(6), 509-525.

Mokdad, A., Bowman, B., Ford, E., Vinicor, F., Marks, J. & Koplan, J. (2001). The continuing epidemic of obesity and diabets in the United States. *Journal of American Medical Association*, *286*(10), 1195-1200.

Moorman, C. & Matulich, E. (1993). A model of consumers' preventive health behaviors: The role of health motivation and health ability. *Journal of Consumer Research*, *20*(2), 208--228.

National Football Association (2012). Play60. http://www.nflrush.com/play60/play60challenge?campaign=ppc_Google_Desktop_Play60_General_12, retrieved on December 30, 2012.

Nejad, L., Wertheim, E. H. & Greenwood, K. (2005). A comparison of the Health Belief Model and the Theory of Planned Behaviour in dieting and fasting behaviour. *E-Journal of Applied Psychology*, *1*, 63-74.

Oliver, R. L. (1999). Whence consumer loyalty. *Journal of Marketing*, *63*, 33-44.

Petty, R. E., Cacioppo, J. T. & Schuman, D. (1983). Central and peripheral routes to advertising effectiveness: The moderating role of involvement. *Journal of Consumer Research*, *10*, 135-146.

Poland, G. (2010). The 2009--2010 influenza pandemic: effects on pandemic and seasonal vaccine uptake and lessons learned for seasonal vaccination campaigns. *Vaccine*, *28*(7), d3-d13.

Posavac, S., Kardes, F., Sanbonmatsu, D. & Fitzsimons, G. (2005). Blissful insularity: When brands are judged in isolation from competitors. *Marketing Letters*, *16*(2), 87-97.

Rogers, E. M. (1995). *Diffusion of Innovation*. New York, NY: Free Press.

Sallis, J., Bauman, A. & Pratt, M. (1998). Environmental and policy interventions to promote physical activity. *American Journal of Preventive Medicine*, *15*(4), 379--397.

Setbon, M. & Raudez, J. (2010). Factors in vaccination intention against pandemic influenza A/H1N1. *Eurpoenal Journal of Public Health*, *20*(5), 490-494.

Shilts, M., Townsend, M. & Horowitz, M. (2002, November). Pilot Study of the EatFit Intervention to Determine Sample Size and Protocol for a Randomized Controlled Trial. Retrieved August 15, 2011, from Center for Advanced Studies in Nutrition and Social Marketing, University of California at Davis: http://ucanr.org/sites/EFNEP_CA/files/47819.pdf

Shiv, B. & Huber, J. (2000). The impact of anticipating satisfaction on consumer choice. *Journal of Consumer research*, *27*, 202-216

Simon, H. (1955). A behavioral model of rational choice. *The Quarterly Journal of Economics*, *69*(1), 99-118.

Sing,V. P., Hansen, K. T. & Gupta, S. (2005). Modeling preference for common attribute in multicategory brand choice. *Journal of Marketing Research*, *42*, 195-209)

Smith, D. K., Grohskopf, L. A. & Black, R. J. et al. *US Department of Health and Human Services*. Antiretroviral postexposure prophylaxis after sexual, injection-drug use, or other nonoccupational exposure to HIV in the United States: recommendations from the US Department of Health and Human Services. Morbidity and Mortality Weekly Recommendations and Reports, *54*(RR-2), 1-20.

Smith, D. K., Grant, R. M., Weidle, P. J., Lansky, A., Mermin, J. & Fenton, K. A. (2011). US Centers for Disease Control and Prevention. Interim Guidance: Preexposure prophylaxis for the prevention of HIV infection in men who have sex with men. *Morbidity and Mortality Weekly Reports*, *60*(03), 65-68.

Srebnik, A. & Brenner, S. (2003). The relationship between the use of sunscreen and health risk behaviors. *Dermatology and Psychosomatics*, *2*(4), 86-88.

Steiner, M., Vermeulen, L., Mullahy, J. & Hayney, M. (2002). Factors influencing decisions regarding influenza vaccination and treatment: A survey of healthcare workers. *Infection Control and Hospital Epidemiology*, *24*, 625-627.

Stokols, D. (1996). Translating social ecological theory into guidelines for community. *American Journal of Health Promotion*, *10*, 282-298.

Suarez, T., Kelly, J. A., Pinkerton, S. D., Yvonne, L., Hayat, M., Smith, M. D., Ertl, T. (2001). Influence of a partner's HIV serostatus, use of highly active antiretroviral therapy, and viral load on perceptions of sexual risk behavior in a community sample of men who have sex with men. *Journal of Acquired Immune Deficiency Syndrome*, *28*(5), 471-477.

Sujan, M. & Bettman, J. E. (1989). The effects of brand positioning strategies on consumer brand and category perceptions: Some insights from schema research. *Journal of Marketing Research*, *26*, 454-467.

Telford, R. & Rogers, A. (2003). What influences elderly peoples' decision about whether to accept the influenza vaccination? A qualitative study. *Health Education Research*, *18*(6), 743-753.

Thaler, R. H. & Sunstein, C. R. (2008). Nudge: Improving Decisions about Health, Wealth, and Happiness. New Haven, CT: Yale University Press.

University of Washington International Clinical Research Center (2011). Pivotal study finds that HIV medications are highly effective as prophylaxis against HIV infection in men and women in Africa. Press Release July 13, 2011. Retrieved from http://depts.washington.edu/uwicrc/research/studies/files/PrEP_PressRelease-UW_13Jul2011.pdf.

Underhill, K., Operario, D., Skeer, M., Mimiaga, M. & Mayer, K. (2010). Packaging PrEP to prevent HIV: An integrated framework to plan for pre-exposure prophylaxis implementation in clinical practice. *Journal of Acquired Immune Deficiency Syndrome*, *55*, 8-13.

Van de Ven, P., Mao, L., Fogarty, A., Rawstorne, P., Crawford, J., Prestage, G., Grulich,A., Kaldor, J. & Kippax, S. (2005). Undetectable viral load is associated with sexual risk taking in HIV serodiscordant gay couples in Sydney. *AIDS*, *19*, 179-184.

Wayman, J., Beal, T., Thackeray, R. & McCormack-Brown, K. (2007). Competition: A social marketer's friend or foe? *Health Promotion Practice*, *8*(2), 134-139.

Weinberg, C. & Ritchie, R. (1999). Cooperation, competition and social marketing. *Social Marketing Quarterly*, *5*(3), 117-126.

Weitz, B. (1985). Introduction to the special issue on competition in marketing. *22*(3), 229-236.

Yancey, A., Fielding, J. F., McCarthy, W. & Breslow, L. (2007). Creating a public health infrastructure for physical activity promotion: A challenge to chronic disease control policy. *American Journal of Preventive Medicine*, *32*(1), 68-78.

Zawislanki, A. & Ulasevich, A. (2003). Eat Smart, Play Hard formative research: Building the foundation brick by brick. *FNS Nutritional Education Conference*. Washington DC, September, 17, 2003.

Zeithaml, V. (1988). Consumer perceptions of price, quality, and value: a means-end model and synthesis of evidence. *The Journal of Marketing*, *52*, 2--22.

In: Psychology of Branding
Editor: W. Douglas Evans

ISBN: 978-1-62618-817-4
© 2013 Nova Science Publishers, Inc.

Chapter 10

BRANDING AND SOCIAL MARKETING

Steven Chapman, James Ayers, Olivier LeTouzé and Benoit Renard[*]

Population Services International, Washington, DC, US

ABSTRACT

Social marketing uses brands and other marketing tools to influence individual behavior in ways that benefit both the individual and society. Branding has played a prominent role in social marketing interventions for public health for nearly 50 years and across more than 100 countries of all income levels, including among audiences that are not a primary target of commercial brands. Social marketing interventions brand categories of products and services, individual products and services, and communications campaigns. Social marketing interventions are designed, implemented and monitored following a process that includes key decision making points for brand development and management. This chapter describes that process beginning with audience insight and ending with evaluation. Each step in brand development and management is illustrated through a case study of condom social marketing in Mozambique.

Keywords: Social marketing, branding, positioning

INTRODUCTION

Social marketing has been wrongly equated with advertising on Facebook, Twitter or other social media in recent years, an unfortunate result of shortening what was originally referred to as social media marketing and of the huge popularity of these channels (Thornely & Hill, 2011). Confusion about social marketing is untimely too: it is happening just as social marketing – a way of influencing socially beneficial behaviors from safe sex to safe driving – is being applied more widely than ever, and just as the role of branding in social marketing is

---

[*] Corresponding author: 1120 19th Street NW, Suite 600, Washington DC, 20036. sec1@icloud.com.

being appreciated, implemented and understood more deeply than ever (Chapman, 2010; Evans & Hastings, 2008).

Social marketing uses branding and other commercial marketing techniques to influence individual behaviors, whose widespread practice would have a social benefit, by making them "fun, easy and popular" (Smith, 1999). The Indian government tried social marketing first in the 1960s to promote the use of family planning, particularly condoms, in an effort to reduce high rates of population growth. Until then, condoms and other contraceptives were available commercially at prices too high for the majority of the population, or for free in public health clinics, but those were few and required both travel and waiting (Harvey, 1999). The government organized a partnership to develop and make popular the Nirodh brand condom, Sanskrit for protection. The partnership provided public funding for condom brand development, procurement, distribution and promotion to private agencies, including large, fast moving consumer goods companies such as Hindustan Latex and Union Carbide. Nirodh condoms were put in small kiosks and shops, where it was easy for low income Indians to get them and where they could do so if they preferred with a high degree of anonymity. Importantly, profit motivations for the distributor and retailer resulted in a high level of availability. Today, more than 40 years later, more than 300 million Nirodh brand condoms continue to be sold at a retail price between US$0.01-0.02 per condom and the Nirodh name is generic for both condoms and, for many, contraception (DKT International, 2012).

Social marketing diffused to other countries slowly in the 1970s and early 1980s, and then more quickly in the 1990s across low-income countries and the United States, Australia, New Zealand, Canada and the United Kingdom, with branding taking two different and incomplete paths (Lefebvre, 2011). Branding remained important in low-income countries where, just like in India, socially beneficial products such as contraceptives, oral rehydration salts, and mosquito nets were given brand names, logos, and slogans and made available through private sector outlets. The extent to which commercial marketing techniques, from audience research to positioning, creating a brand personality and then adhering to these decisions through execution varied greatly. Social marketers with experience in commercial marketing replicated brand development and management procedures to the degree possible in a low resource setting. Mostly, however, these procedures were poorly understood and exceedingly difficult to learn due to the lack of training of social marketing team members in marketing and public health, isolation, and the hidden, proprietary nature of the branding methods used by fast moving consumer goods companies.

Moreover, audience research, which was not routinely conducted, was not closely linked to social-psychological theories of behavior change. Social marketing brands generally differentiated themselves from fear-based campaigns emphasized by health education specialists by focusing on aspiration, including social modeling (Evans & Haider, 2008). The selection of whether to emphasize fear or aspiration was rarely evidence based, and the relevance of aspirational positioning to very poor audiences with few prospects for social mobility was not well understood.

In the United States and other high-income countries, social marketing and branding rarely mixed (C. Lefebvre, personal communication, November 21, 2012). Social marketing campaigns focused on heart health, including smoking, exercise, and diet, substance abuse, and environmental protection behaviors, but unlike in the low-income countries, the campaigns themselves did not introduce and manage products and services, obviating some of the need for brand development and management. These social marketing campaigns did increasingly adopt brands for the campaigns themselves, and, to a far greater degree than occurred in low-income countries, based branding and other communication decisions on social-psychological theories and audience research, and increasingly well articulated procedures borrowed from commercial marketing including positioning relative to competition, personality and execution techniques (Lefebvre, 2011).

Today, social marketing is the dominant behavior change method used in low-income countries and a popular method in a growing number of high-income countries (Chapman, 2010; Blitstein, Evans & Driscoll, 2008). More than one billion dollars per year funds social marketing campaigns for family planning, HIV and AIDS, maternal and child health, smoking and conservation in most low-income countries, with the historically exclusive focus on promoting product-based solutions giving way to clinic and community-based services and communication-only interventions (Schlein & Montagu, 2012). Increasingly, these campaigns select determinants of behavior relevant to audience segments based on social-psychological theory and audience research, and then replicate brand positioning, personality and execution decisions based on methods used by commercial marketing organizations (Evans & Hastings, 2008b; Evans & Haider, 2008). Evaluations have found brand equity in social marketing campaigns to be correlated with willingness to pay for condoms, risk perception and self-efficacy in terms of HIV AIDS prevention, birth preparedness, delaying sexual debut, abstinence, condom use, mosquito net use, and HIV infection (Agha, 2003; Evans & Haider 2008; Evans, Taruberekera, Longfield, & Snider, 2011; Evans et al., 2012).

In high-income countries, branding in public health and environmental protection campaigns is now considered of strategic importance, with campaigns developing brands based on behavioral theory and aimed at changing specific determinants (Evans & Hastings, 2008). In Europe, the United States, and Australia, large-scale, evidence-based, and evaluated public health campaigns relating to tobacco, physical activity, drugs and other behaviors have put a central focus on brand development and execution and the creation of brand equity as a mediator between messaging and behavior (Evans & Hastings, 2008). In Europe, Help was established as a stop smoking brand with the primary purpose of competing directly with tobacco brands (Hastings, Freeman, Spackova, & Siquier, 2008). Help influenced information seeking, coaching and referral behaviors. In the United States, the Centers for Disease Control developed the Verb brand to encourage active play among children aged 9-13 using tactics marketers use for youth-directed brands, including fast-paced visuals, and an imperative slogan "its what you do" that resembled Nike's "just do it." Verb's tracking data showed that the brand achieved good levels of awareness, was viewed positively by the target audience, and influenced beliefs about physical activity benefits, and play during free time (Huhman et al., 2007). Also in the United States, the Truth campaign developed a brand to counter tobacco brands targeting youth and encouraging them to rebel against tobacco marketing that resulted in brand equity and reduced levels of youth and adult smoking (Farrelly and Davis, 2007). The use of brands in environmental protection social marketing has been recently described in a collection of case studies (McKenzie-Mohr, Lee, Schultz, & Kotler, 2012).

Branding in commercial and social marketing has similar aims and principles: to create associations based on aspirations, social modeling and positive imagery, between a product, service, communication or lifestyle, and the consumer using media and other communication channels that ultimately influences purchase, use, and other behaviors (Evans et al., 2007; Evans & Hastings, 2008b). McCormack, Lewis & Driscoll (2008) note however that commercial and social marketing differ in several significant ways that has implications for branding. For example, motives and outcomes differ, with social marketing aiming to influence behaviors that are more difficult to adopt or stop, require community support, and have benefits that sometimes occur years after the behavior is changed or among large populations, such as reduced risk of infectious disease, which may not be noticed by the individual. Bagozzi (1975) characterized the exchange between a consumer and a commercial marketing organization as quid pro quo, money in exchange for a product or service. In contrast, in social marketing, exchanges between a campaign and a target audience member are typically symbolic and complex, with the consumer often asked to make a sacrifice or alter their current behavior in a way that can be viewed as evoking costs or benefits, depending on whether the consumer senses positive reinforcement. In social marketing, brands can apply "upstream" to organizations and government policies, indirectly influencing individual behavior (Evans & Hastings, 2008b). Hastings et al., (2008) point out that social marketing brand development and management lacks the organizational structure, coherence and funding streams that are the standard in the modern commercial fast moving consumer goods company.

The proprietary nature of commercial branding processes and tools, and weak knowledge and skills within social marketing interventions in using those processes and tools that were known, slowed the transfer of branding know how to social marketing. The following sections set forth processes and tools in social marketing brand development, implementation and evaluation used by Population Services International, a global health organization that operates social marketing programs in more than 60 low-income countries. These processes and tools emerged from learning from commercial and social marketing branding and marketing experts, and from trial and refinement in multiple low-income country settings.[1]

SOCIAL MARKETING BRAND DEVELOPMENT

Social marketing brand development consists of four steps, each of which is based on social marketing and commercial marketing principles and analytics, and results in marketing related decisions. These four steps – insight, positioning, personality and execution – are presented in terms of a brand onion, a classic marketing diagram showing that a brand's full identity is layered, with consumers exposed repeatedly to the outside layer, execution, and over time developing an association with the brand that includes the underlying brand layers (Aaker, 1996). In turn, the brand onion is a tool that is of strategic and operational use to the social marketing team. It makes explicit to the team the core identity of the brand and influences execution, implementation, evaluation, and insight over a period of years.

Insight

The first step, insight, defines the core of the brand onion in terms of consumer needs and the problems that the social marketing intervention aims to solve. The insight process consists of audience segmentation and need identification.

---

[1] The Delta Companion, available at www.psi.org, is a tool for social marketing teams to do intervention planning and brand development.

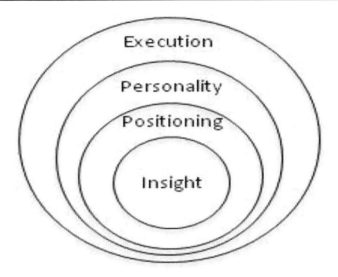

Figure 1. Brand Onion.

Social marketing uses priority-setting tools from public health, conservation or other fields to identify social problems that result from individual behaviors. For example, HIV/AIDS creates health and other social problems for societies and it spreads in part through unprotected sexual intercourse, an individual behavior. Biodiversity sustains ecosystems important to human wellbeing and is reduced by human activities such as deforestation and farming. Social marketing campaigns, for ethical and public funding eligibility reasons, must be based on strong evidence linking individual behavior to a social consequence (McCormack et al., 2008). This evidence also serves to identify which segments of a population are least likely to practice the behavior of interest. Those segments then become target populations.

Social marketing then uses economic, social-psychological and other theories and models to identify perceptions, skills, and household, community and other factors that are negatively or positively associated with the practice of the behavior in the target audience. Once a behavioral correlate is identified, then changing that correlate becomes the immediate objective of the social marketing campaign – the change is expected to trigger the behavior of interest.

Beginning with the Nirodh social marketing campaign in India, household ability and willingness to pay and the community-level availability of a product or service have been both measured and assumed to be highly correlated with the practice of a given behavior in low-income settings (Bagozzi, 1975; Chapman, 2010).[2] Adequate levels of availability of affordable products and services or more generally the opportunity to practice a behavior are a necessary condition in both low and high-income settings for social marketing campaigns (Fishbein & Cappella, 2006; Chapman, 2010).

When the opportunity to practice a behavior is present or achieved, social-psychological correlates relating to individual motivation to practice the behavior are likely to be more important priorities for a social marketing campaign. In public health, the Health Belief Model historically was the primary source for identifying correlates of health related behavior

---

[2] Ability to pay is based on a consumer's household wealth. Willingness to pay is based on consumer responses to survey questions about prices paid or prices that would be paid for specific items.

such as perceived susceptibility, perceived severity of the consequences of the health problem, perceived benefits of adopting the behavior and perceived barriers to doing so (Lefebvre, 2000). Research was conducted among the target audience to determine which of these domains were associated with the behavior. Those that were associated defined the objective of the social marketing campaign. The theories of reasoned action and planned behavior, social cognitive theory, and the transtheoretical model define a large number of additional possible correlates of behavior, including beliefs, for example about one's own self-efficacy in practicing the behavior, attitudes about the behavior, and normative perceptions (Fishbein & Cappella, 2006).

Increasingly, correlates of brand choice are important to social marketers, particularly in low-income settings, within a strategy known as a Total Market Approach (Chapman et al., 2011). As with the Nirodh program, social marketing interventions in most low-income countries used subsidized delivery of products and services through the private sector to increase use over multiple years. At the same time, the same products and services were typically available at no or very low cost through public sector health facilities, and at commercial prices in pharmacies and drug stores. In theory, this resulted in an audience segmentation in which wealthy consumers purchased commercially priced products and services, the very poor received them for free through public sector facilities, and those in between purchased them at subsidized prices (Prata, Montagu & Jefferys, 2005; Hanson, Kumaranayake & Thomas, 2001).

The Total Market Approach is a response to long-standing concerns with social marketing interventions such as the Nirodh program. These concerns included the possibility that the subsidized products were crowding out commercially priced products, thus undermining long-term sustainability of the behaviors being promoted, and that the very poor were unable to afford the subsidized products and unable to access free products and services due to distance or other barriers, thus undermining equity (Chapman et al., 2011; Hanson et al., 2003). By understanding correlates of brand choice, social marketers can use marketing tools in addition to price to focus resources on growing the total market equitably and cost-effectively for a category of socially beneficial products, which is the aim of the Total Market Approach (Blitstein, Evans &Driscoll, 2008; Evans et al., 2011).

In sum, segmentation in social marketing results in at least two audiences with different needs. The first segment are those not currently practicing the behavior of interest, and the social marketing intervention must identify whether that segment has the opportunity to practice the behavior and if so what motivational barriers or triggers exist that the social marketing intervention can influence. The second segment are those currently practicing the behavior, and the social marketing intervention must identify brand choice preferences by ability and willingness to pay to avoid crowding out commercial products and services while encouraging behavioral maintenance among those who need continual subsidy. Preferably, segments and needs are identified using quantitative research approaches (Chapman, 2011).

After audiences are segmented and needs identified, qualitative research strategies are used to discover perceptions, by segment, about the primary problem in meeting the identified need. No one qualitative research strategy is preferred for problem identification, but the use of photo narratives has been a rich source of information for social marketing decision makers in low-income settings (Evans et al., 2011). A digital camera is given to a target audience member who is then asked to photograph his or her day from the bedroom woken up in, to the breakfast eaten, the transport taken to school or work, and the interactions with others had during the day. The photographs are then discussed with a researcher with a view toward understanding why the target audience member is unable to meet his or her needs.

Case Study: Insight

More than one out of 10 adults in Mozambique is HIV positive (UNAIDS, 2012). Condom use is one of the primary means available to prevent HIV transmission and the "Jeito" (meaning way in Portuguese) condom social marketing campaign managed by Population Services International has played a key role in increasing condom use since 1995.[3] Like in India, condoms are available for free in Mozambican government health clinics, while Jeito brand condoms have been available in private sector shops and pharmacies at the subsidized price of just over US$0.02 per condom. The condom market was segmented in terms of price, with the poorest seeking free condoms, the wealthiest high priced commercial brands, and the remainder purchased Jeito. As of 2010, Jeito was distributing about 34 million condoms per year, about half of all condoms used in Mozambique, and commercial brands had a very small market share. The market however was about to change dramatically, leading to a fundamental change in Jeito branding.

Mozambique is extremely poor, but economic development has been rapid in recent years and communications and interactions with other countries occur at an unprecedented rate, leading to changing consumer expectations. Jeito's price had not been adjusted for inflation in years, reducing its real cost by 36 percent, and therefore lowering its value to retailers. International donor funding for Jeito, an essential element to maintaining the subsidized price, was becoming difficult to sustain. These and other considerations led the marketing team in 2010 to increase the price of Jeito to just over $0.05 per condom. Jeito sales plummeted.

The Jeito marketing team faced a serious branding challenge. How could they continue to increase condom use, particularly among low income and highly vulnerable populations, if use of their own brand was declining? And, how could they increase the use of the Jeito brand awhile avoiding crowding out commercial brands, including one, Prudence, at a similar price point to the new one of Jeito? The team designed a series of studies and brand development workshops, based on the star framework, to understand whether, in addition to price, other factors were important to audience segmentation and brand choice.[4] The team concluded that condom purchase and use was mostly driven by purchase and use occasions, the when and where of the star framework, and by brand characteristics other than price, the what.

The research identified four purchase and use occasion based on two dimensions, one whether the purchase was planned or not, and another whether the condom would be used in the short or long term. For example, for planned purchase and long-term use, the team labeled the segment "restock" and noted that the brand significantly influences purchase. Unplanned purchase and short term use was labeled "emergency". Brand is less important here than availability.

For the who of the star framework, the team identified four archetypical audiences based on two dimensions, one whether the user was impulsive or deliberate, and another whether the user was inwardly or outwardly directed. For example, the impulsive, outwardly directed

---

[3] The national demographic health survey showed that condom use at last sex among 15-to-19-year-old unmarried female respondents rose from 34% to 45% between 2003 and 2009. http://www. measuredhs.com/pubs/pdf/ FR161/FR161.pdf

[4] The star diagram is a visual representation of the Five Ws, whose answers are considered basic in information gathering (Wikipedia 2012).

archetype was labeled the party guy, while the deliberate, inwardly directed man was labeled the rationalizer. These archetypes helped the team understand attitudes towards sexuality, values, and habits.

Lastly, for the why of the star framework, needs were divided up into so-called passport factors – the minimum requirements of a condom – and those relating to other desirable functions and emotion. At a minimum, condom brands needed to provide protection, safety and reliability. Other functional needs included affordability, comfort, and enhancements to sexual performance. Other emotional needs included the brand image, experimentation or novelty, attentiveness to partner's needs, and peace of mind during sex.

Figure 2. PSI Mozambique - Social Marketing Condom Distribution Sales Data (1995-2012).

Figure 3. Star Framework.

Figure 4. Purchase and Use Occasions.

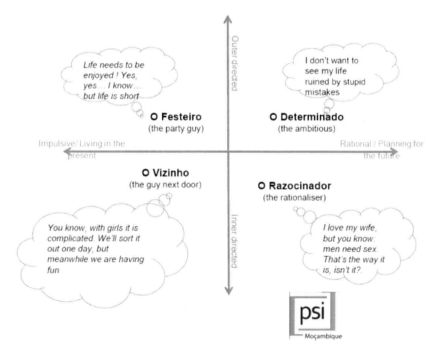

Figure 5. Archetypical Audiences.

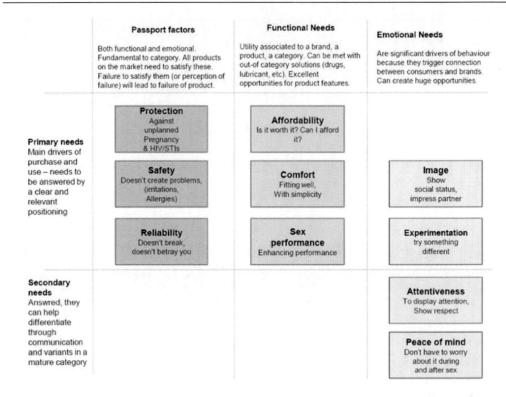

Figure 6. Needs.

The team synthesized data from the star framework in terms of needs (combining the why and the what), occasions (the when and where) as seen in Figure 7. Five segments were identified. Across all occasions, affordability remained an important segment for those seeking "the best value for my money". For emergency occasions only, availability cut across the need states of peace of mind, image, and enhancing sexual performance. Two segments for two occasions met two different needs and were labeled trying something new and special moments. Lastly, the largest remaining segment was labeled "my companion", for routine use, cutting across all occasions, other than emergency, and all three of the four need states, other than affordability.

Positioning

Social marketing brand development after insight relates to brand positioning. Positioning aims to make explicit which association between the brand and related, possibly competing, brands the social marketing team aims to create in each audience segment. Social marketing differs from commercial marketing here in two ways. One "brand" that the social marketing campaign seeks to position itself against is non-use of a product or service or generally not doing the behavior of interest. Positioning against other brands also needs to be done to avoid crowding them out.

As in commercial marketing, social marketing teams use research to identify a compelling and unique benefit that will result from using the campaign's product or service or adopting the promoted behavior. The positioning statement is for the social marketing team and is not seen by the audience, and is written simply and clearly so it remains understood over the long term.

Positioning is a long term, strategic decision for two reasons. One is that existing brands, including generically the behavior being promoted, already hold a position in the audience's mind. For example, the audience will attribute a benefit to exercise such as feeling less stress. Two is that to change a brand's position requires multiple costly exposures, requiring resources that most social marketing campaigns do not have.

The first step in positioning is to determine a frame of reference, which is the range of functional features or benefits that the target audience expects when deciding whether or not to choose the product, service or behavior promoted. The social marketer listens to target audience members to understand whether the range of features and benefits is broader or narrower than expected, whether the social marketer's product, service or behavior delivers those features or benefits at least as well as others – a notion known as points of parity – and whether the social marketer's product, service or behavior is perceived as performing better than all other options – a notion known as points of differentiation (Ries & Trout, 1981).

Research conducted in South Africa, Botswana, Lesotho and Swaziland found that the frame of reference for condoms was narrower than what might be expected – it was simply other condoms; consumers did not think that abstinence or fidelity, two options to condom use for HIV prevention frequently cited by public health professionals, were truly an option (Population Services International, 2012). The points of parity were that the condoms must not break, must fit comfortably, and were preferably a brand known via media or through broad retail level availability. Table 1 shows two examples of frames of reference for technologies to render water safe to drink, and for HIV counseling and testing.

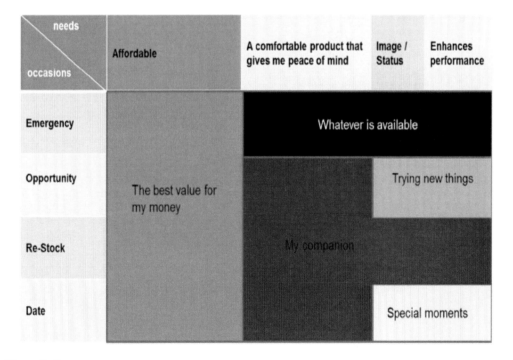

Figure 7. Segments.

The points of differentiation for condoms could be functional (perceived as good for HIV and pregnancy prevention), emotional (perceived as promising novelty or adventure), self-expressive (perceived as communicating the users personality) and or social (perceived as providing benefits to others). Because social marketers seek to increase use of the product, service or behavior generally, avoid crowding out others, and do not usually have a product or service with proprietary technology that can create a functional point of differentiation, emotional points of differentiation are most likely to be chosen. This is also common in commercial marketing (Du Plessis, 2008).

The fewer points of differentiation, the easier it is use to communicate them in ways that will result in strong positioning in the mind of the target audience. Also, the fewer points of differentiation, the easier it is to conclude the last element of positioning, what "reasons to believe" in your positioning the social marketer will be able to communicate to the target audience. Social marketing teams write positioning statements in standard ways, first naming the target audience segment using a memorable label developed during the insight phase, second stating the frame of reference and the point of differentiation. Those are then set against the reason to believe. Table 2 provides examples of three types of positioning statements and reasons to believe, relating to functional features or benefits, technical claims or logic chains.

Table 1. Frame of Reference

	For a safe water brand	For an HIV counseling and testing brand
Broader	All water treatment options, including boiling, chlorine, filters.	All options, including public and private providers and self-monitoring
Narrower	Only store-bought options (excludes boiling)	Only medical options (excludes self-monitoring)

Table 2. Positioning Statements

Type of Reasons to Believe	Examples	
	Brand Positioning	Reason to Believe
Functional features or benefits	For Party Guy Peter, Brand X is the accessory that enhances his sexual experiences, making him feel fulfilled.	• Condom variant with desensitizing lubrication • Lubrication that heats up with friction • Super sensitive condom variant that is extra thin and has lubrication on the inside.
Technical claims on packaging or in media	For Ambitious Anthony, Brand X is the premium condom that lets him express his love for his partner	• "Only condom designed for both his and her pleasure" --e.g. ribs could be near base to stimulate the clitoris, lubrication could be both inside and outside the condom. • "Highest quality latex material" "Triple tested"
Logic chain	For Worried Wilson, Brand X is the HIV testing and counseling clinic that offers him hope.	• If you are HIV+, getting tested now can mean learning your status before you become ill. • If you begin treatment before your CD4 falls below 350, then your long-term chances of survival and leading a healthy life are substantially increased. • If you are HIV-, getting tested at a Brand X clinic means you will learn the skills necessary to remain negative.

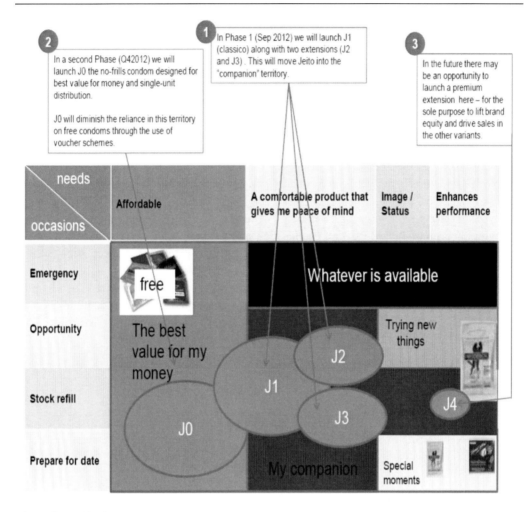

Figure 8. Positioning.

Case Study: Positioning

The Jeito team knew the "my companion" territory was strategic, and that a brand that would be positioned there could both increase use, but would it crowd out other brands? Using consumer research again, the Jeito team was able to place free condoms and the current Jeito brand in the value for money segment. Yet, Prudence, despite being similarly price to Jeito, was occupying the trying new things and special moments segments. In sum, Jeito's positioning – as value for money – was not able to deliver a reason to believe of being the best-priced brand, since it had no price benefit relative to another brand. Notably, no brand was occupying the "my companion" segment.[5]

The Jeito team decided to create four Jeito sub-brands. First, a "Jeito Classico" (J1) would be launched, along with two brand extensions, flavored (J2) and studded (J3) and

---

[5] The "My companion" territory was defined as always being on the side of the customer, during good and bad moments. The key benefit was to make life easier, by proposing a "zero worries" condom that allows 100% success in sexual encounters. The packaging was changed to ensure easier opening of both box and foil. the condom is wider and heavily lubricated and the maximum amount of lubrication allowed by WHO international standards.

positioned in the my companion segment. Second, a no frills condom (J0) would occupy the "best value for my money" territory, in part through single-unit packaging and distribution and targeted subsidies using vouchers that would reduce its price further.

BRAND PERSONALITY

Commercial marketers create archetypical personalities for their brands, often based on one or a blend of 12 such personalities described by the psychiatrist Carl Jung, to make them recognizable and likeable to consumers, and to help marketing teams link the positioning with the brand execution (Mark & Pearson, 2001). Mark and Pearson (2001) described these 12 archetypes in terms of four groups, relating to Change, Self-Knowledge, Order and Group Belonging. In each of the groups, three archetypes are described as in Table 3.

For example, in Mozambique, no brand was occupying the "my companion" segment. In the Group Belonging archetypes, one, "everyman", represents certainty, loyalty, trust and being a best friend. Brands whose personalities reflect the everyman are Toyota and Volkswagen, and celebrities like the Tensing Norkay, who partnered with Sir Edmond Hillary to summit Mt Everest for the first time, or characters such as Samwise Gamgee, who accompanied Frodo Baggins, the hero of the Lord of the Rings, on his journey embody the everyman archetype.

Table 3. Archetypes

	GROUP BELONGING Enjoyment & Sociability		
	Jester (Rebel)	Everyman (Certainty)	Hero (Victory)
Represents	• Amusement • Non-conformity • Surprise • Fun and absurdity	• Loyalty • Trust • Best friend • Belonging to a group	• Courage and honor • Triumph • Steadfastness and fortitude • Inspiration
Popular Brands	• Nandos • Kulula • Fanta • Cell C • M&M	• Toyota • Volkswagon • Wimpy • Castle Lager	• Nike • TAG Heuer • Jungle Oats • Land Rover
Celebrities or Characters Who Embody This Archetype	• Jim Carey • Bugs Bunny • Bart Simpson • Pee Wee Herman	• Tensing Norkay (Mt Everest Sherpa) • Samwise Gamgee (Lord of the Rings)	• Nelson Mandela • Ronaldo • Tiger Woods • Oprah • Michael Jordan

Table 4. What a Brand Is and Is Not

Positioning	Is	Is Not
For Party Guy Peter, Brand X is the accessory that enhances his sexual experiences, making him feel fulfilled	• Sexy • Unpretentious	• Boring • Just for people in relationships

Brand personalities develop directly from consumer research conducted in the insight phase and analysis done for positioning. Brand personalities when strictly drawn and adhered to through execution create the differentiation in the minds of consumers and improve likeability (Mark & Pearson, 2001). The social marketing team should limit the brand personality description to three to six adjectives to remain memorable and easy to communicate.

EXECUTION

After insight, positioning, and brand personality, social marketers need to determine how the brand will be communicated to its target audience. Brand execution should aim to be unique within the consumer's frame of reference in terms of one or more its executional elements, such as color, packaging shape, scent, naming (such as the i in iPhone), logo, symbol, or the product or service itself. Social marketers need to communicate audience executional preferences to creative professionals, usually through completing a creative brief. One helpful exercise is for the social marketing team to be clear in describing what the brand is and what the brand is not. One way to do this to have the team make collages with pictures found in magazines or the internet showing, based on their research and positioning, what the brand is and is not.

Figure 9 shows the executional elements of the rebranded Jeito in Mozambique. In the top right is the packaging for J1, J2, and J3 in primary colors and simple, lower case, lettering. In the top right, a retailer in Mozambique stands with advertising from Jeito, showing the uniqueness of some of Jeito's executional elements. The advertisement in the middle builds on the 1, 2 and 3 in the Jeito brand names by using numbers (549 discos, 2958 bars, and 8172 fun activities) and images to show group belonging. The photo in the bottom left counts 1 man, 1 woman, and 1 love story, sexy and responding to the need for peace of mind in companionship. The photo in the bottom right counts 25000 beaches, 8900 pools, and 47000 bikinis, implying that Jeito is not just for people in relationships.

EVALUATION

Evaluating branding in social marketing ideally begins before a campaign is conducted, but can be conducted later if there is interest in repositioning the brand. Brand evaluation, as in evaluation of social interventions generally, includes formative evaluation to generate insight into the correlates of behavior and brand choice, process evaluation to monitor exposure to the brand, and outcome evaluation to determine whether brand equity has changed over time and whether it influences behavior (Evans, 2011).

Evans et al., (2012) describe a case study of brand evaluation in Madagascar, a first effort by Population Services International to adapt brand equity measures to social marketing interventions in the developing world. In Madagascar, the Prudence Plus condom brand was well known, had high market share, and was positioned to appeal to young people as part of an HIV prevention program, yet program supporters were raising concerns about the brand. Was the brand being managed in ways consistent with a Total Market Approach and therefore growing the market equitably and cost-effectively, and not crowding out commercial brands? And was the positioning correct given the increasing average age of HIV infection?

Evaluators began by integrating brand equity related questioning into the insight stage of brand development. Using photo narratives, consumer statements were used to develop items to be including in a survey aimed at measuring the dimensions of brand equity, including satisfaction, quality, leadership/popularity, value and personality. The items were pre-tested, refined, and then included in a large scale, sample survey of sexually active men aged 18-49. The survey also included questions about message channels used by the target audience, other brand preferences, and current reactions to the brand following Evans, Blitstein, & Hersey, (2008).

Factor analysis was then used to group items into brand equity dimensions and a single brand equity measure. The individual brand equity dimensions and the single brand equity measure were found to strongly predict condom use with partners considered high risk for HIV infection. The social marketing campaign concluded that it needed to more actively manage its brand in order to achieve the objectives of the Total Market Approach.

Figure 9. Jeito Executional Elements.

A similar formative evaluation of brand equity conducted in Zimbabwe produced important conclusions about the relationship of brand equity and willingness to pay for condoms (Evans et al., 2011). There, higher brand equity, especially relating to loyalty, quality and value dimensions, was associated with higher willingness to pay for condoms among users currently receiving free or subsidized products. This information was useful to decision-makers in designing a campaign focused on switching users to higher priced brands, increasing the efficiency of condom promotion there.

Process evaluation in social marketing branding is also similar to commercial marketing, focusing on exposure to the brand, and reactions to messages. For example, Agha (2003) found that those exposed to branded advertising messages liked those messages and were significantly more likely to consider themselves at higher risk of acquiring HIV and to believe in the severity of AIDS. Exposure to branded messages was also associated with a higher level of personal self-efficacy, a greater belief in the efficacy of condoms, a lower level of perceived difficulty in obtaining condoms and reduced embarrassment in purchasing condoms. Process evaluation information of this nature guides social marketing decision makers in terms of channel selection and media campaign duration.

Outcome evaluation in social marketing branding is primarily concerned with the influence on behavior and brand choice of changes in brand equity over time. Outcome evaluations conducted repeatedly over the course of a multi-year health-related social marketing intervention could influence for example whether investments to increase brand equity or to communicate non-branded threat related information would be preferred.

CONCLUSION

Branding in social marketing is now considered an essential, strategic tool for influencing behavior and brand choice. Social marketers today benefit from the substantial learning in commercial marketing about the psychology of branding and how commercial marketers develop and manage brands. Brand related research and evaluation tools that are relevant to social marketing have been developed and tested in both low income and high-income settings. Increasing evidence is emerging about the effectiveness of branding in social marketing, and that evidence is beginning to be used for decision-making and evaluation in social marketing. As shown in the Mozambique case study above, the need for increased use of branding in social marketing is higher today in some settings than ever before as markets evolve and the role of social marketing brands becomes more targeted within the context of a Total Market Approach.

Nevertheless, branding and social marketing remain at its beginning stages. In low-income countries, many social marketing brands have existed for years and may have developed significant brand equity, though the extent to which that is so is neither measured nor managed (Evans, 2011, Evans et al., 2012). Recent examples of social marketing and branding in the United States and elsewhere indicate that brand measurement and management is becoming more routine and important, yet challenging due to the slow pace of behavior change and the high cost of exposing target audiences to brand related messages. Many social marketers have no experience developing and managing commercial brands, rendering branding concepts, processes and metrics difficult to master, particularly translating behavioral and brand choice insights into positioning statements.

Insight resulting in correlates of brand choice, and emotional, cognitive and behavioral responses to positioning and personality elements present in brand execution is the scope of the psychology of branding in social marketing. The most important implication of the approach set forth here is the need to continue to evaluate the role of brand equity as a single factor and in terms of its dimensions on behavior. Other implications include the need to develop and use theory to generate brand correlates to test within the context of the Total Market Approach and the need to evaluate whether different types of executions result in different outcomes over time.

REFERENCES

Aaker, D. (1996). *Building strong brands*. New York: Simon and Shuster.

Agha, S. (2003). The impact of a mass media campaign on personal risk perception, perceived self-efficacy and other behavioral predictors. *AIDS Care*, *15*, 749-762.

Bagozzi, R. P. (1975). Marketing as exchange. *Journal of Marketing*, *39*, 32-39.

Blitstein, J. L., Evans, W. D. & Driscoll, D. L. (2008). What is a public health brand? In W.D. Evans & G. Hastings (Eds.) *Public health branding: Applying marketing for social change* (25-41). New York: Oxford University Press.

Chapman, S. (2010). Evaluating Social Marketing. In M. Thorogood and Y. Coombes (Eds.) *Evaluating Health Promotion* (105-120). Oxford: Oxford University Press.

Chapman, S., Jafa, K., Longfield, K., Vielot, N., Buszin, J. Ngamkitpaiboon, L. & Kays, M. (2011). *Sexual Health*, *9*(1), 44-50.

Du Plessis, E. (2008). *The advertised mind: Ground-breaking insights into how our brains respond to advertising*. London: Millward Brown and Kogan Page Limited.

DKT International. (2012). 2011 Contraceptive Social Marketing Statistics. Retrieved from http://www.dktinternational.org/wp-content/uploads/2011/11/2011-Statistical-Mktg-Rpt2.pdf.

Evans, W. D. (2011). Public health brand research: Case studies and future agenda. *Cases in Public Health Communication & Marketing*, *5*, 48-71.

Evans, W. D., Blitstein, J. & Hersey, J. C. (2008). Evaluation of public health brands. In W.D. Evans & G. Hastings (Eds.) *Public health branding: Applying marketing for social change* (43-72). New York: Oxford University Press.

Evans, W. D., Blitstein, J., Hersey, J. C., Renaud, J. & Yaroch, A. (2012). Systematic review of public health branding. *Journal of Health Communication: International Perspectives*, *13*(8), 721-741.

Evans, W. D. & Haider, M. (2008). Public health brands in the developing world. In W.D. Evans & G. Hastings (Eds.) *Public health branding: Applying marketing for social change* (215-232). New York: Oxford University Press.

Evans, W. D. & Hastings, G. (2008a). Public health branding: Recognition, promise, and delivery of healthy lifestyles. In W.D. Evans & G. Hastings (Eds.) *Public health branding: Applying marketing for social change* (3-24). New York: Oxford University Press.

Evans, W. D. & Hastings, G. (2008b). Future directions for public health branding. In W.D. Evans & G. Hastings (Eds.) *Public health branding: Applying marketing for social change* (87-296). New York: Oxford University Press.

Evans, W. D., Longfield, K., Shekhar, N., Rabemanatsoa, A., Snider, J. & Reerink, I. (2012). Social marketing and condom promotion in Madagascar: A case study in brand equity research. In R. Obregon, & S. Waisboard (Eds). *Handbook of Global Health Communication,* (330-347). New York: Wiley.

Evans, W. D., Renaud, J., Blitstein, J., Hersey, J., Connors, S., Schieber, B. & Willett, J. (2007). Prevention effects of an anti-tobacco brand on adolescent smoking initiation. *Social Marketing Quarterly, 13*, 19-38.

Evans, W. D., Taruberekera, N., Longfield, K. & Snider, J. (2011). Brand equity and willingness to pay for condoms in Zimbabwe. *Reproductive Health, 8*, 29.

Evans, W. D., Wasserman, J., Bertolotti, E. & Martino, S. (2002). Branding behavior: The strategy behind the truth [sm] campaign. *Social Marketing Quarterly, 3*, 17-29.

Farrelly, M. C. & Davis, K. C. (2008). Case studies of youth tobacco prevention campaigns from the USA: Truth and half-truths. In W.D. Evans & G. Hastings (Eds.) *Public health branding: Applying marketing for social change* (127-146). New York: Oxford University Press.

Fishbein, M. & Cappella, J. N. (2006). The role of theory in developing effective health communications. *Journal of Communication, 56* (s1), S1-S17.

Hanson, K., Kumaranayake, L. & Thomas, I. (2001). Ends versus means: The role of markets in expanding access to contraceptives. *Health Policy and Planning, 16*(2), 125-136.

Hanson, K., Kikumbih, N., Armstrong-Schellenberg, J., Mponda, H., Nathan, R., Lake, S., Mills, A. & Lengeler, C. (2003). Cost-effectiveness of social marketing of insecticide treated nets for malaria control in the United Republic of Tanzania. *Bulletin of the World Health Organization, 81*(4), 269-276.

Harvey, P. (1999). *Let every child be wanted: How social marketing is revolutionizing family planning programs in the developing world.* Westport: Auburn House

Hastings, G., Freeman, J., Spackova, R. & Siquier, P. (2008). Help: A european public health brand in the making? In W.D. Evans & G. Hastings (Eds.) *Public health branding: Applying marketing for social change* (93-108). New York: Oxford University Press.

Huhman, M., Potter, L. D., Duke, J. C., Judkins, D. R., Heitzler, C. D. & Wong, F. L. (2007). Evaluation of a national physical activity intervention for children: VERB campaign 2002-2004. *American Journal of Preventive Medicine, 32*, 38-43.

Lefebvre, R. C. (2000). Theories and models in social marketing. In P. Bloom & G. Gundlach *Handbook of marketing and society* (506-518). Thousand Oaks: Sage Publications.

Lefebvre, R. C. (2011). An integrative model for social marketing. *Journal of Social Marketing, 1*, 54-72.

Lefebvre, R. C. (2012). *Personal communication*, November 21, 2012.

Mark, M. & Pearson, C. (2001). The hero and the outlaw: Building extraordinary brands through the power of archetype. New York: McGraw-Hill.

McCormack, L. A., Lewis, M. A. & Driscoll, D. (2008). Challenges and limitations of applying branding in social marketing. In W.D. Evans & G. Hastings (Eds.) *Public health branding: Applying marketing for social change* (271-286). New York: Oxford University Press.

Huhman, M., Potter, L. D., Duke, J. C., Judkins, D. R., Heitzler, C. D. & Wong, F. L. (2007). Evaluation of a national physical activity intervention for children: VERB campaign 2002-2004. *American Journal of Preventive Medicine*, *32*, 38-43.

McKenzie-Mohr, D., Lee, N. R., Schultz, P. W. & Kotler, P. (2012). Social marketing to protect the environment: What works. Thousand Oaks: Sage Publications.

Population Services International. (2012). *The delta companion*. Washington, DC: PSI.

Prata, N., Montagu, D. & Jefferys, E. (2005). Private sector, human resources and health franchising in Africa. *Bulletin of the World Health Organization*, *83*(4), 274-279.

Ries, A. & Trout, J. (1981). *Positioning: The battle for your mind*. New York: Warner Books

Schlein, K. & Montagu, D. (2012). *Clinical social franchising compendium; An annual survey of programs*. San Francisco: The Global Health Group, Global Health Sciences, University of California, San Francisco.

Smith, W. A. (1999). Marketing with no budget. *Social Marketing Quarterly*, *5*(2), 6-11.

Thornely & Hill (2011). *Social Marketing vs Social Media Marketing Infographic*. Retrieved from www.thornelyhill.co.uk/social-marketing-vs-social-media-marketing-infographic/

UNAIDS. (2012). *AIDSInfo*. Retrieved from http://www.unaids.org/en/ dataanalysis/ datatools/aidsinfo/

Wikipedia. (2012). *Five Ws*. Retrieved from www.en.wikipedia.org/wiki/ Five-Ws.

In: Psychology of Branding   ISBN: 978-1-62618-817-4
Editor: W. Douglas Evans   © 2013 Nova Science Publishers, Inc.

Chapter 11

BRAND ALLIANCE OF D.A.R.E. AND *KEEPIN' IT REAL*: A CASE STUDY IN BRAND DISSEMINATION PRACTICES

Michael L. Hecht[1] and Jeong Kyu Lee[2]
[1]Department of Communication Arts and Sciences
Pennsylvania State University, University Park, PA, US
[2]Centre for Health Initiatives
University of Wollongong, New South Wales, Australia

ABSTRACT

This chapter discusses the brand alliance of the Drug Abuse Resistance Education (D.A.R.E.) Program with Penn State University's *keepin' it REAL* (*kiR*) substance abuse prevention curriculum. In 2009, D.A.R.E. licensed *keepin' it REAL* as its new middle school curriculum. What began as "co-branding" emerged into a true alliance as *keepin' it REAL*'s creators and D.A.R.E. America worked together to merge the two brands. This was accomplished by combining the brand image of a non-user, capitalizing on the brand loyalty toward D.A.R.E. and the D.A.R.E. officers and the brand equity of the kid-centric *kiR* approach. Using this case, we examine how brand alliances can create compelling sales points and build positive brand images/identities in the context of substance use prevention. We also provide implications and strategic considerations of brand alliances in health prevention and promotion.

Keywords: Brand alliance, public health brand, substance use prevention, D.A.R.E., *keepin' it REAL* curriculum

Public health has matured into a domain that offers a number of evidence-based programs and practices. This maturity brought with it issues of dissemination. While the dissemination of some programs is planned from the beginning (e.g., Legacy's truth[sm] Campaign), others start as NIH or foundation supported research that is conducted in a university setting. As a result, dissemination often requires partnerships or alliances between the intervention developer and dissemination channel. These partnerships are more than just paperwork.

Instead, success may require an alliance between two public health brands. This chapter discusses brand alliance, using the partnership between Pennsylvania State University's *keepin' it REAL* (kiR) substance abuse prevention curriculum and D.A.R.E. America as a case study to illustrate the process. We begin with a theoretical discussion of brand alliance and then apply the discussion to the alliance between these two exemplar public health brands.

WHAT IS A BRAND ALLIANCE?

In the commercial domain, brand alliances are an effective marketing strategy that attempts to create synergy between two brands where the resulting brand is more powerful or effective than either individually. Brand alliances are defined as mutual agreements between companies that merge two or more individual brands into a joint product or service, or that market together in some fashion (Rao & Ruekert, 1994; Rao, Qu, & Ruekert, 1999; Simonin & Ruth, 1998). Well-known examples of brand alliances or co-branding include Sunkist, known as a juice brand with soda, candy, and vitamin products, Star Alliance network with 27 different international airlines and so on.

Brand alliances should be distinguished from co-branding as two related ways of partnering brands that vary in the integration of the companies involve. While co-branding is often seen as physical linkage between two or more brands (e.g., using both logos combined in some ways in promotions such as Winston cigarettes and NASCAR), brand alliances usually go beyond mere physical connection of brand execution components such as logo, symbol, or trademark (Keller, 2007; Rao & Ruekert, 1994). In this chapter we use the term, *brand alliances* to describe strategic partnerships between companies that allow them to capitalize on the complementary resources and features of the partner brands.

Types of Brand Alliances. Brand alliances occur in a number of ways. Bundling is one of the most common types of alliances, combining two or more distinct brands. For example, different General Mills' cereal brands are bundled and sold in a single package or multipack (Keller, 2007). Joint sales promotion is another type of brand alliance. These alliances generally involve making and presenting two or more products/services with the same or different brands (Hadjicharalambous, 2006; Leuthesser, Kohli, & Suri, 2003). More typical combinations involve merging two or more brands into a single end product. A variety of branded combinations represent this type of alliance such as Shell MasterCard from Citi Card and the Star Alliance network among 27 member airlines. A third approach, ingredient branding, is a special case of brand combination that involves retaining some branded components, parts, or materials within another co-branded product (Keller, 2007, p 298; Norris, 1992). *Intel-Inside* featured in personal computers is one of the most famous instances of ingredient branding. In this type of alliance, ingredients such as the Intel processor brand serve as a signal of certain quality characteristics for an overall computer brand.

Brand alliances also coordinate one or more components of marketing execution between companies. Companies form joint ventures where the alliance extends into research and product development through financial cooperation. The recently announced joint venture among Ford, Daimler, and Renault-Nissan to develop hydrogen cells to power cars is an example of this type of alliance strategy. For smaller firms, distribution agreements with existing larger and successful ones can extend their distribution system (Kotler & Keller, 2006).

There are several advantages to forging partnerships that combine two or more brands that are presented jointly to consumers. One of the major advantages is that companies can position their co-branded products more convincingly as well as differentiating their products by providing quality assurance to consumers (Keller, 2007; Rao & Ruekert, 1994). Additionally, brand alliances can help companies reduce the cost of product promotion by utilizing two or more allied brands' well-known images, reputations, or resources (Kotler & Keller, 2006). Also, partnering with successful brands provides valuable opportunities for companies to learn more about how the partner companies approach consumers and market their products (Keller, 2007). For these reasons strategic alliances often lead to more positive consumer evaluations and greater market sales (Keller, 2007; Park, Jun, & Shocker, 1996; Suh & Park, 2011).

Recently, the concept of strategic brand alliances has been applied to health promotion and prevention. In 2008, *The Heart Truth* created a comprehensive alliance among several corporate, media, government, and non-profit groups to place the Red Dress symbol on products and create joint promotional events. For example, *The Heart Truth* and Diet Coke announced a promotional partnership to expand the audience of women that the Red Dress campaign messages reach (Long, Taubenheim, Wayman, Temple, & Ruoff, 2008). The partnership included featuring the Red Dress brand on Diet Coke packages and conducting a sweepstake to win a red dress Heidi Klum wore to the Academy Awards.

This type of strategic collaboration is becoming crucial in health promotion social marketing campaigns (Harding, 2010). In this chapter, we introduce the case of a brand alliance between two public health brands in the youth-targeted substance abuse prevention field, the Drug Abuse Resistance Education (D.A.R.E.) program and the *keepin' it REAL* (kiR) curriculum.

D.A.R.E.'S STRATEGIC PARTNERSHIP WITH PENN STATE'S *KEEPIN' IT REAL*

D.A.R.E. and *keepin' it REAL* (kiR) represent two very successful brands in the substance abuse prevention field. D.A.R.E. America has been the leading provider of substance abuse prevention education for over 25 years and *keepin' it REAL* (kiR) emerged as a leading multicultural prevention program for middle schools in the mid-1990's. This chapter discusses how these two brands came to form a successful alliance to capitalize on their combined brand equity.

D.A.R.E. was founded by the Los Angeles Police Department (LAPD) in 1983 in an effort to stem the increase in adolescent substance use. The Monitoring the Future (MTF) Survey (Johnston, O'Malley, Bachman, & Schulenberg, 2009) tracked this trajectory and other research documented their costs in health and other outcomes (Pettigrew, Miller-Day, Krieger, & Hecht, 2012). LAPD recognized that schools were the logical site for prevention work because of universal education and targeted elementary and middle school students in order to intervene prior to the time when most initiation occurs as well as during early onset of use. The decision was made to teach drug information using uniformed police officers to lend credibility to the program and because they believed that if students learned about the consequences of substance use from officers they would be less like use substances.

As has been documented, D.A.R.E. was rapidly and widely disseminated (Rogers, 2002) for a variety of reasons. As a police-led intervention, the program had great credibility among education decision makers such as school boards, superintendents, and principals. It also gained great visibility and popularity in the community due to extensive publicity that news media were happy to provide this law enforcement education initiative.

What emerged was a D.A.R.E. brand that represented a police-school partnership. D.A.R.E. logos and products, especially t-shirts that became ubiquitous (see figure 1). At the same time, many students came to see D.A.R.E. as officers presenting drug information and telling stories. For some, this was a positive image, but for others, particularly those initiating or likely to initiate, the brand may have taken on a less positive image. Unfortunately, the program, which had modified or created its own curriculum several times, did not achieve the prevention outcomes it desired (e.g., West & O'Neal, 2004).[14] The prevention community and popular press began to portray D.A.R.E. as a failed program and its brand equity was tarnished in some areas. This was particularly true as federal and state governments began demanding that their funds only be used on "evidence-based" interventions or those that had proven scientific efficacy or merit.

This lead D.A.R.E. America to rethink what its brand represented. They sought to rebrand D.A.R.E. as a dissemination vehicle rather than a prevention curriculum. Their officers were shown to be more credible and effective teachers of prevention materials (Hammond et al. 2008) and despite the decline in equity D.A.R.E. was still the most widely disseminated program in the world; although admittedly with smaller enrollments than at its peak. They still had an extensive training and distribution network that allowed for rapid and wide dissemination if they could partner with an effective curriculum. After conducting an extensive evaluation of prevention programs, D.A.R.E. selected Penn State University's *keepin' it REAL* (kiR) program as their partner and a licensing agreement was established in 2009.

The *keepin' it REAL* (kiR) brand, itself, had a long history. Begun as part of the National Institute of Health funded Drug Resistance Strategies Project by Drs. Michelle Miller-Day and Michael L. Hecht, kiR had established an identity and reputation as an "evidenced-based" prevention program. Consultation with Albie Hecht, then President of Television and Film at Nickelodeon and an industry branding expert, lead Miller-Day and Hecht to build the kiR brand around "REAL" – initials that began as an acronym for four strategies youth were found to use to resist drug offers (refuse, explain avoid and leave) and later came to stand for the idea that kiR was "from kids through kids to kids". The idea was to identify "real" youth narratives that portrayed drug free lives in a positive way (Lee & Hecht, 2008) and present resisting peer pressure in drug offers through REAL as "cool." This and other formative research enabled the DRS project team to create branded messages targeting drug resistance skills and efficacy to resist drug offers through social modeling that was culturally grounded (Hecht & Miller-Day, 2009; Lee & Hecht 2011). A logo (see figure 2) was developed by youth to create a "real" look and youth-produced narrative videos and other activities attached socially desirable images and peer role models to the brand. As a result, the multicultural kiR

---

[14] To be fair to D.A.R.E., to the authors' knowledge no other prevention program has been subject to national evaluation by researchers external to the development team.

curriculum developed unique brand awareness and associations (i.e., brand equity) in the prevention field (Hecht & Lee, 2008; Lee & Hecht, 2011). Consistent with pervious literature (Aaker, 1996; Blahut, Evans, & Price, 2004), Lee and Hecht (2011) found that the kiR brand had a hierarchical structure of equity consisting of four sub-dimensions: brand awareness, leadership/popularity, brand personality, and brand loyalty. They also suggested that more favorable and stronger brand associations with kiR enhanced students' confidence in their ability to resist drug offers as well as to make healthy choices (Lee & Hecht, 2011). At the same time, kiR came to be known within the prevention community as the first effective or evidence-based multicultural curriculum (Hecht & Miller-Day, 2009; Miller-Day & Hecht, in press) giving it wide applicability to schools around the country.

It was these qualities that attracted D.A.R.E., but truthfully kiR's branding as "evidence-based" by the prevention community on the federal government's National Registry of Evidence-based Programs and Practices, known as "the list", was probably the key brand element in D.A.R.E.'s eyes. The alliance allowed the D.A.R.E. brand to enhance its equity by leveraging the *keepin' it REAL* brand. More specifically, through the licensing and adoption of the kiR curriculum, the D.A.R.E. brand can be linked to the kiR brand giving it unique brand knowledge and associations. At the same time, the alliance gave kiR access to D.A.R.E. experienced educators, trainers, and officer implementers.[15] The initial vision was a brand in which kiR was the content provider and D.A.R.E. was the delivery mechanism.

Figure 1. D.A.R.E. Logo and t-shirt.

Figure 2. Original kiR Logo.

---

[15] Many thanks to all the D.A.R.E. staff who made this possible, but particularly Anita Bryan, Commander Bobby Robinson, Frank Pegueros, and Benita Calahane.

In this way the D.A.R.E. program could rebuild its brand equity by leveraging kiR brand though the alliance and kiR gained a reliable and credible dissemination network. Both organizations were committed to an adaptation that capitalized on this by staying true to kiR's prevention strategy but recognized that a "DARE-ification" process was needed in order for the lessons to be effectively taught by officers rather than teachers. It was anticipated that this would allow the brand to be sharpened in ways that immediately improved its content.

THE D.A.R.E. AND *KEEPIN' IT REAL* BRAND ALLIANCE

While this common vision was ultimately realized, as D.A.R.E. and kiR began its negotiations to merge the brands it became clear that a number of issues had to be dealt with. First, kiR was owned by Penn State and its creators, Miller-Day and Hecht, were concerned about maintaining the scientific integrity of the curriculum. kiR required a narrative-based, highly interactive delivery. The prevention strategy involved skill development through a highly engaging implementation style. Its content was based on stories, teaching decision making, risk assessment, communication and relationship skills. This view was potentially in conflict with some of the commonly held perceptions of the D.A.R.E. brand that was based on drug information and lecturing. It turned out the two brands were really not that far apart. D.A.R.E. America was committed to maintaining the scientific validity of the kiR's evidence-based approach and had begun to transition to a facilitative delivery style over the past decade.

kiR and D.A.R.E. team members worked to "DARE-ify" kiR. This process was smoothed by the special skills and emerging friendship of Margaret Colby and Anita Bryan who took the lead on this task with input from Commander Bobby Robinson and Michael Hecht, among others. The agreement was to retain the core structure and elements of kiR lessons, with modifications to accommodate teaching by officers rather than teachers as well as the updating of stories and examples. The key to this was their perceiving a common audience. Here a new series of challenges arose.

Both programs saw youth as their primary audience. They shared a common dedication to the health and well being of the students who receive the curriculum. They both acknowledged the presence of the prevention field that "validates" curricula by designating them "evidence-based" if they meet rigorous standards for scientific research. D.A.R.E. was attracted to kiR because of the brand image it presented to youth by providing positive models of safe and drug free youth through stories. However, the "from kids through kids to kids" kiR philosophy and brand was a bit of a challenge for D.A.R.E, whose previous curriculum was more officer-centric than kid-centric. Fortunately, the D.A.R.E. educational and training staff bought into this new model and worked to convey it to the officers by building on the previous D.A.R.E. move to "facilitative" teaching style rather than lecture. More problematic, however, was the reliance on stories in kiR rather than D.A.R.E.'s more didactic style of teaching of "drug information." Didactically presenting drug information potentially serves to communicate moralistic (drugs are wrong) and fear (i.e., "you will get sick", "you will become a criminal", "you will die") messages rather than the rebranded narrative about drug-free youth that kiR sought to convey. This uneasy tension between the two brands still exists, to some degree, and may never fully be resolved in the alliance.

A second common audience are the schools, themselves. Both focus on the schools because they provide access. However, at this point a new awareness of D.A.R.E.'s target audiences was required to build the alliance. The primary difference between kiR before and after D.A.R.E. is the delivery mechanisms. The original kiR was designed for teachers who require fewer instructions about classroom and interaction management. D.A.R.E. Officers receive 80 hours of initial training and then full day updates on new curricula.[16] However, their primary jobs are in law enforcement, not education. So the kiR-D.A.R.E. team had to rethink how it saw itself both in terms of training and the kinds of activities that could be accomplished in a classroom. In a sense, this required a clearer focus on the brand image and what was essential to its equity. This resulted in a sharpening of the brand, particularly the messages in five curriculum videos there were reshot and updated.

Teachers remain present in the D.A.R.E. system but do not deliver the curriculum, as they did in previous version of kiR, and thus typically fill a secondary role. However, they play important roles as gatekeepers, along with principals and school boards. Thus, the brand alliance must appeal to teachers, principals, and school boards and this required a clear explanation of kiR as the curriculum and D.A.R.E. as the delivery mechanism.

What was totally new to kiR was the presence of the law enforcement community (and its culture). The D.A.R.E. structure is more complicated than first meets the eye. D.A.R.E. America is the national organization, still located in Los Angeles. It has a small primary staff with a larger, diffuse network of regional coordinators (typically law enforcement officials), educators (typically teachers), and trainers (typically former D.A.R.E. Officers). In addition, there are state and regional D.A.R.E. organizations and, within these, D.A.R.E. Officer Mentors. These elements of the constituency were all at different levels of agreement with the kiR brand, especially the issue of how much drug information to provide and how forcefully to assert a moral and legal stance rather than a guided, kid-centric and narrative discussion. This created a complex task in establishing common messaging about D.A.R.E.'s kiR curriculum, particularly when some within the centralized D.A.R.E. America structure and training network appear to share these reservations.

A final participant in the brand is the distribution network. D.A.R.E. licenses its materials to private companies who provide them to officers and schools. Currently the D.A.R.E. Catalog is the vehicle distributing and, at the same time, elaborating the D.A.R.E. and D.A.R.E.- kiR brand. This company sells Officer Guides and Planners (student workbooks) used to implement the curriculum. These are created by D.A.R.E. and kiR with design help (see figure 4). However, the catalog also has rights to use the logo and images on a variety of other products including T-shirts, caps, sweat shirts and pants, jackets, coffee cups, pens, etc. (see DARECATALOG.com). D.A.R.E. and kiR exercise limited control over these other uses of the images, complicating control of the brand image. Fortunately, to date these other uses have been consistent with the overall brand image.

Throughout these challenges there was the common realization that this alliance was focused on the youth and what was best for them, and that both brands prospered through the alliance. Adopting kiR allowed D.A.R.E. to answer critiques by pointing to scientifically valid studies that showed kiR's effects on substance use (Hecht, Graham, & Elek, 2006). kiR represented a continuation in D.A.R.E.'s transition from police officer-led didactic teaching

---

[16] It should be noted that this is another advantage the alliance brought to kiR. This level of training would never have been possible without D.A.R.E.

style that focused on drug information to a more facilitative, narrative and kid-centric approach. The new approach adopted from the kiR curriculum presented an appealing identity and social benefits of drug resistance though multiple components. One of the key learning tools was a series of engaging, narrative style classroom videos created based on students' real stories. In addition to the videos, a variety of fun activities such as role plays, discussions, etc. lead students to actively engage in learning as well as to promote interactions between officers and students. Hence partnering with the kiR enabled D.A.R.E. to build more beneficial and attractive brand for consumers. It is, however, telling that the one brand that had potential for contributing to this alliance, the Penn State brand, was not really integrated in the alliance and thus was not capitalized on due to administrative and ideological issues within the Penn State hierarchy.

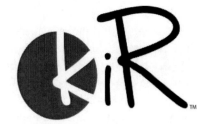

Figure 3. kiR Rural Logo.

Figure 4. Combined D.A.R.E. and kiR logos.

The brand alliance allowed D.A.R.E. to stop the erosion of its network. In other words, the alliance allowed D.A.R.E. to position its program more convincingly in the market by licensing the core contents of the kiR curriculum and with it the claim to be "evidence based" and on "the list" (see www.nrepp.samhsa.gov) as well as its narrative, multicultural, kid-centric strategy. kiR recognized that D.A.R.E placed the program in front of millions of youth in the U.S. as well as those in 43 countries around the world. D.A.R.E. also provided an impressive training network and an array of experts who understand students, schools and prevention. Thus, the alliance provided a leveraging of kiR through the D.A.R.E. brand.

In fact, the alliance appears to be a success so far. The erosion of D.A.R.E.'s market share seems to have been halted and the program appears to have recaptured some of its previous market share. Since D.A.R.E.'s kiR program was implemented in middle schools in fall 2009 enrollment increased from 125,000 to over 800,000 in the US and the number of international partners increased to 23 countries. While outcome evaluation will occur at a future date, the market, itself, seems to have responded favorably. In fact, the partnership was so successful that an elementary school kiR was launched through D.A.R.E. in fall of 2012.

CONCLUSION

In the public health domain, brand alliance is a promising strategy that appeals to consumers (Harding, 2010) because they can reinforce the products' attribute profiles and differentiate the products by offering quality assurance (Park et al., 1996; Rao & Ruekert, 1994). The brand alliance between D.A.R.E. and *keepin' it REAL* demonstrates how two public health brands can work together for youth substance abuse prevention. It also underscores some of the challenges these alliances face.

Research on brand alliance/co-branding indicates that effective alliances can have positive effects on consumer brand evaluations (Keller & Aaker, 1992). Several factors affect consumers' favorable evaluations, including prior attitudes toward brands in the partnership, perceived fit of the products/brands, and partner compatibility. Customers' perceptions of product fit are one of the key factors since consumers may not favorably assess brand alliances if they perceive the allying brands' products as incompatible (Rao & Ruekert, 1994). Additionally, partner compatibility is crucial in the success of brand alliances. In alliances between brands of equal or similar weight, partners tend to make contributions equally to the alliance and spillover effects are split equally between the brands. Previous studies suggest that alliances can be effective when partners are chosen carefully, and the projects are relevant and well selected (Todd, 1997; Rao & Ruekert 1999).

Penn State University's *keepin' it REAL*, was designed as a multicultural, narrative-based substance abuse prevention program through rigorous formative and narrative research (Hecht & Miller-Day, 2009). It proved effective in reducing drug use in a scientific, randomized clinical trial (Hecht et al. 2006) resulting in market demand without a reliable vehicle for dissemination. The curriculum was successfully adapted to the D.A.R.E. program through the partnership. While it was originally thought that the brand roles were separate (kiR as content; D.A.R.E. as dissemination and implementation) it quickly became clear that both elements benefited from the alliance. The alliance was initiated out of mutual and complementary need but was successful due to the cross fertilization it provided. Campaign designers and practitioners should consider the perceived fit of the products/brands and partner compatibility in social marketing programs to maximize the benefits.

There are some challenges related to alliance formations in social marketing campaigns. Brand alliances sometimes dilute the respective brand equities of partnering brands, primarily due to poor attitudes toward one of the allying brands prior or during the alliance. In addition, the "Free-Riding" problem can hinder the success of brand alliances. Alliances between partnering brands of unequal weight tend to result in unequal contributions and limit the synergy. When creating and designing brand alliances in social marketing campaigns, campaign designers need to consider these problems in order to avoid negative consequences of brand alliances. The challenges and affordances are apparent in the D.A.R.E. – kiR brand alliance and this case study can, we hope, inform future public health alliances.

REFERENCES

Aaker, D. A. (1996). *Building strong brands*. New York; The Free Press.

Blahut, S., Evans, D. & Price, S. (2004). A confirmatory test of a higher order factor structure: Brand equity and the truth campaign. *Social Marketing Quarterly*, *10*, 3-15.

Hadjicharalambous, C. (2006). A typology of brand extensions: Positioning cobranding as a sub-case of brand extensions. *Journal of American Academy of Business*, *10*, 372-377.

Hammond, A., Sloboda, Z., Tonkin, P., Stephans, R., Teasdale, B., Grey, S. F. & Williams, J. (2008). Do adolescents perceive police officers as credible instructors of substance abuse prevention programs? *Health Education Research*, *23*, 682-696.

Harding, S. (2010). *The Heart Truth campaign: Exploring the success of the Red Dress*. Master thesis, American University, Washington, D.C.

Hecht, M. L., Graham, J. W. & Elek, E. (2006). The drug resistance strategies intervention: Program effects on substance use. *Health Communication*, *20*, 267-276.

Hecht, M. L. & Lee, J. K. (2008). Branding through cultural grounding: The *keepin' it REAL* curriculum. In W. D. Evans & G. Hastings (Eds.), *Public health branding: Applying marketing for social change* (161-179). Oxford, UK: Oxford University Press.

Hecht, M. L. & Miller-Day, M. A. (2009). The drug resistance strategies project: Using narrative theory to enhance adolescents' communication competence. In L. Frey & K. Cissa (Eds.), *Routledge handbook of applied communication* (535-557). London, UK: Routledge.

Johnston, L. D., O'Malley, P. M., Bachman, J. G. & Schulenberg, J. (2009). *Monitoring the future national results on adolescent drug use: Overview of key findings, 2008* (NIH publication no. 09-7401).

Keller, K. L. (2007). *Strategic brand management: Building, measuring, and managing brand equity*. Upper Saddle River, NJ: Pearson Prentice Hall.

Keller, K. L. & Aaker, D. A. (1992). The effects of sequential introduction of brand extensions. *Journal of Marketing Research*, *29*, 35-50.

Kotler, P. & Keller, K. L. (2006). *Marketing management*. Upper Saddle Review, NJ: Pearson Prentice Hall.

Park, C. W., Jun, S. W. & Shocker, A. D. (1996). Composite brand alliances: An investigation of extension and feeback effects. *Journal of Marketing Research*, *33*, 453-466.

Pettigrew, J., Miller-Day, M., Krieger, J. & Hecht, M. L. (2012). The rural context of illicit substance offers: A study of Appalachian rural adolescents. *Journal of Adolescent Research*, *27*, 523-550.

Leuthesser, L., Kohli, C. & Suri, R. (2003). 2+2=5? A framework for using co-branding to leverage a brand. *Brand Management*, *11*, 35-47.

Long, T., Taubenheim, A., Wayman, J., Temple, S. & Ruoff, B. (2008). "The Heart Truth:" Using the power of branding and social marketing to increase awareness of heart disease in women. *Social Marketing Quarterly*, *14*, 3-29.

Miller-Day, M. & Hecht, M. L. (in press). Narrative means to preventative ends: A narrative engagement approach to adolescent substance use prevention. *Health Communication*.

Norris, D. G. (1992). Ingredient branding: A strategy option with multiple beneficiaries. *Journal of Consumer Marketing*, *9*, 19-31.

Rao, A. R., Qu, L. & Ruekert, R. W. (1999). Signaling unobservable quality through a brand ally. *Journal of Marketing Research*, *36*, 258-268.

Rao, A. R., Qu, L. & Ruekert, R. W. (1994, Fall). Brand alliances as signals of product quality. *Sloan Management Review*, *36*, 86-97.

Rogers, E. (2002). Diffusion of preventive interventions. *Addictive Behaviors*, *27*, 989-993.

Simonin, B. L. & Ruth, J. A. (1998). Is a company known by the company it keeps? Assessing the spillover effects of brand alliances on consumer brand attitudes. *Journal of Marketing Research*, *35*, 30-42.

Suh, J. & Park, S. (2009). Successful brand alliance and its negative spillover effect on a host brand: Test of cognitive responses. *Advances in Consumer Research*, *36*, 243-247.

West, S. L. & O'Neal, K. K. (2004). Project D.A.R.E. outcome effectiveness revisited. *American Journal of Public Health*, *94*, 1027- 1029.

Todd, S. (1997). The effects of partner and relationship characteristics on alliance outcomes. *Academy of Management Journal*, *40*, 443-461.

In: Psychology of Branding
Editor: W. Douglas Evans

ISBN: 978-1-62618-817-4
© 2013 Nova Science Publishers, Inc.

Chapter 12

BRANDING AS A STRATEGY TO BUILD COMMUNITY ENGAGEMENT IN HEALTH PROGRAMS

*Nicholas Goodwin**

Goodwin Collaboration, Washington, DC, US

"In the minds of each lives the image of their communion"
Benedict Anderson

ABSTRACT

This chapter aims to show that understanding and building brand communities will help ensure the success of your work. It examines the global evidence and experience of brand communities from research and practice – in both the commercial and public sectors. It begins with an overview of traditional approaches to branding, marketing and communications, then introduces the disruption caused by new technologies and ideas. Next it examines ideas of community found in a variety of fields, including psychology, sociology and anthropology. It introduces Muniz and O'Guinn's idea that the brand community is "a specialized, non-geographically bound community, based on a structured set of social relationships among admirers of a brand. It is specialized because at its center is a branded good or service. Like other communities, it is marked by a shared consciousness, rituals and traditions, and a sense of moral responsibility."

This chapter then describes how to understand and build more effective brand communities. It draws on community psychology, which provides an ecological perspective with the person-environment dynamic as the focus of research and action to address a commercial or social issue. It also introduces the idea of a "sense of community" as a way to understand these dynamics. Within groups, change agents, e.g. opinion leaders, peer educators, community facilitators, counsellors, outreach workers etc., can assist in building and strengthening brands, influence relationships and can shape behavioural norms. We know from work done on sustainability that involving the intended beneficiaries of the program and their communities is important, however why and how this is done is critical.

---

* Corresponding author: Nicholas Goodwin is Director of Goodwin Collaboration, PhD Candidate at The University of Sydney, and Research Scholar at The George Washington University. E: nick@goodwincollaboration.com.

The chapter then examines how working with a variety of partners from the private sector, industry groups, government agencies and community organizations brings to the table new resources, expertise and networks to help build a brand community. It shows that capacity building for brand communities is a process of strengthening the abilities of individuals, organizations and systems to sustainably and effectively respond to their needs. The chapter draws on the author's experience managing and researching projects in Asia and Australia. One of the cases covered is Hello Sunday Morning, an online community changing the culture of alcohol in Australia. Another is on approaches to building a brand community in Indonesia to improve sanitation. From the commercial sector, new technologies are making it possible to reach new consumer markets, lift more people out of poverty and provide access to communities previously out of reach – bringing change and highlighting commonalities. The chapter closes with a discussion of the implications for brand communities and recommendations for more effective marketing and stronger brands to enable commercial success and improved social impact.

INTRODUCTION

Traditional approaches to marketing and communications are being broken down across commercial and public policy domains. One-way advertising and top-down public campaigns are considered less effective than in the past.[1] The individual consumer has dominated marketing for so long and only relatively recently have practitioners and policymakers begun the task of understanding how groups form around brands and the most effective ways to engage them. A brand community is a group of people who come together in the physical or virtual/mediated worlds to interact with a brand and each other. As you will discover, sometimes this brings a positive result for a brand, sometimes a negative one. This chapter shows that understanding and building brand communities is essential to the success of marketing and the brands with which you work.

This chapter examines the global evidence and experience of brand communities from research and practice – in both the commercial and public sectors. It identifies two main issues facing practitioners and policymakers – control and participation – and seeks to provide new ways to address them. It does this by offering key insights into brand community building that can be applied to social and behaviour change, primarily for the public and community sectors, which are also useful for commercial initiatives. The chapter also examines the role of technology in brand communities, including the promise of new ways of connecting and the possibility of reclaiming practices lost. To bring these issues to life, it will refer to initiatives from the commercial sector, including the Harley Owners Group, Apple and European car clubs, as well as those from the public sector, including an Australian organization focused on alcohol harm, Hello Sunday Morning, and two Indonesian sanitation projects, "Fantastic Mom" and "High-5", which aimed to reduce infant mortality and improve community health. Combining the latest evidence from social and community psychology with learnings from the practices of commercial marketing, sustainability and community development, this chapter will provide a better-stocked toolbox for researcher and practitioner alike.

---

[1] Hopkins, J. L. (2012), Can Facebook be an effective mechanism for generating growth and value in small businesses?, *Journal of Systems and Information Technology*, 14(2), 131-141.

TRADITIONAL APPROACHES TO BRANDING, MARKETING AND COMMUNICATIONS

The role of commerce as an engine for change is well documented. Advancing consumer culture is often covered in discussions of modernity and the impact it brings to individuals and their communities.[2] The emergence of a consumer culture is one in which branded goods replaced generic commodities, where mass advertising replaced personal selling, and where the individual consumer replaced the communal citizen. Helping to drive this change is marketing, which has been defined as a "social and managerial process by which individuals and groups obtain what they need and want through creating and exchanging products and value with others."[3] Marketing aims to build a relationship between the consumer and a brand, which may include a product, service or behaviour, by providing added value.[4] Central to this culture is the individual consumer. This culture is often blamed, either in part or in its entirety, for the loss of traditional notions of community. As purchasing power expanded, branded products became ubiquitous and took center stage as the symbols of this shift in human consciousness and the resultant loss of community. The brand, therefore, has a central and prominent place in the discourse of modernity, community and society.[5]

This discourse was dominated by consumer-centric views of marketing and brands, which saw the brand-consumer relationship as its foundation. These views define the quality of the brand relationship as the degree to which the consumer views the brand as a satisfactory partner in their continuing relationship.[6] They describe a two-way relationship between the consumer and the brand with the impact on broader communities as a collateral externality. Many communication programs are designed to change an individual or community by delivering messages to mass or local audiences with little regard for the nature of the communities in which they exist.[7] Understanding the structure, dynamics and history of these communities is essential to the success of programs designed to change or harness them. As we learn more about consumer behavior and social change, the discourse on branding has begun to shift. Increasingly marketers are turning to psychology and sociology for answers on understanding, engaging and building communities.

CONCEPTS OF COMMUNITY

Ideas of community can be found in a wide variety of fields, including psychology, sociology and anthropology. The intellectual history of the concept of community is lengthy and abundant. A 1953 study by Hillery identified 94 definitions of community in which the

---

[2] Lasch, C. (1991), *The True and Only Heaven: Progress and Its Critics*, New York: Norton.

[3] Kotler, P., Roberto, N., & Lee, N. (2002). *Social marketing: improving the quality of life* (2nd ed.). Thousand Oaks, Calif.: Sage Publications, p. 6.

[4] Evans, W. D., & Hastings, G. (2008). *Public health branding: Applying marketing for social change*: Oxford University Press, USA.

[5] Muniz, A. M., & O'Guinn, T. C. (2001), Brand community, *Journal of Consumer Research, 27*(4), p. 413.

[6] Algesheimer, R., Dholakia, U., & Hermann, A. (2005), Interplay between Brand and Brand Community: Evidence from European Car Clubs, *Journal of Marketing, 69*(3), p. 23.

[7] Valente, T. W., & Davis, R. L. (1999), Accelerating the diffusion of innovations using opinion leaders, *The Annals of the American Academy of Political and Social Science, 566*(1), p. 56.

only common factor was people.[8] A sprint through the history of community would encounter German sociologist Tonnies and his two forms of human association: *gemeinschaft* (community) and *gesellschaft* (society);[9] Weber's concept of social action;[10] Simmel's references to sociability and social boundaries;[11] Dewey's groups of citizens "created" by communication;[12] Durkheim's "collective conscience" which sat in opposition to the notion that a society was nothing more than an assembly of individuals;[13] Park's notions of group solidarity in crowds and publics;[14] Wirth's work on urban social lives;[15] Anderson's imagined communities, where "in the minds of each lives the image of their communion";[16] Stokols' development of the social ecological approach;[17] and the research of Cruz and Lewis on media audiences and culture.[18] McLuhan asserted that it is the masses that mediate individual and social change, by affecting both the medium and the message.[19]

At this stage we should remind ourselves that the concept of community is a contested one that features prominently in discussions of modern society. Muniz and O'Guinn describe how many saw the changes brought by industrialization as not just challenging community, but damaging and ultimately destroying it.[20] The idea of modern society was positioned largely in opposition to the traditional community. When Tonnies presented his ideas on *gemeinschaft* and *gesellschaft*, he marked the differences between the traditional, ancestral, collective, emotional rural community and the technological, legalized, individualistic, rational urban society. His basic idea was that the community – as something more natural and real – was being replaced by modern society – a more mechanical, mass produced, and disconnected type of human experience. It was feared that it would be lost forever. Yet community has persisted, not in the traditional form described by Tonnies and others, but as a set of needs, practices and aspirations.

As a contemporary alternative to the traditional form, the concept of community identity lends itself well to this project of considering the dynamics of brand communities. "Community identification is an individual's desire to belong to a particular community and behave according to established norms and values. Within this desire, the search for a "social identity," to create and foster one's personal identity, is a valuable aspect of such

[8] Hillery, G. A. (1955), Definitions of community: Areas of agreement, *Rural Sociology, 20*(2), 111-123.

[9] Tönnies, F., & Loomis, C. P. (1957), *Community & society (Gemeinschaft und Gesellschaft)*, East Lansing,: Michigan State University Press.

[10] Weber, M., & Runciman, W. G. (1978), *Max Weber: selections in translation*, Cambridge; New York: Cambridge University Press.

[11] Simmel, G. (2007), The Social Boundary, *Theory, Culture & Society, 24*(7-8), 53-56.

[12] Dewey, J. (1927), *The public and its problems*, New York,: H. Holt and Company.

[13] Durkheim, E., & Halls, W. D. (1984), *The division of labour in society*, New York: Free Press; Durkheim, E., Solovay, S. A., Mueller, J. H., & Catlin, G. E. G. (1938). *The rules of sociological method* (8th ed.). Chicago, Ill.: The University of Chicago press.

[14] Park, R. E. (1972), *The crowd and the public, and other essays*, Chicago,: University of Chicago Press.

[15] Wirth, L. (1938), Urbanism as a Way of Life, *The American Journal of Sociology, 44*(1), 1-24.

[16] Anderson, B. R. O. G. (2006), *Imagined communities: reflections on the origin and spread of nationalism*, (Rev. ed.). London, New York: Verso, p. 6.

[17] Stokols, D. (1992), Establishing and Maintaining Healthy Environments: Toward a Social Ecology of Health Promotion, *American Psychologist, 47*(1), 6-22.

[18] Cruz, J., & Lewis, J. (1994), *Viewing, reading, listening: audiences and cultural reception*, Boulder: Westview Press.

[19] McLuhan, M., & Lapham, L. H. (1994), *Understanding media: The extensions of man*, MIT Press Cambridge, MA.

[20] Muniz & O'Guinn (2001), pp. 412-3.

affiliations."[21] People can belong to multiple communities and therefore assume multiple identities. These can overlap and reinforce, as well stand in competition, especially in the context of the products, services and behaviors provided through brand relationships. In addition to identity, we can draw upon community psychological to examine relationships between individuals and their communities, including as predictors of behavior change.

BRAND COMMUNITIES

For decades, especially since Muniz and O'Guinn and others introduced the idea of the brand community, practitioners and researchers have worked to understand how groups of people form around their products, services and behaviors.

> "A brand community is a specialized, non-geographically bound community, based on a structured set of social relationships among admirers of a brand. It is specialized because at its center is a branded good or service. Like other communities, it is marked by a shared consciousness, rituals and traditions, and a sense of moral responsibility."[22]

Algesheimer et al draw on social psychology to describe the process of identification with a brand community as both cognitive and affective.[23] With the cognitive, the individual formulates and maintains a self-awareness of his or her membership of the community, emphasizing the perceived similarities with other members and dissimilarities with non-members. The affective component implies a sense of emotional involvement with the community, which social psychologists have described as an "affective commitment"[24] and which brand community research has depicted as "kinship between members."[25] Identification with a brand community means that the individual agrees with its norms, traditions, rituals and aims as well as promotes and defends its wellbeing.[26]

However, it is important to consider the notion that identification with a brand community can have both positive and negative consequences for consumers – and for brands. On the positive side, McAlexander et al show that participation in a "Jeep Brandfest" event increased consumers' attachment to their cars and to the Jeep brand significantly.[27] On the negative side, Muniz and Schau reported that even six years after Apple had discontinued its Newton personal digital assistant (PDA) product, the members of its brand community still

---

[21] Heere, B., Walker, M., Yoshida, M., Ko, Y. J., Jordan, J. S., & James, J. D. (2011), Brand Community Development Through Associated Communities: grounding community measurement within social identity theory, *The Journal of Marketing Theory and Practice, 19*(4), p. 408.

[22] Muniz & O'Guinn (2001), pp. 412.

[23] Algesheimer et al (2005), p. 20.

[24] Ellemers, N., Kortekaas, P. and Ouwerkerk J.W. (1999), Self-Categorization, Commitment to the Group, and Group Self-Esteem as Related but Distinct Aspects of Social Identity, *European Journal of Social Psychology*, 29 (2-3), 371-89.

[25] McAlexander, J. H., Schouten, J. W., & Koenig, H. F. (2002), Building brand community, *The Journal of Marketing*, 38-54.

[26] Bhattacharya, C.B., Rao, H. and Glynn, M.A. (1995), Understanding the Bond of Identification: An Investigation of Its Correlates Among Art Museum Members, *Journal of Marketing*, 59 (October), 46-57.

[27] McAlexander, Schouten, and Koenig (2002).

continued to use it, support one another and advocate the product's use to outsiders.[28] These Newton communities continued to thrive in 2012.[29]

People's need to feel connected to their communities helps drives their choices, decisions and behaviors. How people differ in their views of brands depends on where they are, their emotions and their history of engagement. As an example, the interactions of members of the Harley Owners Group (HOG) provide not only support in the form of motorcycle riding and maintenance advice but also social support through experiences of learning, community activism and fellowship. Participation in a HOG has been found to increase members' affection for the Harley brand, making them committed, dependable, and, in many cases, even evangelical consumers. However some HOG members also report feeling uncomfortable with the behaviors expected by the community, eg. mocking owners of other brands, leading to what psychologists describe as "reactance", where people seek to assert their individual independence in contrast to the demands of the community.[30] Similarly in Indonesia, Johns Hopkins' Fantastic Mom hand washing campaign engaged the community of parents and caregivers of children by providing an inspirational platform of change. This platform, discussed in more detail later in the chapter, not only provided accurate information on health issues related to sanitation but provided a fun social setting and opportunities for people to interact with each other. Johns Hopkins provided the foundations for the platform, however its success was derived from the ability of partners and their communities to access it and make it relevant and interesting to them.

The impact of social norms on behavioral intentions provides insight into the complex nature of brand community building. It's not a straightforward case of strengthening or changing social norms. Reactance is more likely to occur the greater pressure there is on members to conform to the brand community's norms and aims, and the more troubling and negative the association is with the brand community.[31] Not surprisingly, people can become less willing to engage in community-related activities. In contrast to this punishment approach is community engagement, which represents the positive and self-instigated aspects of the brand community's influence and is likely to be experienced more positively. Unsurprisingly, members are often eager to repeat behaviors that lead to positive rewards, and they should have higher levels of behavioral intentions as a result. Reactance is also likely to have a negative effect on future use of the brand. Analyzing these complexities will help you to understand and build effective brand communities.

HOW TO BUILD EFFECTIVE BRAND COMMUNITIES

In order to build an effective brand community, it is important to first establish a vision of success for your marketing. An effective community is a successful outcome which, in turn, leads to an impact for the brand. That impact can be measured in a variety of ways, including brand equity, sales and behavior change. During the process of achieving these things, we can also measure the intent to purchase commercial goods and services, as well as

---

[28] Muniz, A.M. and Schau, H.J. (2005), Religiosity in the Abandoned Apple Newton Brand Community, *Journal of Consumer Research*, 31(4), 737-47; Algesheimer et al (2005), pp. 20-21.

[29] See http://myapplenewton.blogspot.com/. Accessed December 11th, 2012.

[30] Algesheimer et al (2005), p. 19.

[31] Algesheimer et al (2005), pp. 22-23.

knowledge and awareness of new behaviors. Similarly, the success of a brand community is not just measured in terms of numbers of participants or the positive views of a brand but the quality of the community. This quality can be measured in terms of who the membership is and what they do, as well as the members' overall sense of community. In essence, it's not enough for members to just say good things about a brand, they must remain engaged and involved in the brand's development.

There are proven ways to build genuine participation and identify the most appropriate and effective allies to help you do this. Community psychology provides an ecological perspective with the person-environment dynamic as the focus of research and action to address a commercial or social issue. This differs from attempts to change either the person or the environment to address an individual problem. Community psychology bases these interventions in empiricism, which is one of its major differences from the qualitative approaches of sociology and anthropology. Methods from psychology have been adapted for use in building communities that recognise value-driven, subjective research involving community members.[32] One such method is based on the idea of a psychological "Sense of Community".

Sense of Community

The concept of a psychological "Sense of Community" (SOC) was formally developed by Sarason in his work in mental health.[33] It was further developed by Doolittle, MacDonald and Glynn before being more fully defined by McMillan and Chavis.[34] The SOC, as defined by McMillan and Chavis, aimed to "strengthen and preserve the community." It was based on work done in community psychology and sociology, building on definitions of community advanced by Hillery and others. The McMillan and Chavis definition of SOC has four interrelated elements:

1. Membership: a feeling of belonging and sharing relatedness
2. Influence: of the individual over the group and vice versa
3. Needs: fulfilment of the individual's needs by the resources of the group
4. Connection: the belief that group members share personal experiences and emotional associations

This framework employs an empirical approach to analyse a subjective and relative measurement of a member's attitude or perception of their communities, rather than attempt to measure the objective strengths or characteristics of the community itself. The Sense of Community Index (SCI) has been used as a quantitative measure of sense of community in

---

[32] Rappaport, J. (1977). *Community psychology: values, research, and action*. New York: Holt, Rinehart and Winston.

[33] Sarason, S. B. (1974). *The psychological sense of community: Prospects for a community psychology*: Jossey-Bass.

[34] Doolittle, R. J., & MacDonald, D. (1978). Communication and a Sense of Community in a Metropolitan Neighbourhood: a factor analytic examination. *Communication Quarterly, 26*(3), 2-7; Glynn, T. J. (1981). Psychological Sense of Community: measurement and application. *Human Relations, 34*(9), 789-818; McMillan, D. W., & Chavis, D. M. (1986), Sense of community: A definition and theory, *Journal of Community Psychology, 14* (January).

North and South America, Asia, the Middle East, as well as in many different contexts, e.g. urban, suburban, rural, tribal, workplaces, schools, universities, recreational clubs, online communities, etc. Earlier work has established the SCI as a robust measure of the psychological sense of community of a member towards a nominated group.[35] The latest version, 'Sense of Community 2 (SCI2)', has been demonstrated to be a strong predictor of social and behavior change.[36] Ideas around community engagement and participation also draw on a wealth of evidence from the fields of community and sustainable development.

SUSTAINABILITY, ENGAGEMENT AND PARTICIPATION

The concept of sustainability originated in the context of the debate around renewable resources, such as forests and fisheries.[37] Sustainable development subsequently evolved to become the basis for new approaches to poverty and social change – one that grew from its environmental and development origins and incorporated the latest thinking and practice from political science, psychology, economics, anthropology, sociology and many more fields. Countries and communities receiving services, long dictated to through top-down delivery of public programs, have resisted their lack of control and demanded a greater role in decisions affecting them. At a more individual level, disadvantaged and marginalized people at the local level became suspicious of the motivations of donors and national elites and have increasingly called for their needs and opinions to be incorporated into the development process. One element that has emerged from this, becoming almost compulsory in a discussion of sustainable development, is that of participation.[38]

There are many ways to distinguish participatory approaches from those it seeks to supersede, however there is no universal agreement on its definition. A suggested method is to examine two key elements – the actor (or participant) and the type of participation.[39] The actors are the intended beneficiaries of the program and their communities. The second

---

[35] Chavis, D., Lee, K. S., & Acosta, J. D. (2008), *The Sense of Community (SCI) Revised: The Reliability and Validity of the SCI-2*, Paper presented at the 2nd International Community Psychology Conference, Lisboa, Portugal; Fisher, A. T., Sonn, C. C., & Bishop, B. J. (2002), *Psychological sense of community: research, applications, and implications*, New York: Kluwer Academic/Plenum Publishers; Tartaglia, S. (2006), A preliminary study for a new model of sense of community, *Journal of Community Psychology, 34*(1), 25-36; Glynn, 1981; McMillan & Chavis, 1986; Sarason, 1974;

[36] Chavis et al (2008), p. 1.; Finlayson, T. J. (2007), *Effects of stigma, sense of community, and self-esteem on the HIV sexual risk behaviors of African American and Latino men who have sex with men* (PhD), Georgia State University; Graham, B. C. (2011), *Residence hall sense of community in physical and technology-based spaces: Implications for alcohol-related attitudes and behaviors* (PhD), DePaul University, Chicago, Illinois (UMI Number: 3491555); Hystad, P., & Carpiano, R. M. (2012), Sense of community-belonging and health-behaviour change in Canada, *Journal of Epidemiology and Community Health, 66*(3), 277-283; Xu, Q., Perkins, D. D., & Chow, J. C. C. (2010), Sense of community, neighboring, and social capital as predictors of local political participation in China, *American Journal of Community Psychology, 45*(3), 259-271.

[37] Khang & Moe (2008), p. 74.

[38] Goodwin, N. (2013 in press), Sustainable Change Marketing: learnings from development and communications programs in Indonesia and beyond, In L. Brennan, J. Fien, L. Parker, H. Duong, M. A. Doan & T. Watne (Eds.), *Growing Sustainable Communities: a development guide for Southeast Asia*. Melbourne, Australia: Tilde University Press.

[39] In relation to "actor," the literature refers to "people's participation" (McCall, 1987), "community participation" (Midgeley et al., 1986), "people's own development" (Swantz, 1986), "community development" (Gow and Vansart, 1983), and "self-help" (Verhagen, 1987). See Campbell, L. M., & Vainio-Mattila, A. (2003), Participatory development and community-based conservation: Opportunities missed for lessons learned?, *Human Ecology, 31*(3), 417-437.

element – the type of participation – refers to the positioning of initiatives on a continuum, with manipulation at one end and empowerment at the other.[40] Manipulating participation is carried out to secure the actor's involvement for the achievement of externally identified project goals. Empowerment of the actors means that they define the goals themselves, as well as make decisions on the strategies and actions required to achieve them. This means a shift from a passive voice to an active one for the targeted individuals and their communities.[41]

In the context of brand building, the difference between the two ways is that manipulation considers participation as a means to an end for brand success, while empowerment views participation as an end that, when achieved, will result in long-term engagement by those involved in the brand. Proponents of participatory approaches have criticized the old model of participation on the grounds that it promoted a top-down, ethnocentric and paternalistic view of communities. Individuals and their communities were not involved in choosing, designing and implementing the products, services or behaviors, which were developed with the view of consumers as passive receivers of decisions made outside of their influence.

In building brand communities, we should automatically ground our work in response to the real-life circumstances of individuals and their communities, not our hopes or wishes for what might be. Kotler and Zaltman advised, "Careful thought be given to the manner in which manageable, desirable, gratifying and convenient solutions to a perceived need or problem are presented to its potential buyers."[42] Hearing and responding to local voices is a key feature of the empowerment approach. It is essential for the people directly experiencing a brand to voice their perspectives, experiences, analysis and ideas as a central part of planning and implementing steps that lead to improving or expanding the brand.[43]

THE ROLE OF CHANGE AGENTS

There is evidence that interpersonal communication is necessary for marketing and social programs to be successful.[44] Beginning in the 1950s and early 1960s, several hundred diffusion studies supported the idea that interpersonal communications is an important influence on behaviour change.[45]

Gaps in a community's structure can restrict the flow of information disseminated for the purposes of effecting change. This change may be to a person's choice of commercial products or to an individual's behaviour around a social issue. These gaps can be bridged with relationship building, effectively enlarging the social network. Change agents, e.g. opinion leaders, peer educators, community facilitators, counsellors, outreach workers etc., can assist in building and strengthening these influence relationships and can shape behavioural

---

[40] Arnstein's "Ladder of Citizen Participation" is an example of this continuum.
[41] Goodwin (2013 in press).
[42] Kotler, P., & Zaltman, G. (1971), Social marketing: an approach to planned social change, *The Journal of Marketing*, p. 10.
[43] Goodwin (2013 in press).
[44] Valente (1998), p. 99.
[45] Rogers, E. M. (2003), *Diffusion of innovations* (5th ed.), New York: Free Press.

norms.[46] Change agents can also be leaders, as approximately 15 per cent of the members of a community are early adopters of an innovation. However, leaders won't always pass on new information, their choice of a "protect or propagate" response depends on what they determine is important for the group. The success of change agents in dissemination of information can be influenced by several factors – education, financial incentives, social norms, skills training, power, age and others.[47]

Many commercial marketing and public programs make use of change agents – e.g. brand ambassadors, peer educators, counsellors, opinion leaders and community health workers – to disseminate messages within target communities. These change agents can be either remunerated or voluntary. One form is the concept of peer education, which is based on the assumption that some individuals will act as role models and opinion leaders within their communities and can be important determinants of rapid and sustained change.[48] This assumption has been tested as part of interventions, with opinion leaders shown to be effective at decreasing the rate of unsafe sexual practices[49] and at decreasing the rate of cesarean births.[50] These findings imply that maximizing the effectiveness of change agents can accelerate the rate of diffusion of information within a community.

This evidence leads us toward two further questions. First, how can we identify and select change agents? Second, how do we choose the change agents who are more likely to be more effective in influencing change in the community in which they are active or to which they have been assigned?

Valente and Pumpuang researched the role of change agents in programs as diverse as HIV/AIDS prevention and tobacco prevention in schools.[51] They collected and reviewed the ten most common techniques for identifying opinion leaders as well as the advantages and disadvantages of each one.

These methods of identifying change agents focus on who they are connected to and how the community feels about them. Research currently underway also examines how the change agents feel about their communities and how this affects how information is disseminated.[52] These techniques are important in building brand communities as change agents can play a major role. We can see how this works in the development of Hello Sunday Morning, a community to change the role of alcohol in the lives of Australians.

---

[46] Kempe, D., Kleinberg, J., & Tardos, E. (2003), *Maximizing the spread of influence through a social network*, Paper presented at the Ninth ACM SIGKDD international conference on knowledge discovery and data mining, New York, NY, USA.

[47] Valente, T. W., & Saba, W. P. (1998), Mass Media and Interpersonal Influence in a Reproductive Health Communication Campaign in Bolivia, *Communication Research, 25*(1), 96-124, p. 99.

[48] Valente, T. W., & Davis, R. L. (1999), p. 57.

[49] Kelly, J. A., St Lawrence, J. S., Diaz, Y. E., Stevenson, L. Y., Hauth, A. C., Brasfield, T. L., Andrew, M. (1991), HIV risk behavior reduction following intervention with key opinion leaders of population: an experimental analysis, *American Journal of Public Health, 81*(2), 168-171.

[50] Lomas, J., Enkin, M., Anderson, G. M., Hannah, W. J., Vayda, E., & Singer, J. (1991), Opinion leaders vs audit and feedback to implement practice guidelines, *JAMA: the journal of the American Medical Association, 265*(17), 2202-2207.

[51] Valente, T. W., & Pumpuang, P. (2007), Identifying Opinion Leaders to Promote Behavior Change, *Health Education & Behavior, 34*(6), 881-896.

[52] Goodwin, N. (2011), *Community: the missing ingredient in the social marketing mix*, Paper presented at the World Social Marketing Conference, Dublin, Ireland.

HELLO SUNDAY MORNING: A COMMUNITY CHANGING THE CULTURE OF ALCOHOL IN AUSTRALIA

Hello Sunday Morning (HSM) is an Australian non-profit organisation that has built a brand community to enable people to develop a healthier relationship with alcohol. Participants in HSM programs choose to go for an extended period without consuming alcohol, usually three, six or 12 months. These individuals not only reduce their own alcohol use but also act as change agents in their communities, reducing overall harm from alcohol. HSM is therefore a brand community driven by a movement towards a better drinking culture. Their purpose is to provide a platform for individuals to create meaningful change in their lives through a period without alcohol. By sharing their story with the "HSMer" community online, each person's experience is a unique and essential contribution to a better drinking culture. HSM does not operate a clinical service and is not a traditional intervention or population health campaign. HSM takes a networked approach to health promotion, rather than create and disseminate messages to an audience, HSM has constructed a communication network across blogging and social networking platforms.[53]

HSMers communicate with each other as they attempt to change their own drinking behaviours and broader cultural attitudes to alcohol. The blogging community is highly connected to the HSM brand and made up of individuals who discuss the process of challenging individual behaviours and cultural practices of alcohol consumption. These community connections are evident in the activity on the website with – on average – five new blog posts posted each day, several with very active comment threads attached to them. Often blog posts take on a very personal narrative and focus on the specific life events of the HSMer. HSM recruits 'Community Moderators' to act as change agents in the broader HSM community, by providing support to those undertaking an HSM program. These Community Moderators answer questions from current and potential participants, comment on blogs and provide feedback to HSM management. HSM recruits new members through online communities, events and social networks.

The HSM community helps build the brand by defining what a safe drinking culture is and engaging with its development. In the two years to mid-2012, over 4,300 people have signed up to take a break from drinking through HSM. By the end of 2015 HSM aims to find 100,000 people who are ready to take on the challenge.[54]

PARTNERSHIPS

Engaging partners across government, community and private sector is also critical to the success of brand communities.[55] Working with a variety of partners from the private sector, industry groups, government agencies and community organizations brings to the table new resources, expertise and networks to help build a brand community. In the public sector, the

---

[53] Hamley, B., & Carah, N. (2012), *One Sunday at a time: evaluating Hello Sunday Morning*, Sydney: Foundation for Alcohol Research and Education.

[54] Hamley & Carah (2012).

[55] Lefebvre, R. C. (2006), Partnerships for social marketing programs: An example from the National Bone Health Campaign, *Social Marketing Quarterly, 12*(1), p. 52.

complexity and interconnectedness of social issues requires us to move beyond long-held assumptions about what government, business and non-profits should do. Solutions to persistent problems require a flexible and innovative approach that draws on a range of capabilities, no matter in which type of organization these are found. Local community need, capability and decisions will determine which partners are needed for what issues.[56] In the private sector, alliances with like-minded brands and their communities provide the potential for expansion of the existing brand community and opportunities for growth in new markets.

Community centered social marketing approaches incorporate many of these ideas on partnerships and participation. Of these, the most recognized are Bryant et al with 'community based prevention marketing'[57], which borrows from community organizing and capacity building approaches. Another is Doug McKenzie-Mohr's 'community based social marketing' which "merges knowledge from psychology with expertise from social marketing"[58] and provides recommendations for program design and evaluation at the community level. These approaches take us from implementing marketing programs *in* a community to *with* a community.

The most successful projects are those that combine a core of marketing with the enabling environment of partnerships and transform these into movements for change. Examples include Thailand's 100% Condoms program,[59] Australia's Hello Sunday Morning movement on healthy alcohol use and the Heart Truth campaign of the USA's National Heart, Lung and Blood Institute. To enable brand communities to sustain this type of movement for change, we must build capacity to ensure impact beyond the life of the project.

CAPACITY AS CULTURE

In the context of brand communities we can think of capacity building as a process of strengthening the abilities of individuals, organizations and systems to sustainably and effectively respond to their personal needs and those of their community. Successful approaches are centered in helping ensure that companies, governments, donors and other brand leaders invest in building capacities that both have direct and immediate applications to sustain themselves. These investments must also contribute to capabilities that have broader and long-term importance, enabling communities to evolve and respond to issues as these arise. The most successful are those that approach capacity strengthening as culture building.[60]

Capacity building is often described as an external organization or group providing tools and training to individuals and groups with a lack of resources. However, capacity is not something that is provided or produced and then passed on. Rather, it is best and most effective when it is "home-grown," that is, when it builds on and strengthens something that already exists in some form. Capacity building efforts grow from and seek to strengthen

---

[56] Goodwin (2013 in press).

[57] Bryant et al (1999), Community-based prevention marketing, *Social Marketing Quarterly,* 5, 54-59.

[58] McKenzie-Mohr, D. (2000), New Ways to Promote Proenvironmental Behavior: Promoting Sustainable Behavior: An Introduction to Community-Based Social Marketing, *Journal of Social Issues*, 56, p. 546.

[59] Ainsworth, M., Beyrer, C., & Soucat, A. (2003), AIDS and public policy: the lessons and challenges of 'success' in Thailand, Health Policy, 64(1), 13-37.

[60] Goodwin (2013 in press).

existing resources, skills and knowledge. In effect, through capacity building we nurture and grow "seeds" that already are planted among the individuals, organizations and systems we seek to support. Asset mapping of what already exists – tools, processes and knowledge – can be useful for this purpose.[61]

Capacity building as culture

1. Improving the ability of individuals to effectively design, execute, and evaluate programs and to foster this ability in others.
2. Improving the performance of groups and organizations – their management and processes – to support effective programs, continuous learning and adaptation.
3. Improving the systems in which organizations and individuals function, including policies, structures and standards that support effective programs.

The approach to capacity building as culture reflects a commitment to continuous improvement both in people and the activities undertaken, directed by a process owned by both the brand leader and the community itself. Targeted communities should be approach the work as empowered participants in the production process. They are expected to identify and implement changes needed to ever-improve the quality of their work – and the efforts of those seeking to help them – as a matter of course. The result is steady and significant improvements in efficiency, effectiveness and results for individuals, organizations and systems. Brands can work with individuals, groups and organizations to build capacity through an iterative process of analysis, design, implementation, assessment and redesign. Brand planners and practitioners can draw on existing tools and training resources that have been tested, and develop new ones as needed. Ongoing assessments and process evaluations provide information about which tools and approaches work best and how they should be modified, and feed into the overall body of knowledge concerning capacity building.[62]

TWO APPROACHES TO BUILDING A BRAND COMMUNITY IN INDONESIA

This section of the chapter will examine these issues in relation to two case studies from Indonesia – the Fantastic Mom" and "High-5" projects on sanitation. It will show two approaches to building a brand community around a behavior change and highlight the issues of control and participation. In 2003, Indonesia was at a crossroads. The nation had begun to emerge from the Asian Financial Crisis and the ensuing social and political turmoil. However it faced persistent problems that demanded attention in order that the country could continue to lift many of its people out of poverty, including lowering infant mortality rates. At that time Indonesia ranked 76 in the world, with 41 children for every 1,000 born dying before their fifth birthday. A group of public health policymakers and practitioners in Jakarta, including USAID, had been analyzing the most effective and cost-effective approaches. USAID decided to design a project that included technical assistance for a national campaign,

---

[61] Goodwin (2013 in press).
[62] Goodwin (2013 in press).

grants for community partners and capacity building to support local organizations. And so the Fantastic Mom project[63] was conceived – designed to reduce infant mortality by changing hand washing with soap behaviors among mothers and caregivers in poor communities in priority provinces. But USAID and partners faced significant challenges – people saw hand washing as an "old" behavior that had already been taught, mothers were tired of negative health campaigns, people faced numerous problems and funds were limited – all of which meant a weak brand community.[64]

USAID provided funds to the US-based Johns Hopkins Centre for Communication Programs (CCP) and the Jakarta-based Coalition for a Healthy Indonesia (KuIS) – an alliance of NGOs, community groups and the private sector – to design and execute the project. USAID also funded several international NGOs, such as Save the Children, to integrate the project into their existing development programs. CCP and KuIS also worked with local partners, including NGOs, universities and religious groups, especially those in the project's priority provinces. Other international agencies, such as the World Bank and UNICEF, collaborated and shared results.[65]

At the individual level, CCP research found that diarrhea affected three in every 10 people in Indonesia. And it was the number two killer of Indonesian children under five, causing 13.2% of total deaths. The research found low awareness among mothers and caregivers of the benefits of washing hands with soap to prevent diarrhea. Whilst soap was relatively affordable and available, hand washing was considered an old or learned behavior, something that people had already heard about at school or in the community. However, the connection in people's minds to diarrhea was not well understood. Getting people to use soap and clean, running water was a challenge.

At the community level, mobilizing action by stakeholders proved difficult. The Indonesian government, whilst committed to this project, was challenged by restricted funds and limited capacity to coordinate several departments at national and local levels, plus coordinate international agencies and local organizations. Other health and social issues, such as natural and human-made disasters, a growing HIV/AIDS epidemic, poor education, corruption and deforestation, also challenged Indonesia. The NGO community was mobilized but lacked capacity and access to the funds to make the impact they desired. The private sector was engaged, especially well known companies and their brands such as Unilever's Lifebuoy soap.

The traditional approach might have been to distribute information through health workers and government agencies. The existing market would take care of the provision of soap and associated products. However, a different approach was required to overcome the significant inertia acting as a barrier to adoption of the new behaviors. The project required the creation of sustained collective action through a branded hand washing movement that galvanized the parents as well as the key influencers and partners. This included creating the central and aspirational brand of the "Fantastic Mom", who was an inspiration for all mothers. Loved by her healthy children, supported by her capable husband and admired by her neighbors – who wouldn't want to be a Fantastic Mom?

---

[63] The author managed the Fantastic Mom project on behalf of Ogilvy, the communications and marketing agency engaged to help with design and execution.
[64] Goodwin (2013 in press).
[65] Goodwin (2013 in press).

Strengthening and supporting this brand platform was a community mobilization program and a media campaign to provide the surround sound effect for the program. Messages on hand washing with soap were delivered through a jingle, music and dance competitions, radio spots and other media. Mothers and other members of the community were able to experiment with soap and the new behaviors at carnival-style roadshows. These featured local and national celebrities and hand washing competitions. Many of these activities were made possible with the participation of members and volunteers from local community and religious groups, engaged as partners in the movement by KuIS.

The international agencies and local organizations were funded to incorporate the messages and materials in their existing programs. CCP convened a working group of international agencies to coordinate this work, often attended by USAID. Limited effort was made to engage the national and local governments. KuIS mobilized its network of NGO and private sector members, including through roundtable discussions and funding partnerships. These local organizations were given the opportunity to attend learning sessions on the campaign, which were generic classes on how to use the materials and tools developed by the project. While effective on this level, the learning sessions were not tailored to the specific needs of the individuals and organizations, nor did these activities take into account other needs of these organizations nor the dynamics of building system-wide capacity.

The roadshows and media activities helped the messages reach more than 10 million people in the two priority provinces. The evaluation at the end of the first year recorded an increase of those who reported practicing hand washing with soap from 35% to 56%. There was also an increase in audience awareness of the benefits of hand washing with soap from 45% to 85%.[66] Two large companies, Unilever and Wings, launched soap product campaigns utilizing the project's messages in areas not already reached, working with KuIS and partners. Government support for expansion of the project proved to be weak, partly reflecting limited human and financial capacity. The preference of the international development partners to work with international NGOs might be the reason that national and local government involvement, and therefore support, was limited. A lack of government support can also create a vicious cycle that leads back to a lack of donor support. Programs need to account for and where appropriate be responsive to government strategies and development priorities.[67]

Despite the success of the Fantastic Mom and other health projects, diarrhoea remains a major public health problem in Indonesia. The second most common cause of mortality among children under the age of five, it is also one of the two main causes of undernourished children across the country. One of the weaknesses identified in evaluations was the lack of engagement by local communities. It wasn't enough to create and communicate a strong brand like the Fantastic Mom, it needed the community to mobilise themselves around it and track its progress. In response to this issue, the Government of Indonesia launched the STBM (Community Based Total Sanitation) strategy to ensure ownership by the local population. STBM had an integrated approach dealing with five key sanitation behaviours including: 1) eliminating open defecation; 2) hand washing with soap; 3) household water treatment and storage; 4) solid waste management; and 5) waste water management.

[66] Rimbatmaja, R., Pooroe-Utomo, N., Semiarto, A., Adri, A., Lestari, A., Amini, F., & Figueroa, M. E. (2007). *Health and Hygiene Behaviors in Indonesia: results of the formative research*, Jakarta, Indonesia: Environmental Services Project (ESP).

[67] Goodwin (2013 in press).

To support the government's STBM, the Cipta Cara Padu (CCP) Foundation designed the 'High 5' project to be implemented from 2012-2014. CCP is an Indonesian non-profit focused on improving Indonesians' quality of life through strategic communication for social development focusing on health communication and capacity building. The "High 5" Kelurahan project aimed to improve hygiene and sanitation practices at the household and community levels in urban areas in Indonesia with high diarrhoea prevalence. The project would contribute to the achievement of the national sanitation campaign and citywide sanitation strategies in three major cities: Medan, Surabaya and Makassar. High 5 would benefit about 12,000 households or 48,000 people; 12,000 of whom are children under the age of five.[68]

One of the interesting aspects that differentiates the design of the High-5 project from that of the Fantastic Mom project is the approach to building the brand community. The High-5 brand was based on the functional aspects of the five behaviors or pillars, whereas the Fantastic Mom brand was an emotional one. Also, High-5 identified, surveyed and engaged a group of change agents from the project areas. These change agents are both health workers and other prominent members of the community. The change agents have been organising into district-level working groups (*pokja*), which meet on a regular basis and have responsibility for implementing and tracking the project activities in their areas. The *pokja* organise themselves by allocating tasks in two ways. First is that at least one member of every *pokja* has responsibility for one of the five behaviors or vertical pillars of the project. The second way is that they also group themselves into three horizontal teams – mobilization, socialization as well as monitoring and evaluation.

The change agents then undertake various activities in the local neighbourhoods (referred to as RW and RT). One activity is individual visits to each household, where they provide information and track any infrastructure and other resource needs, eg. septic tanks. The change agents also organise community gatherings, often attached to other local events such as religious festivals.

The High-5 *pokja* monitoring and evaluation team then track their progress, reporting back on a monthly basis to the *pokja*. The change agents are unpaid, however some resources are available, eg. materials for septic tanks. Local High-5 staff reported that some *pokja* members were more active than others and that this participation varied over time. They attributed this to the personalities of the change agents. Both the High-5 and Fantastic Mom projects sought to engage the mass media, including through journalist forums and training. In contrast to the Fantastic Mom project, High-5 does not use community festivals or other forms of engagement.

The High-5 project is approaching its mid term evaluation so the results are not yet available for discussion. However, it is likely that the phenomena of reactance was at play in this brand community, as some change agents sought to assert their individualism in the face of pressure from the *pokja* to participate. This is likely influenced by their involvement in other community programs and the demands of family and other aspects of daily life. The lack of a strong emotional element to the High-5 brand, especially compared with the Fantastic Mom, suggests this may be a weakness to the program. We know that it is important to consider what consumer and community characteristics affect the brand community's

---

[68] CCP. (2011), *Technical Application - 'High 5' Kelurahan project*, Jakarta, Indonesia.

influence on its members.[69] Both projects featured highly centralized control of the brand messages, although the Fantastic Mom project allowed some personal adaptation. Both projects demonstrate the need to combine strong brand identities with participation through effective community mobilization, including through engaging change agents.

CHANGES AND COMMONALITIES FROM TECHNOLOGY

We have seen an enormous expansion in the availability and functionality of new ways to communicate and connect, including through the Internet, mobile phones and social media. These technologies are making it possible to reach new consumer markets, lift more people out of poverty and provide access to communities previously out of reach. However, as Mangold and Faulds report, "in the era of social media, marketing managers' control over the content, timing, and frequency of information is being severely eroded."[70] These changes have had a distortive effect on the influence exerted on and by brands. Certain voices online do not have the same power offline and communities created online are both distinct from efforts on the ground and reflective of them.

These technologies enable real-time feedback, including online, enabling more accountability and a greater demand on resources. We can make use of services like social networks and tools such as mobile phone applications to lower costs and expand the scale of impact. For example in a country like Indonesia, which has extremely high social media usage and mobile phone access, providing a rich source of opportunities to build brands.[71]

These conceptualizations of community and what it means to be social had been largely agreed and lay undisturbed until the rapid emergence and dominance of new Internet-based technologies and services. Emerging in the late 1990s and early 2000s, these came to be referred to collectively as social media and ever since then have captured the public imagination. The numbers of users for the largest platforms and services are staggering, with Facebook amassing over one billion registered users since its inception in 2004.[72] Twitter has over 500 million registered users as of 2012, generating over 340 million tweets daily and handling over 1.6 billion search queries per day.[73] Global mobile phone subscriptions grew from fewer than 1 billion in 2000 to over 6 billion now.[74] Social network phenomena can be exploited to disseminate positive behaviors in brand communities, e.g. for health, "whole connected clusters within the social network stopped smoking roughly in concert"[75] and other drug taking behaviors. The possibilities enabled through these new technologies seem endless and hold great promise for commercial and public organizations.

---

[69] Algesheimer et al (2005), p. 23.

[70] Mangold & Faulds (2009), p. 360.

[71] Goodwin (2013 in press).

[72] http://www.pcmag.com/article2/0,2817,2410560,00.asp; Accessed 18 January 2013

[73] http://www.mediabistro.com/alltwitter/500-million-registered-users_b18842; http://blog.twitter.com/2012/ 03/ twitter-turns-six.html; Both accessed 18 January 2013;

[74] http://www.worldbank.org/en/news/2012/07/17/mobile-phone-access-reaches-three-quarters-planets-population; Accessed 18 January 2013.

[75] Christakis, N. (2011). Putting the social into science. Forget about nature vs. nurture. The answer lies in between. *Time, 178*(24), p. 8; Valente, T. W., Gallaher, P., & Mouttapa, M. (2004). Using social networks to understand and prevent substance use: A transdisciplinary perspective. *Substance use & misuse, 39*(10-12), 1685-1712.

IMPLICATIONS FOR BRAND COMMUNITIES

The preceding evidence and experience raises questions about the nature of brand communities in practice and the different approaches to building them. It is clear that there have been important and rapid changes taking place. In the traditional approach to brand building, the marketing organization and its agents, including professional communications agencies, developed messages and disseminated these to potential consumers, who may or may not have been willing participants in the process. The control over the production and distribution of information was in the hands of the marketing organization. The traditional elements of the promotion mix – advertising, public relations, sales and direct marketing – were the levers through which control was asserted.[76] It was a one-way street.

The implications for researchers, practitioners and policymakers are that traditional forms of influence have been challenged, including the rise of so-called "strangers with experience" and word-of-mouth marketing. Traditional approaches to marketing and communications are being broken down due to new technologies, the increasing complexities of modern operations and the constant pressure for organizations to maintain their success. As a result, "more and more companies are attempting to build deep, meaningful, long-term relationships with their customers."[77] A vital part of success in this endeavor is to remove the individual-brand relationship from its altar and introduce a community-based approach. This enables a broader understanding of this processes enabling social and behavior change and provides marketers with increasingly accurate perspectives on the complexities that shape identification with a brand community.[78]

Making use of tools from psychology and sociology, such as the Sense of Community Index, will enable to us to understand how brand communities feel about themselves and which areas can be targeted for intervention. Engaging change agents is vital as they the people who often make protect or propagate decisions on innovations affecting their communities. Ultimately the use of these tools should be focused on finding the right balance between control and participation, with the likely scenario requiring a loosening of the former and a boosting of the latter. This is not just a nice-to-have but is fast becoming the new normal thanks to the disruption of new technologies.

There is also much that we can recognize in the behaviors and practices that new technologies enable. Connecting with friends and family, sharing news, joining causes and many other similar activities have taken place for millennia and continue to expand all over the world. In many respects, social media enable people to do what they have always wanted to do, but not had the opportunity to do so.[79] But social media has also enabled people to share and connect with an intensity and frequency that has never been seen before. With such a high volume of information being produced, shared and utilized by so many people in so many places, it wasn't long before marketing practitioners and researchers began to notice and harness its potential for building brands.

---

[76] Mangold, W. G., & Faulds, D. J. (2009), Social media: The new hybrid element of the promotion mix. *Business Horizons, 52*(4), p. 364.
[77] Bhattacharya and Sen (2003), p. 76.
[78] Heere et al., 2011, p. 408.
[79] Shirky, C. (2010), Cognitive surplus: Creativity and generosity in a connected age, ePenguin.

The potential pitfalls of this new technology and the change it brings are only just beginning to emerge. We know that the increased competition and constant need for improvement could drive some brands to look for shortcuts and low hanging fruit. This may mean an overly great emphasis on short-term indicators, such as likes, shares, awareness and positive brand perceptions, instead of more meaningful markers, such as brand equity, engagement and behavior change. Also the displacement of the individual-brand from the altar of marketing does not mean the individual doesn't matter. Inevitably, individuals still make the final decisions on purchases and behavior change and so their wants and needs must be central to any marketing program.

Additionally, new media habits show that we can't just build it and they will come. Embedding engaging messages in content that these individuals will enjoy and use and in contexts that engender a positive mindset offer greater potential to reach this group, for example through social networking websites, digital games and podcasts.[80] Using healthcare as an example, patients can be effective partners in their own wellbeing and communities can participate in reshaping the health system to meet their needs. These new technologies enable individuals and their brand communities to be more involved in decision-making that affects them, strengthening ownership and ensuring change is more likely to succeed. Therefore the idea of empowering brands and their communities with a culture of capacity building will help ensure that useful innovations are more readily developed and adopted. We can remember from Tonnies that the idea of modern society was positioned largely in opposition to that of the traditional community, meaning that change brings good or bad depending on how you see it.

CONCLUSION

Governments, non-profits and businesses need to better understand how a community influences people's choices, decisions and behaviors in order to sustain their efforts to make their brands successful. Change in technology – and the human demand that drives it – shows us that complete control is no longer possible, and it was never effective. It is important to purposely select, initiate, manage and direct interactions among customers when facilitating brand communities. New technologies, including the rapid expansion of access to the Internet, mobile phones and social media, have enabled people to connect in new ways and interact with an intensity not seen before. The expansion and utilization of these technologies is driven by old needs and practices. Directing change is possible and desirable – especially with the help of change agents. To ensure success in brand communities, participation of its members must be genuine, not engineered purely for manipulation. The psychological sense of community has an important influence on people in the commercial and public domains and can be useful as a tool to identify change agents who are more likely to succeed in disseminating information.

---

[80] Della, L. J., Eroglu, D., Bernhardt, J. M., Edgerton, E., & Nall, J. (2008), Looking to the future of new media in health marketing: deriving propositions based on traditional theories, *Health Marketing Quarterly, 25*(1-2), p. 159.

Often there is a general assumption that building a brand community will have a positive and controlled effect on behaviours or decisions – the reality is often much more complex. Communities can resist and promote change; individuals can participate or seek personal freedom. Underpinning a brand community's success is attention to the capacity of the individuals and the group. Partnerships with other brands sharing similar values related offer additional resources and new constituents. Effective brand communities offer a fresh and effective approach to building brands in the saturated, highly competitive information environment. Practitioners and policymakers may do well to take advantage of the opportunities that brand communities present.

REFERENCES

Algesheimer, R., Dholakia, U. & Hermann, A. (2005). Interplay between Brand and Brand Community: Evidence from European Car Clubs, *Journal of Marketing, 69*(3).

Anderson, B. R. O. G. (2006). *Imagined communities: reflections on the origin and spread of nationalism* (Rev. ed.), London, New York: Verso.

Bhattacharya, C. B., Rao, H. & Glynn, M. A. (1995). Understanding the Bond of Identification: An Investigation of Its Correlates Among Art Museum Members, *Journal of Marketing*, *59* (October), 46-57.

CCP. (2011). *Technical Application - 'High 5' Kelurahan project*, Jakarta, Indonesia.

Chavis, D., Lee, K. S. & Acosta, J. D. (2008). *The Sense of Community (SCI) Revised: The Reliability and Validity of the SCI-2*, Paper presented at the 2nd International Community Psychology Conference, Lisboa, Portugal.

Christakis, N. (2011). Putting the social into science. Forget about nature vs. nurture. The answer lies in between, *Time, 178*(24).

Cruz, J. & Lewis, J. (1994), *Viewing, reading, listening: audiences and cultural reception*, Boulder: Westview Press.

Della, L. J., Eroglu, D., Bernhardt, J. M., Edgerton, E. & Nall, J. (2008). Looking to the future of new media in health marketing: deriving propositions based on traditional theories, *Health Marketing Quarterly, 25*(1-2), 147-174.

Dewey, J. (1927). *The public and its problems*, New York: H. Holt and Company.

Doolittle, R. J. & MacDonald, D. (1978). Communication and a Sense of Community in a Metropolitan Neighbourhood: a factor analytic examination, *Communication Quarterly*, *26*(3), 2-7.

Durkheim, E. & Halls, W. D. (1984). *The division of labour in society*, New York: Free Press.

Durkheim, E., Solovay, S. A., Mueller, J. H. & Catlin, G. E. G. (1938). *The rules of sociological method* (8th ed.), Chicago, Ill.: The University of Chicago press.

Ellemers, N., Kortekaas, P. & Ouwerkerk, J. W. (1999). Self-Categorization, Commitment to the Group, and Group Self-Esteem as Related but Distinct Aspects of Social Identity, *European Journal of Social Psychology*, *29* (2-3), 371-89.

Evans, W. D. & Hastings, G. (2008). *Public health branding: Applying marketing for social change*, Oxford University Press, USA.

Finlayson, T. J. (2007). *Effects of stigma, sense of community, and self-esteem on the HIV sexual risk behaviors of African American and Latino men who have sex with men* (PhD), Georgia State University.

Fisher, A. T., Sonn, C. C. & Bishop, B. J. (2002), *Psychological sense of community: research, applications, and implications*, New York: Kluwer Academic/Plenum Publishers.

Glynn, T. J. (1981). Psychological Sense of Community: measurement and application, *Human Relations*, *34*(9), 789-818.

Goodwin, N. (2013 in press). Sustainable Change Marketing: learnings from development and communications programs in Indonesia and beyond; In L. Brennan, J. Fien, L. Parker, H. Duong, M. A. Doan & T. Watne (Eds.), *Growing Sustainable Communities: a development guide for Southeast Asia*. Melbourne, Australia: Tilde University Press.

Goodwin, N. (2011). *Community: the missing ingredient in the social marketing mix*, Paper presented at the World Social Marketing Conference, Dublin, Ireland.

Graham, B. C. (2011). *Residence hall sense of community in physical and technology-based spaces: Implications for alcohol-related attitudes and behaviors* (PhD), DePaul University, Chicago, Illinois. (UMI Number: 3491555)

Hamley, B. & Carah, N. (2012). *One Sunday at a time: evaluating Hello Sunday Morning*, Sydney: Foundation for Alcohol Research and Education.

Heere, B., Walker, M., Yoshida, M., Ko, Y. J., Jordan, J. S. & James, J. D. (2011). Brand Community Development Through Associated Communities: grounding community measurement within social identity theory, *The Journal of Marketing Theory and Practice*, *19*(4), 407-422.

Hillery, G. A. (1955). Definitions of community: Areas of agreement, *Rural Sociology*, *20*(2), 111-123.

Hopkins, J. L. (2012). Can Facebook be an effective mechanism for generating growth and value in small businesses?, *Journal of Systems and Information Technology*, *14*(2), 131-141.

Hystad, P. & Carpiano, R. M. (2012). Sense of community-belonging and health-behaviour change in Canada, *Journal of Epidemiology and Community Health*, *66*(3), 277-283.

Kelly, J. A., St Lawrence, J. S., Diaz, Y. E., Stevenson, L. Y., Hauth, A. C., Brasfield, T. L. & Andrew, M. (1991). HIV risk behavior reduction following intervention with key opinion leaders of population: an experimental analysis, *American Journal of Public Health, 81*(2), 168-171.

Kempe, D., Kleinberg, J. & Tardos, E. (2003). *Maximizing the spread of influence through a social network*, Paper presented at the Ninth ACM SIGKDD international conference on knowledge discovery and data mining, New York, NY, USA.

Kotler, P., Roberto, N. & Lee, N. (2002), *Social marketing : improving the quality of life* (2nd ed.), Thousand Oaks, Calif.: Sage Publications.

Lasch, C. (1991). *The True and Only Heaven: Progress and Its Critics*, New York: Norton.

Lomas, J., Enkin, M., Anderson, G. M., Hannah, W. J., Vayda, E. & Singer, J. (1991). Opinion leaders vs audit and feedback to implement practice guidelines; *JAMA: the journal of the American Medical Association, 265*(17), 2202-2207.

Mangold, W. G. & Faulds, D. J. (2009). Social media: The new hybrid element of the promotion mix, *Business Horizons*, *52*(4), 357-365.

McAlexander, J. H., Schouten, J. W. & Koenig, H. F. (2002). Building brand community, *The Journal of Marketing*, 38-54.

McLuhan, M. & Lapham, L. H. (1994). *Understanding media: The extensions of man*, MIT Press Cambridge, MA.

McMillan, D. W. & Chavis, D. M. (1986). Sense of community: A definition and theory, *Journal of Community Psychology*, *14* (January).

Muniz, A. M. & Schau, H. J. (2005). Religiosity in the Abandoned Apple Newton Brand Community, *Journal of Consumer Research*, *31*(4), 737-47.

Muniz, A. M. & O'Guinn, T. C. (2001). Brand community, *Journal of Consumer Research*, *27*(4), 412-432.

Park, R. E. (1972). *The crowd and the public, and other essays*, Chicago: University of Chicago Press.

Rappaport, J. (1977). *Community psychology: values, research, and action*, New York: Holt, Rinehart and Winston.

Rogers, E. M. (2003). *Diffusion of innovations* (5th ed.), New York: Free Press.

Sarason, S. B. (1974). *The psychological sense of community: Prospects for a community psychology*, Jossey-Bass.

Shirky, C. (2010). Cognitive surplus: Creativity and generosity in a connected age, ePenguin.

Simmel, G. (2007). The Social Boundary, *Theory, Culture & Society, 24*(7-8), 53-56.

Stokols, D. (1992). Establishing and Maintaining Healthy Environments: Toward a Social Ecology of Health Promotion, *American Psychologist, 47*(1), 6-22.

Tartaglia, S. (2006). A preliminary study for a new model of sense of community, *Journal of Community Psychology, 34*(1), 25-36.

Tönnies, F. & Loomis, C. P. (1957). *Community & society (Gemeinschaft und Gesellschaft)*, East Lansing,: Michigan State University Press.

Valente, T. W. & Pumpuang, P. (2007). Identifying Opinion Leaders to Promote Behavior Change, *Health Education & Behavior, 34*(6), 881-896.

Valente, T. W., Gallaher, P. & Mouttapa, M. (2004). Using social networks to understand and prevent substance use: a transdisciplinary perspective, *Substance use & misuse, 39*(10-12), 1685-1712.

Valente, T. W. & Davis, R. L. (1999). Accelerating the diffusion of innovations using opinion leaders, *The Annals of the American Academy of Political and Social Science, 566*(1), 55-67.

Valente, T. W. & Saba, W. P. (1998), Mass Media and Interpersonal Influence in a Reproductive Health Communication Campaign in Bolivia, *Communication Research, 25*(1), 96-124.

Weber, M. & Runciman, W. G. (1978), *Max Weber: selections in translation*, Cambridge ; New York: Cambridge University Press.

Wirth, L. (1938). Urbanism as a Way of Life, *The American Journal of Sociology, 44*(1), 1-24.

Xu, Q., Perkins, D. D. & Chow, J. C. C. (2010), Sense of community, neighboring, and social capital as predictors of local political participation in China, *American journal of community psychology, 45*(3), 259-271.

INDEX

D

E

Q

R

S